UNTIL JU ⠀⠀⠀⠀⠀ JMES

STORIES ABOUT JAMAICAN MEN

ALSO BY OPAL PALMER ADISA

Eros Muse, poems & essays
Caribbean Passion, poems
Leaf-of-Life, poems
It Begins With Tears, novel
Tamarind and Mango Women, poems
Bake-Face and Other Guava Stories, stories

ACKNOWLEDGEMENTS

Special thanks to Bert Nepaulsingh for reading this manuscript in its earlier draft, and for confirming that I was on the right track, and had captured the men's voices.

Special thanks also to the members of my writing circle, Devorah Major, Aya de Leon & James Cagney, for their invaluable insights that helped me to flush out the latter stories, especially "Trying Words", "Ebenezer's Watermelon Knee" and "Bad-Boy".

Thanks too to Ken and our conversation about Caribbean men and life.

Thanks always to my mother, Catherine, who I frequently telephoned to check certain Jamaican references or missing bits of information.

And a special thanks to Jeremy and Peepal Tree Press for *getting* these stories, for really understanding what and how I was writing and making this collection a reality after ten years of working and reworking.

Special thanks to the Sacatar Institute where I spent two months in residence (December 2005-February 2006) and where the title story was reworked and came together.

Thanks to those who rejected this manuscript, those who didn't get it, and those who didn't even try.

Thank to these characters who didn't give up on me, and thanks to my own perseverance for not giving up on them.

Thanks to time and life and love.

OPAL PALMER ADISA

UNTIL JUDGEMENT COMES

STORIES ABOUT JAMAICAN MEN

PEEPAL TREE

First published in Great Britain in 2007
Peepal Tree Press Ltd
17 King's Avenue
Leeds LS6 1QS
England

ISBN 1 84523 042 6
ISBN13: 1 978 184523 042 5

ACKNOWLEDGEMENTS

'The Brethren' (Published in *The Caribbean Writer*, Volume 9,
1995; winner of Canute A. Brodhurst Prize, April 1996); 'De
Myal Man' (Published in *The Caribbean Writer*, Volume 14, 2000).

Peepal Tree gratefully acknowledges Arts Council support

DEDICATION

men walk with a swagger
men fold away their tears
men see the sun
and take it inside themselves
men hide their dreams
and call pain women's foolishness
men with ready smiles
bottle their fear
men who shine despite the times

In memory of:
Richard Samuel James, my maternal grandfather
whose smile shone through his eyes
&
Ezikel Laberton Palmer, my paternal grandfather
who was firm and saved his pennies

For Orlando Melahado Palmer, my father who always loved
himself and me too
For Ewan (Keith) Caddle Palmer & Stratton Andre Melahado
Palmer, my brothers
and to the nameless and countless men of Jamaica who have
always worked at something, always loved their women and
children, always believed in the beauty of life; those men who
smiled at me, raised me on their backs and shoulders, helped
me with my load, gave me words of encouragement, believed
in me, I sing you these word songs

shirtless men wearing sweat like silk
men in starched whites and ambition ties
men who plowed and men who lead
men whose masculinity celebrates
the heart

TABLE OF CONTENTS

THE WHEREOF OF *UNTIL JUDGEMENT COMES* AND THE MEN I LOVE: AN INTRODUCTORY DISCLAIMER

My father is the first man I ever loved. This should be a truism, and perhaps it is, but I suspect for me, for who I am and have always been, to say that my father is my first love is too easy and predictable.

When I close my eyes and go back into time, the first man I ever loved has no face, but his back is as prominent as the whites of my eyes. Except his back is the colour of night, one without stars, the sort of night that pulls you into its depth. It is naked, his back, he is naked, and his muscles are washboard hard, his arms are tree branches, and he is a mountain for me to lean on – he glows with his strength borne from the labour of love. This is my first love. I know him; feel his presence, experience him reciprocating, loving me back, unreserved, without boundaries, transcending distance and time.

To say that I love men would be an understatement. I love men. Love the manliness of them. Love their posture and stance. Love their sugar raw, tamarind smell. Love their boastful laughter, and the way they all, regardless of class or caste, cup their manhood as if it might fall off and disappear. Love their foibles. Love their gestures and yanking. Love how they mask their fears (because so many of them have lost hold of their wants). I love the lust that bleeds from their eyes, the way they purse their lips to whisper lewd remarks. Love how fresh their hands are to grab behinds and breasts without so much as an introduction. I love men because they are not me, and despite or perhaps in spite of

9

all their idiosyncrasies they make me still want them. Love to feel their arms about me – not only in sexual embrace; love to rest my head on their chest; love to press my body into theirs, love to hold and caress and help them to love themselves so they can love me back. Loving men is easy with me. I don't fear them, and I allow them to come to me as they are, undressed, without pretence or guile. With me they can, if brave, find themselves in my presence; with me they are able to walk towards love with wild abandonment.

Perhaps that's why Jacob, Edmond, Ebenezer, Jeremiah, Padee, Sheldon and Devon aka Bad-Boy, these men of this collection, came to me, this avowed feminist, this independent woman who doesn't need a man to accomplish her goals, but who seeks the company of men, and basks in their friendship, their playful flirtation and love. Yet these men are not the sort of males I would seek out as partners or lovers, and even more importantly these men would not seek me out – I would not be one of their women because my sense of self would too aggressively force them to interrogate who they are and how they are being with me. Yet I am attracted to them in some intrinsic way because I love each of them. For many, many years I have felt their pull, heard them calling me, sensed them pulling me out of the arms of other men; have experienced them dogging me, relentlessly, inviting me into their most private as well as their public spaces, tugging, grasping, fondling and pleading. "Come nuh man, come nuh. How long yu want we fi wait. Come nuh gal, come woman, come." So I yielded to the call of their love. I visited with them and laid down with them, and ate with them and slept with them, and loved them even when I vehemently disagreed with who they were being at any given moment. I loved them, and will always love them for opening up and being able to be vulnerable in my presence. We love each other, each of them, as that was the only way I could get inside their heads and hearts so they would tell me their stories. I gave up judging them. I gave up criticizing them. I gave up wanting them to be someone they were not. I just listened and loved them. I just listened and helped them to find an outlet for all their pain. I just helped them to see that regardless of the past, regardless of their mistakes, they too were deserving of love and deserved a second or third or as many chances as we all do. I just loved them, and didn't try to dress them up or make them into the ideal man I have been seeking, and in doing so they became the ideal – because love is that powerful, that miraculous.

Jacob manifests and infuses such a love. Jacob tries so hard to stay the course, to see beyond the immediate, to work towards change, to love himself, his woman and his family despite the colonial oppression that would try to amputate his sense of manhood and thwart his progressive ways. I love him, and encourage him on his struggle, so was very honoured when he came to me, insisting that I go with him on this journey, and I did. I am so thankful that I did because he has taught me so much about the frustrating struggles of Jamaican/Caribbean/African/ working-class men whose spirit and energy get so tired that they give in to the bottle and give in to domestic violence, unable to find their way out of the prison of poverty and lack of resources, foremost of which is lack of education. But Jacob forges ahead. Jacob's love has not turned sour. Jacob continues to work out of love.

And there is nothing more sexy, but also potentially more lethal than a man who knows what he wants. Initially, that was what caused me to love Edmond, who knows what he wants and gets it. But like so many men who when faced with women's ardour become fearful and run or deliberately mess up so they can be driven away, Edmond almost does that – he comes close. Thankfully, however, he pauses, he reflects, then he allows himself to see and accept that what he has is actually what he has always wanted, so he is able and willing to make the minor adjustments necessary so he can have his love. I celebrate Edmond and love that he is my friend and confidant.

What I love most about Ebenezer is that he is smart enough to know that he does not know how to love a woman intimately, that he doesn't want to be with a woman, so he avoids the pitfalls that could lead him to an unhappy situation. But Ebenezer loves himself enough to know that he wants a son, so devises a way to have what he wants, while keeping women at bay, except as un-interfering friends. Ebenezer is a man that I can visit, even stay at his house, have him take care of me, without any demands.

He does not even require that I speak, yet we share an unspoken love.

The love I feel for Jeremiah is as complex and entangled as the several tributaries of a river that enter the mouth of the sea at the same point. His love sometimes burns, leaving scars, making for disconcerting pauses. I had to really struggle to keep loving Jeremiah, consequently I was many years writing him, learning about him, forgiving him so I could set him free to find his way to love again.

Padee, was just the opposite of Jeremiah. He was easy to love even though it was clear he was a wanton womanizer. He is the man that women are doomed or fated to love. Padee is based loosely on my maternal grandfather and snatches of stories I heard about him from my mother, and her sisters and brothers, and from my own vague memory of him, since he died when I was about thirteen. Even though many women loved Padee, he couldn't find his way to the avenue of love. He sought refuge between the thighs of many women, and he fathered thirteen children, yet Padee with his ready smile and irresistible charisma, did not love himself. Perhaps women intuitively recognized this and tried to love him into loving himself – Padee who treated women like newspaper, which was never to be thrown away, but saved to wrap something in the future. And I love Padee back like a newspaper that I keep and will never toss because, he more than the others, has taught me about the enormous magnanimity of women and the deeper, truer meaning of unconditional love.

Sheldon, too, requires a love that is a balm but that also hurls him back into the recesses of his memory where love once lived boldly and ferociously. Sheldon, because of the era in which he was born, and the hurdles he has had to scale, forgets this fact, and is therefore unable to love himself, unable to love anyone else, unable to love his history or heritage. He seeks refuge in his intellect, and this eventually turns on him and the vacuous life he insists on leading. My love went and rescued Sheldon, but he is still in great need of love to heal himself from years of self-imposed isolation.

And I couldn't help but love Devon, aka Bad-Boy. Had to shower him with love, wrap him with love, talk to him with love, look at him through the eyes of adoration, because Devon is like far too many boys whose mothers, hurt by their children's fathers (who were unable to live up to their promise), take out their anger and frustration on their sons, and destroy their capacity to trust and/or love other women. And because I didn't want Devon to be added to the list of such men who too often become rapists, misogynists, murderers, woman-beaters, I had to fight for him. I had to drop everything so I could love Devon, love him hard, love him relentlessly so he would feel and breathe my affection and find his way into the arms of caring without hurt or hurting. Love unmitigated, open, honest. Love of each of these men.

I know I am blessed because I have known and still know the love of good men. Notwithstanding the years of separation and the subsequent feeling of abandonment I experienced with my father, I know he loves and cares for me, and I love him back. I know that my brothers love and admire me. I know uncles who love me. I know these loves as sustaining and varied as yams. And I have known passionate loves with my first boyfriend, Patrick, with my second husband, Tarik – their love like jackfruit that sticks and stains and marks you for life. And there are those familial loves that grow fast and sturdy like bamboo in the persons of my nephew, Paul, my son, Jawara, and my grandnephew, Irie Boy aka Patrick. I know the love of my dear friends Neville, Ian, Don, LeRoy, Bilalh, Skip, Bert, Earl, Acklyn, Ken, love that is both a hybrid like a Seville orange and a staple like rice, and a delicious treat such as pone that is wrapped and baked in banana leaf. It is from this love and knowing of men that these stories were spawned. They drip sweat, they lead in the dance and pull me on their laps; I sip beer from their bottles, throw back my head and laugh as they hug me around the waist. Because we have loved, and we will continue to love each other.

Opal Palmer Adisa,
Daytona, Florida, June 2006

TEACHMENT I:

"Every man gwane be judge by him actions at the end of him life".
That's what Papa always used to tell me. He wasn't really my papa, he was my grandpapa, but he was the only one I knew. My papa, his son, went to Panama to build the canal when I was just one year old. He never did come back and we never did find out why. At first he used to send money, Papa says, then he stopped, and he didn't hear from him any more. Papa wrote letters, even to the Governor General, to ask them to inquire, but nobody did anything. Papa died with a great big hole in his heart wanting to know what happened to his son, my father.

I didn't know my mama either. She left before I was two years old, to some place in Europe. Papa says it was no place he ever heard of. She had been working for some rich white people and a friend of theirs from some far-far place in Europe came to visit and invited her to be a nanny for their children. Papa says he told her not to go, but she said from she was girl she wanted to know some place other than this little island so she going for a year and then come back. But cold kill her dead-dead, that's what Papa say and it was too much to bring her body back here to bury, so she dead alone over there, in some place in Europe the name of which Papa and me don't know.

Well Papa dead too. Long-long time now. Seems like he held on until I turn woman, then he died, quiet-quiet so. I had just turn eighteen and the house he was building just finish, the same house I live in now and have since then. Throughout all my life, growing up with Papa, he would always say, "Every man will be judged." He was a sweet wise man, and I miss him, but not too much because I feel as if he is always with me.

So you wondering why I telling you all of this? Where this story going? Well settle yourself and all will be made plain. You see I grow in a place call Potosi in St James with Papa. But this here is where my mother did grow, St Catherine. Papa says since she dead the land is mine, so he build me this house. When I moved here, is only bush for miles. It didn't clear out yet, and people didn't start to live here then, but in time more and more come. My house was the first house, and then about half a mile from my house was Jacob house. Is really his story I want you to hear, but let me tell you how I know him.

As I said, for almost three years only me live down here, then Jacob who is a cane-cutter on one of the sugar estates come and build a little house for he and his wife. They had baby on the way, and since is only the two of we live around here, we shout howdy to each other and talk. Now Jacob's wife was a quiet woman, so sometimes he would come and sit down in my yard and we have some deep-deep talk about life, and what's fair and all those things. Well as time go on Jacob grew angry bad about the condition of cane-cutters. He showed me his hands, how them rake-up and cut-up from cutting cane, and yet still he hardly had enough to feed his family. He was a man that had a vision for better and he wanted to do something to help not just himself, but others. I encouraged him to talk with the other workers. Next thing I know Jacob make plan and dream dreams. He was a man who had no need to fear the judgment Papa speak of.

BRETHREN

The sun perches on the hill swaying like a pendulum.
The sun plays hopscotch with the trees cooing a wistful tune.
Look homeward, cane-cutters, look homeward.
Drag your weary bodies to rest.
Jacob's back is to the sun. It has been a gigantic orange ball
filling up the sky, turning the place into a steaming oven that drags
sweat from dark bodies.

Syncopated melodies – *Limbo, limbo like me... Coconut woman
is comin out... Day de light an a wanna go home...* all rolled into one,
ring through the air while Jacob continues his tiresome bend-
down, pick-up dance, and the flaming ball in the sky twirls, and
twirls, spewing more heat from its body.

A trickle of sweat makes Jacob close his eyes and for a minute
he dreams, his body still against the stifling heat.

The frantic flapping of a bird's wings rouses him, but he still
stands transfixed, watching the heat send up steam from the
melting tar under his feet. In worn, black rubber boots he feels his
feet burning like a wasp caught in bubbling molasses. A trickle of
sweat drips onto his shirt. Jacob stirs, his swollen feet treading
over cane-stalks, dirt, trash, while the orange ball splashes pink
and tangerine streaks all over the sky. Before Jacob reaches home
the ball will fall over. The workday is done, oh.

Let de music play
Watch how they dance
Sugar in they waist
Rum in they heads
Molasses cruising through they veins
Let de music play

Jacob's clothes, like those of the other cane-cutters, are torn, blotched, stained, darned together just enough to conceal his maleness, which might offend the placid middle-class women on their way to and from shopping.

Sugar in their waist. Sugar. Sugar. Sweet and bitter. Sugar for your pastries. Sugar for your punch. Sugar for your honey who wrap you in love. They do not wait for the aftertaste, the bonbon that lingers at the back of the throat and the abortive, gurgling attempts to dislodge the irritating saccharine.

Jacob dances, but it's no celebration. No sweetness here. Life is the dance being pantomimed. The sun wanes.

Slavery done and gone
But him brother still here
Slavery done and gone
But him uncle still around
Slavery done and gone
But him relatives still here.

Jacob brushes dirt from his clothes, and trash from his hair. He is not a pretty sight. His cutlass is grimy and sticky. His hands are blistered. His back feels like a train track. A honest day's work for meagre pay. Sugar cane ruin your life.

Jacob walks ahead of the other cane-cutters; a half smile plays at the corners of his mouth. Even among themselves they are just work objects – men who survive by their muscles, their machetes, the crosses they bear staggering home.

Sugar is sweet, but what good is it if an army of ants invade, collapse under the sweetness and lie dead in the heaped spoonful ready to be stirred into a cup of tea?

Jacob walks alone so that he can think. He must think, sort out his endless days and try to see an end in sight. He wants the other cane-cutters' companionship, but he dreads their common fear, their united refusal to look beyond their lot. How not to split a cane in half to see the veins running through the middle? How to refuse the momentary sweetness that will quench your thirst and send shivers rippling through your body as the sticky liquid stains your chin and the syrup pumps energy into your body. He walks alone.

Jacob doesn't need to look back; he hears the thud, thud of his brothers' feet, hard, yet weary, large black rubber boots dragging on the road, sounding like a bursting dam. The season just started so they walk an avenue through the cane, thick and swaying to their left and right, blocking out everything else, acres and acres of cane that they must plough through, chop into pieces, raising the dirt that will plug up their throats. They can never escape the cane: their bodies reek of it; their children beg for it; their women wear it as perfume; some is sprinkled on everything they eat; their children drop the hard brown crystals in their beds, so they sleep grated by it. They are entombed by this sweet bitterness even when they attempt to run from it.

Four years ago Jacob had tried; he went to work on the wharf loading sugar bound for England. One day he stumbled and the large fifty-pound crocus bag spilled open, burying him in sugar. They dismissed him and returned him to the fields.

Jacob looks all around him, and all he sees as far as the horizon are stalks of cane dancing in the breeze, swirling through the air, their leaves sounding rhythms in the wind; cane everywhere. He inhales deeply, but the pungent smell of cane is like mucus stifling his breathing. He coughs and cane-juice jets from his throat. "Aaaaah!" he wails, tossing his machete in the air – which misses him by a hair's breadth as it lands. "Aaaah!" Jacob writhes, kneading his sticky palms on the ground. The other cane-cutters step around him, continuing their journey home as he knew they would. The season has just begun; too soon for the sugar to fly to his head and send him off. They too have women and children to feed. The cane is their master and their daily bread. To deny that truth is to invite starvation. Besides, they're tired, and already too much blood has been shed. That's why they frequently curse each other: *You blood-claat! Man, you bumbu-claat! Kiss me backside, you rass-claat, you.*

They bleed like poinsettia trees when leaves are plucked from their branches; they bleed every day in the fields when cane leaves slice into their hands, prickle their feet, bruise their faces. But who knows this? To whom can they complain? They must withstand until... When? So the cane-cutters pass Jacob by and shake their heads. He should know better, should have learned to hide his feelings like a snail in its shell. Frustration should not be paraded like a peacock's fan. "Look pan me! Look pan me!" Jacob demands of the broad-shouldered backs that are retreating from him. For a moment, the cane-cutters stumble over invisible pebbles; they pause; linger; continue silent, their eyes distant and red, their necks held stiff, their chests pushed out. Jacob will have to pick himself up as many other cane-cutters have done in the past, and some will surely have to do before this season is over. If Jacob wallows in his anger, he will become nothing more than a caution, a warning to them to bear up stronger. So they walk on, not glancing back. He will pick himself up and join them.

Sugar cane mek
you bitter so
Sugar cane mek
you bad-minded so
Thought you was sweet
til a boil blister me mouth
Sugar cane mek
you bitter so

Jacob's eyes are like charred cane-stalks burning. Beady crystals run down his forehead and neck, his muscles ripple, yet he feels spineless. "Is who me workin fa?" He looks around, but no eyes meet his. "Fa what?" Silence, then a rush of wind rustles the cane fields. "To dem, me is not man; to dem me is boy; cane-cutter is boy." He rests on one knee, both hands clutching his machete that is stuck in the ground. The creases dissolve from his forehead; a glow transforms his face into varnished mahogany.

"Is what we get fa all we toilin? Bread an butta an suga water? Is really who de damn blast me a work fa?"

Jacob squats on his haunches and uses his forearm to wipe the sweat from his eyes. He looks to the sky for the orange ball that is already close to drop behind the hill.

Thirteen years! Thirteen year he has been cutting cane, and he wouldn't be able to recognize the face of the man who owns this sugar estate, the man who in fact owns him since he owns his labour. All he knows is that the man is younger than he, is white and most likely is from England. Why doesn't he stay in England and grow cane?

Jacob remembers many years ago when a fellow cane-cutter pointed out the owner to him. They had just finished a field and the cane stalks were heaped high like a hill and he and a few others had climbed on top of the pile. They didn't see the Land Rover until it stopped behind them, dirt swirling all around. Jacob doesn't remember the man's face, except that it was red, not pink like his tongue, but red, burning red. What he remembers is how clean the man looked in a white shirt, short khaki pants, a felt hat and shiny brown boots. Jacob had looked down at himself, and at the other cane-cutters and felt dirty, ashamed. The owner never spoke to them. He spoke to the overseer, a flabby brown man who was always picking at his teeth with a piece of cane trash. But Jacob remembers that the owner half waved at them just before he sped off in his Land Rover, sending up more dirt to obliterate their existence.

Jacob sits squarely in the dirt, then on impulse he rolls and bathes himself in it. His tongue curls inside his mouth; he bites it trying to deaden its sweet taste. Blood spurts. Jacob spits; bees quickly buzz for the sugar in his saliva. Jacob is tormented by the memory of the owner, and agonizes over all the hopes he had for himself, his woman, his children. A shadow looms over him; he looks up and meets the sympathetic gaze of Efton, the Joban lad of seventeen who is just two weeks fresh from the parish of Trelawny. The youth extends his arm to Jacob, who raises his right hand and Efton pulls him up, then helps him to brush the dirt from his clothes and arms. Jacob pulls a piece of cane skin from the boy's black-pepper-seed hair and together they walk, arms around each other's waists.

"Boy, you fresh, you is new blood. Me give you time, den you will walk on by wid de oders," Jacob warns, squeezing Efton's shoulder. The youth says nothing, but his eyes tell Jacob *never*. Jacob accepts the bond, welcomes a kindred soul; their feet move in tune to a marching-rhythm, heading homeward bound to rest their weary bones.

The sun dips behind the hill.

The cane leaves and the wind continue their maddening drumming, and the cane-cutters' voices resound with chatter.

Jacob shifts his machete to his left shoulder, the blade away from his neck, the tip pointing backward to the hot, dusty fields that they just left. Evening has crept out slowly like a caterpillar

21

travelling along an unfamiliar branch. In a likewise manner Jacob and Efton walk, conceding that tomorrow will be another day, and maybe, just maybe, it will be their day if they are not too afraid to claim it. "He dat sow shall reap" is like a song playing in Jacob's head and he murmurs just audibly, "Fa thirteen back-breakin years me cuttin cane. Thirteen years!"

During the off-season Jacob had worked as a "yard-boy" for one of the backras – billing grass, raking leaves, shining shoes, mending fences, doing whatever needed to be done, doing what he has to, to help put food on the table and buy school uniforms for his children to go to the government school.

"Me no reap fi me own yet, boy. All dis time, an me still no reap fi me own."

Working at such odd jobs, Jacob has to contend with the backras' children, who frequently disrupt his chores by asking questions for which he has no answers, but which he tries his best to respond to, being careful to punctuate his reply first with "Mas John or Miss Pam", to children who sometimes don't even come up to his waist.

Jacob reflects on the time he came close to chopping off the little brown boy's head. If he had done so, it would not have had anything to do with the child, nor would his action have freed him. The little boy was merely the loudspeaker. The person who was blaring the noise was hidden. Destroying the loudspeaker would not stop the person whose orders would still determine his life. Jacob had to find the person responsible for setting the chain of events in motion. "Imagine. Big man like me, dis little boy orderin about like me an him de same size."

Jacob's machete now swings freely as he talks, cutting the enclosing night with its sharpness. He stops in his track and shouts at Efton.

"You listenin to me? Hear what a tellin you. Dis little brown picknie tell me fi stop rakin de yard and gi him donkey-ride like me is mule."

It wasn't just humiliation that Jacob felt, it was something deeper; the child's order felt like knives being stuck into his flesh. He was powerless and the child knew it. He had to do what he was told because he was afraid not to. The jarring pain Jacob felt reached to his marrow causing him to tremble in the eighty degrees heat. How to say no? No was not a word he had practice using with the likes of this child or his father. The word for them was always yes, accompanied by a smile, so Jacob complied and became a mule for the greater part of the afternoon, until he felt the tear which stung his cheek.

Jacob leaned his machete against the mango tree in the yard, and the boy, Master John, jumped on his back after ordering him to go on all fours. After that, Jacob was forced to crawl around the hard ground, full of prickly weeds and stones, while John nudged him in his side and rode him in earnest like a mule, all the while demanding that he go faster. Then Jacob felt a tear sting his cheek, and his children rose in a vision before him, ashamed for themselves and for him, or perhaps it was the vision of his children that prompted the tear. Whichever, he saw them right before him and he stopped suddenly and the boy, caught off guard, fell from his back and laid there looking up at him with a startled, but angry look. Jacob moved toward his machete, and curled his fingers around the handle. The child was still on the ground as he clutched his machete, and he knew he was going to raise it.

Man is a hard
person to be
Man is a hard
person to achieve
Each day when you bend down
to cut cane
Man is a hard
person to be

The boy's accusing stare was replaced with disbelief and fear. As Jacob raised the machete over his head, the backra drove up in a flurry and the boy scampered to the safety of his father. But Jacob remained ready, standing firm even after the backra had ordered him to go and pick some jelly-coconuts. For more than a minute Jacob stood there, the machete raised above his head, chest heaving, jaws moving, the veins in his neck pulsing, unable to move, to think beyond what he was about to have done. The backra, seeing Jacob like that, went quickly inside to the safety of his house, pulling his son along. When Jacob left that afternoon – without picking any coconuts – he was given five shillings and told by the maid, one of his sisters by lot, that his services were no longer required. For the next two weeks following that incident, Jacob and his family had very little to eat.

Again, Jacob stops in the middle of the road, the memory of that day alive in his mind. "Backra did 'fraid me, did 'fraid me that day," he declares to Efton, who has been listening intently. Jacob's pride swells with the memory; he feels strong. Efton, too, is proud and happy of this new friendship. Jacob is a man of action, he says to himself. Perhaps the other cane-cutters can become men of action too, tired of constantly bowing to others, ready to declare a new day, like Paul Bogle whom he learned about in school. Such are Efton's thoughts as he and Jacob walk more quickly to catch up with the others. After all, when they wield their machetes in the cane-fields, whilst the power of each man's singular action could be breathtaking, their collective force was awesome. In the fields they were men, strong and forceful. No one could deny that, though the backras tried, speaking to them as if they were children or, worse, animals without feelings. But when they were in the midst of the cane, in the middle of motion, there was only the whoosh-sounding force that their machetes made, blade against cane, anger against task.

Yes. Efton does not regret having declined his cousin's offer to join him in Spanish Town in a vagabond existence of purse snatching and stealing fruits from the market women. He is prepared to sweat his life into a noble manhood.

Jacob's thoughts are different. His moments of rest, the momentary pauses when his thoughts crowd in on him, make him angry, especially because he cannot say exactly what he's feeling and he doesn't know how to change things, how to make his life a little sweeter. If only he could be a cane-stalk that was carried to the factory, juice squeezed out into the vat, then boiled until it turned into steaming black molasses, then changing to wet brown sugar, before crystallizing into pine-coloured sugar that sweetens the most bitter medicine. How to change himself like that?

Jacob shakes his head.

"Dat evenin, when me get home, afta me lose de backra work, Dacas seh me fi mek sure me no tun wutliss man dat no mind dem picknie."

Jacob had expected a rebuke from the backras but didn't get one. He had shared his pain with Dacas, and here was his woman, mother of his five children, disregarding all he said since it did not relate to food or money for her and the children.

Damn blasted woman!

Jacob and Efton walk for a while, engrossed in their separate thoughts, their feet moving in synchronized rhythm. However, Jacob's memory will not stay quiet any longer; he taps Efton on his shoulder, words reeling from his mouth.

"Me ask she if it didn't matter that the brown picknie ride me like mule? You know wha she answer me?" Jacob pauses, turns to Efton, not really expecting a reply. Efton shakes his head expectantly, switches his machete to his left shoulder, fans at mosquitoes buzzing around his head, spits on the rough, partially tarred road in front of him, then looks again to Jacob for the answer.

"She say almost every day when she pan she knees scrubbin dem floor, one a de picknie dem jump pan she back." Jacob looks at Efton as if to say, "Imagine dat. All a we is nothin more than mule to dem."

He had not thought that Dacas' life in those comfortable homes, which she often bragged about – though it made her feel more dissatisfied in their own cramped, miserable quarters – was nothing more than daily abuse and self-denial. Their lot was the same, but neither took the time to acknowledge this.

It was indeed true what old people said, "De ground no level for true." He pauses, pondering the thought.

"Dat's why woman lay unda we at night time; dem is true ox wid dem roarin silence, dem lip push out like full pot a soup boilin over."

Jacob's eyes turn toward home, the matchbox-size room whose floor always glows from Dacas' efforts on her knees with a coconut-husk brush. What Jacob has been patiently waiting for is to receive his due, but now taking it is the only thing that seems practical.

Jacob has seen the backras' house, not all of it, but enough, and the maid described the rest in detail: all five bedrooms, three bathrooms, living and dining room, kitchen, large breezy front and back veranda, and a pantry almost the size of the entire one-room that he and his family occupy.

"De backra house big like de whole cane-field. Upstairs an downstairs, swimmin pool an more room fi get lost in." Jacob pauses, looks around. "Tell me, man, you think dat fair?"

It is not a question and Efton just nods his head. Then, going against everything his mother taught him, he ventures, "An dem only have two picknie?" Jacob's reply is punctuated by a gush of spit which flies through the air.

"The meek shall inherit the earth is a lie."

That's why Jacob has given up going to church; even God was not on his side. The pastor always condemning him and his kind for sinning, urging him to be more humble than he already was, telling him to bow down lower than he had already, his mouth eating dirt, never giving him credit for his patience and long-suffering, placating him with the Beatitudes about the poor and the meek inheriting the earth. Which earth was this? The man who owned him, the backra, never seem to bow down. They not only had inherited the earth, they and their kind lived like kings.

Memories merge and compete inside Jacob's head. He remembers how readily he would smile whenever the overseer was around. He didn't want to lose his job. There were too many other hands waiting to replace him. That was until he heard an overseer say that he was one of the good ones who knew his place, didn't question, gave respect; he would be especially grateful for the bonus due at the end of the crop season.

Jacob had grinned. A bonus. Rewarded for reaping a good crop. He had joined with many of the other cane-cutters who had taken off their work-stained caps, humbled themselves, their teeth showing. "Tenk you, Massa! Tenk you. You is good boss man."

They did not believe these lies that spilled out their throats, but they knew what was expected of them, so they bowed and shuffled, desperate to secure the bonus promised, the money already spent on sweets for their children, a piece of cloth for their women and a rum to knock back for themselves.

Jacob feels he can never find his face nor himself anywhere. The backras don't drink the same water – too many women and children pushing and shoving with their pots and pails to catch water from the one standpipe that often yielded only drips or sputtered in spurts. The backras didn't speak the same language. Most times he didn't understand what they said, but he knew what they felt, their eyes darting everywhere except to meet his eyes – and he heard their laughter, which sounded like a cough or a loud belch from a full stomach, and guessed that it was at his expense. Gestures like the bonus were just a way for them to ease their conscience. If he could name his grief, his anger would spill like a flood over the banks of a canal. The backras wouldn't understand; they would be surprised that he thought, that he hurt, that he reflected on his pain.

But it was mostly about the day-to-day that Jacob's anger found words. "So we a go get bonus Christmas. But wha bout now? Me woman need fi put pot pan fire today. Me picknie dem need drawers fi cova dem backside. Me back need rest. Wha bout today, now?"

Sampson had tried to pacify him. "Tek it easy, man. Fi we day a come, and soon too; we a go tek it soon, so save you sweat fi de time when it produce food."

The cane-cutters knew very little about Sampson, except that he was the strongest among them, the most able, yet also the most gentle, the most willing to share whatever he had. They admired the way he never bowed to the backras, even joking with them sometimes. At first, the men often excluded him from their private talks because he was one of the very few among them, and certainly not the youngest, who did not have a woman or any children. This marked him as different, so their admiration was mixed with reservation. For no matter that they complained about having to work hard to provide for their children and their women, their children were central to them. They were testaments to their manhood and for that they were prepared to withstand another day under the sun, bow yet again to the overseer. Most of all, the children made them believe in the possibility of change – for all their feelings that having children bonded them to labour. Their children would be that change; with children there was always hope. But Sampson did not seem to need this hope; he lived alone, cooked his own food, washed his own clothes, and did not have to answer to any woman about the money he spent on rum or gambling. Sampson challenged them. He would join them as they were quietly enjoying their meagre lunches, or during the mid afternoon when they sat shaded by the cane-stalks, humming, smoking, just dreaming of a better life, he would join them and tell them, gently yet persistently, about another estate where he'd worked where the workers had organized, demanded more wages and got them. How the workers had taken their time to cut the cane until it started to rot, and their demands were met. They'd tied up those cane-cutters who still sped along as if their very lives depended on how much cane they cut. Sampson seemed to have worked on many estates and been in the midst of several uprisings. Some of the cane-cutters had heard bits and snatches of such events, but since they did not read the newspaper, and didn't have radios, they only knew about what happened close by. But Sampson's stories fired some imaginations. There were those who thought: *If only we would do that* – and silently cursed the way they competed to see who could cut the most cane, even betting on each other from their small wages. This, though, they no longer did since that time they'd bet on Sampson against another cutter, Nesta. Sampson found out and refused to cut cane that day, which led to a big fight in the fields. That was the first and only time they saw him angry; he shouted at them that the backras had a right to cheat them since they didn't have sense enough to help each other.

Now at lunch or afternoon break, they spoke less of their endless woes, their women, their children and more of how to get more wages, who should approach the backras, how to get all the cutters to agree to go slow. During these talks, Sampson was always present, seemingly on the periphery, but guiding the discussion, and if they stumbled or drifted, his quiet but firm voice could be counted on to refocus them. Lately, though, Sampson was speaking less, and Jacob more, so that it was agreed that Jacob should be the one to speak to the backra on their behalf. Sampson encouraged Jacob to take the lead.

Although Jacob did not know the reason for Sampson's pain, he was the only one who saw the sadness that often crept in his eyes, and the tremble of his lips. What Sampson had told no one was that once his life had been no different from theirs. He started as a boy of eight cutting the small patch of cane that his family grew on their few acres of land, but as the children grew there was less food to feed the family so the older boys all drifted away to find jobs. Sampson had been walking on the road, when a truck loaded with men pulled alongside him and the driver asked him if he knew how to cut cane, and if he wanted to work. He said yes, and joined the other young men in the back of the truck. That had begun his life almost thirty years ago when he was fifteen. Like all the other young men, he'd had several girls, until he met Nicey, a strapping girl, brown like wet sugar, who was also a cane-cutter. They fell in love, set up house and were looking forward to a family. But one day a fight began in the field between Nicey and another woman about who had cut the largest heap of cane. Soon they were tearing at each other's clothes. When the other woman saw that Nicey was getting the better of her, she ran for her machete, hoisted it and slashed away Nicey's arm at the shoulder. Sampson was far away in another part of the field. By the time he arrived, his sweetheart lay bathed in blood. No overseer or backra was around. No vehicle, not even a donkey cart was available. By the time the men made a makeshift stretcher and started for the nearest clinic fifteen miles away Nicey was close to death. Even jogging at top speed, five miles into their journey she bled to death, her severed arm coming loose from the cloth that was holding it in place. That was the last time Sampson cried. He bawled for days, unashamed. The cane-cutter who had killed Nicey got ten lashes with the cat-o-nine-tail switch and ninety days' hard labour. It was then that Sampson quietly began organizing the cane-cutters, urging them to redirect their anger and channel their energies for their own benefit.

Jacob knew none of this, but as he and Efton neared home, having walked almost six miles, he was thinking about what Sampson had told them. It stirred him, and though he felt he still didn't have the words to speak, he wanted to talk and be listened to.

He thinks about the weapons they have: sharp blades which can slice heads from necks, limbs from bodies. He recalls limbs lost over a threepence borrowed and not repaid, over insinuations against someone's woman or just teasing to release tension. But why turn their anger on each other? His palm itches where the machete has made contact with his skin. "Why we mus always cut-up one anoder over nutten?"

Nearing home, Jacob thinks about how Dacas will greet him. She is his only love, yet the moment he walks in the yard, he can be sure a frown will crease her forehead and her lips will move, not in greeting but rapid exclamation. Still he can't complain; she always manages to cook him a piece of yam, a little salt-fish simmered in plenty Puritan oil with onions and thyme the way he likes it. He appreciates her, but the words are not there, and often when he tries to show it through gesture, his strong hands fall hard on her and she shoves him away, complaining and pleading, "Why you must be so rough, Jacob?"

Every time he opens his mouth to say, *Is cause me want touch you, feel you*, nothing comes out. It isn't easy to feel her; her skin isn't like the cane whose fibrous tegument is rough against his hand. So he has to grab her firmly, trying to get under her skin so she will know he loves her; but when they are through he mostly feels they are no better than dogs in heat pumping each other.

They pass a dead goat. Jacob spits; the stench of decaying flesh in his nostrils. "Evryting in me life is like de damn yard me cage in."

He surveys the tenement yard with its slimy gutters, and many children always playing the fool, seeming as multitudinous to their parents as the John-crows that clamour over the remains of dead animals.

"Chups!" Jacob and Efton kiss their teeth. "If is not dead dog, is a puss or goat. Rich people in dem motor car no care dat animal is de poor man riches."

Jacob takes out his cloth, stained with cane-juice, perspiration, and blood, and wipes his face; Efton does likewise.

Jacob has so much to say, so much he wants to explain to his fellow cane-cutters, to Dacas, and even to the overseers and the backras. How can he explain his suffering if the backras pretend to not see it, refuse to share it? How can he shape his words, cut them clear out of the confusion that surrounds him? Where can he find the privacy and peace to do that? In the tenement yard, his children sleep in the same room with he and Dacas, seeing and hearing them at it, at everything. Where is the place where he can go to find his voice? Yet, Jacob knows that he must begin to speak with Dacas who is closest to him, the one most inclined to listen to him, even if she misconstrues what he says as mere complaining. He has to try and explain it to her, tell someone before he explodes, for then it will be too late.

Jacob counts a flock of birds – nine of them including the leader – in a formation like the base of a sling-shot, awesome against the pink sky.

"Fly, fly little black birds, fly home to rest..."

He hears the children in the yard singing this song as he watches the birds. He raises his tattered felt hat (a gift from one of the overseers for his hard work) in salute to the birds, regretting that he isn't one of them. He's the one left behind because of its broken wing. He points to them. "You see dem birds; dem fly for food; we walk fah bread."

Jacob realizes that they are near Mister Thomas' bar. "Walk up, man," Sampson, the lion of a cane-cutter, shouts back to Jacob and Efton. "Walk up if you want fi off a flask wid me."

Jacob can already feel the sting of the over-proof white rum gliding down his throat, sending a momentary fire in his belly. He must ease his mind, drink his pain calm, though he can hear Dacas accusing – *Jacob, you mean you drink off the little money?* – her lips going like bees maddened by the scent of sugar. He wants to resist, but does not. A few of the cane-cutters continue towards home, but Jacob, Sampson and Efton and the others turn into the shack-bar which is already packed with men. Entering, they raise their caps to swipe the sweat that has tangled their matted, dust-filled hair.

Grumbles, salutes, shifting of chairs, banging of dominoes greet them and, of course, the smell of rum, raw and powerful. Jacob is suddenly bothered by a familiar stench of the bar so he seats himself away from the midst of the activities, calling attention to himself in the small, tightly packed room. Sitting alone, he feels the men's eyes on him – like he's sipping his rum like a woman who can't hold her liquor.

"Wha de rass oonu lookin pan?" he hisses like a wasp stinging an innocent bystander. The men bang their dominoes loud, gulp their rum. Occasionally, they steal glances at Jacob, cautioning him to not force them, this Friday evening, to look at themselves, at their lives. They want him to join them in drinking, in denial, in blocking their pain, in oblivion.

Wha mek you must question
an cause trouble fah all a we?
Wha mek you must question
an force we hand?
Bite you lip
Bite out you tongue
Mek de day end happy
Mek de day end as always.

But Jacob refuses to let himself or the other cane-cutters off the hook. When was it that a day of theirs ended happily? Sampson sits back observing the men, confident that Jacob cannot be stopped now; he will not turn back and run.

"Oonu no understan. Me nah drink out de last two shillings so me 'oman can cuss me how me wutliss."

It's out. An accusation directed at all of them, but it also provides relief. The men stare openly at Jacob, for a moment their dominoes and rum glasses held in mid air. They know how hard it is to go home to the slime-green yards where bickering is the only thing guaranteed to be in abundance. Jacob gazes into his empty glass. Sampson nods at Jacob who takes heart. He gets up and stands with his back to the bar.

"All a we deserve more dan we been getting. We men. We deserve a honest day pay for a hard day labour. We no wutliss. We no lazy. We men, and we wuk hard. We deserve more." Jacob walks back to his seat; the men are quiet, deep in thought; no joke interrupts the mood. Sampson, not having a woman of his own to go home to, makes a generous gesture toward Jacob.

"Broda T, pass anoda half flask; put it unda me name in you book."

Jacob gulps down the offering, until the tension in his back from the bend-down, rise-up, pile-and-load cane in ganuh tractors for factory bound, bend-down, rise-up-till-you-tumble-down dance disappears. He relaxes and for a moment enjoys the brutality of his life. Suddenly, he craves a scoop of wet sugar eaten from his palm. The men resume their domino playing, rum drinking and friendly bantering, although their tone is less boisterous.

Jacob rises from the table, violently pushing back the old wobbly chair, causing it to fall on the ground, ringing a warning through the bar. The rum working on his bladder forces him to go and piss on the side wall next to the lot of land the community has taken over for the pasturing of goats and cows. It all adds to the stench of the bar. As Jacob pisses he spits in disgust and swears at himself, and others like him, "Nega wutliss, sah!" But for the first time he doesn't really believe what he says. All his life he has been told how worthless he and others like him are so that words like these come easily to his mouth. But Jacob knows, with the rum spreading fire through his body, that he is no more a no-good scoundrel than are the other men in the bar. They work hard, six days a week, from sunrise to sunset. Though they often drink too much come Friday night, it is the only time that they are permitted a moment's idleness, an opportunity to celebrate their lives.

He re-enters the bar, thanks Sampson and Efton, then heads home. His life is like a huge pile of cane-stalks that must be heaped up in a tractor then taken to the factory to be ground into cane juice. Oh, to be such sweetness, without any bitter aftertaste.

As he greets the night, Sampson shouts after him, "We de children of Israel, Broda Jacob; we de children." Sampson and Efton head in the opposite direction.

At last the humming that has been travelling through his body takes form and reverberates inside his head.

Hang down you head, poor workers,
Hand down you head and bawl
Hang down you head, poor workers,
Good boy you not gwane die!

Jacob rambles on, oblivious to the starless night and the stagnant air, which sticks to his skin like a cobweb. Gradually the tune changes before he is even aware of the words he sings.

Raise up your arms, cane-cutters,
raise up your arms and reap.
Raise up your arms, cane-cutters,
stand up for what you reap.

Jacob stops by a roadside Revival meeting with the devotees

dressed in long, white, gathered-waist skirts and shirts with blue sashes wound around their waists and turbans on their heads. Tonight Jacob, too, will be saved. He joins in the circle, everyone holding each other around the waist, as they urge the spirits to come and lead them – give them directions out of the wickedness into which they had been thrown, and in which they have wandered much, much too long. At first in jest, Jacob follows the devotees, then a force sweeps through his body and he convulses, reeling around the circle, his head heavy as a ganuh tractor loaded with cane. His spirit surges and bubbles like boiling molasses, and his possession becomes a dance, more buoyant than his tiresome bend-down, rise-up toil.

The Mother and officers of the bands see Jacob is travelling and gradually guide him to the centre of the circle. The women with tambourines beat them against their thighs which immediately begin to prickle. The other devotees clap their hands, pound their feet, moving only the upper half of their bodies. The meeting has truly begun. Jacob weaves in and out of the circle of worshippers; agile and sinewy; he is the Cutter. Then Jacob's movement changes and the Shepherd sees that Jacob has become the Hunter. He brandishes his machete, and water and rum are poured on the ground in front of his feet. Calm, swaying from side to side, the Shepherd declares in a firm, monotonous voice, "Blessed are de poor in spirit..." The Hunter seizes the words and reworks them, "Blessed are de poor in spirit, but de brave in deeds..." The phrase seems incomplete, and the wind takes up the words, and together the Hunter and the wind fling those words at the devotees, "Blessed are de poor in spirit, but de brave in deeds..." and immediately the devotees respond, "For de land dat dey work will be deirs." On and on the Hunter and the devotees talk to each other. The Hunter's voice is like the baying of a goat. He bays, "Blessed are the merciful" and the devotees intone, "We are de merciful, and we'll not cast a hand against those who have done us no wrong." On and on they converse, the Hunter raising a chant that the devotees pick up and play with until it becomes a new song, until light starts to sneak through the darkness. Then the Hunter gathers his knife and his goatskin clothes and enters the bushes and the devotees turn to each other in wonder. Never before had a spirit so strong come amongst them for such a long time. They disperse without their usual closing ritual, but all go to rest their hands on Jacob's shoulder before stumbling home.

Finally, Jacob is relieved of the Hunter's spirit, and his body is returned to him. He saunters home drenched but feeling energized. Dacas is in bed and the room is suffocating with the loud smell of bay rum. From the sound of her breathing, Jacob knows she isn't sleeping, but much about her presence tells him to tread cautiously, that tonight she is an iron left on the stove too long. Although the fire is cold, the kerosene from the one-burner competes to perfume the room. Jacob's fingers open and close, he cracks his knuckles noisily. Dacas turns on her side, her face to the wall. Jacob looks around and meets a surprising glow of white, the wide-open eyes of his third son staring out at him from the dark, too bold to feign sleep. Jacob feels the blood travelling through his veins; he shouts in the dark, "Me did wuk hard. When me cup gwane run over?"

Dacas turns to him, conciliatory: "Come to bed. Nuh wake de picknie dem."

Jacob will not be stilled tonight; his voice echoes on and Dacas sits up in bed, her arms folded over her breasts.

Perhaps if he hadn't seen the shiny gadgets that the backras have in their homes he wouldn't feel so cheated. He wasn't allowed inside the backras' house, although they permit him to eat in the kitchen on a chair by the back door. One day he could not help himself. When Pauline, the maid, was summoned upstairs by the missus, he'd ventured into the rest of the house, gingerly craning his neck into the dining room, astonished at all he saw, not recognizing most of what his eyes beheld or their functions. Everything looked shiny, brand new. There was lots of space; everything smelled wholesome like when he visited the country, especially after an early morning shower and the earth was bathed in the luxury of clean water. Then he understood why most evenings Dacas seemed vexed with the world. Why shouldn't she, after working all day in a world so different from her own? Why shouldn't she think him worthless if all his efforts could not provide her with a place remotely like the one in which she was forced to slave? As he looked, pain took hold of his body and he could not will his feet to move, not even when he heard Pauline coming and saw her surprised look at seeing him standing there. He had glimpsed another world. But how did the backras possess it? They did not work nearly as hard as he did. In fact he'd never seen them raise their hands, except to enforce their orders, and while it might be true that running an estate took a great deal of skill – which he envied – Jacob knew that if it weren't for his muscles and sweat, the estate would close down and all the backras' fancy talk and education would not yield a pound of sugar. Pauline must have read his thoughts because she shoved him roughly and shouted at him, "So wha you did expect, bruk-down junk like we have?" For a minute they had both forgotten where they were until the madam's voice jarred them back. Pauline's and Jacob's relationship was never the same again. She took to putting the chair outside the kitchen door, and handing him his food without so much as a *Here*.

Dacas brings Jacob back to the present. "You not content fi come home late like you is sportin, boy, you have fi wake up de baby an de boys dem." She thrusts out her arms in the direction of the children, the four boys cramped on the three-quarter bed against the other wall. As if on cue, eight eyes open and seek him. The baby on the bed beside Dacas lets out a shriek. Jacob feels terribly wronged by Dacas' accusation, and stomps loudly on the floor. "Alright, mek we done wid it dis night."

He orders the children to sit up in bed. They look pleadingly at their mother, then turn to their father and sit up, rubbing their eyes, looking down at the bed, afraid, not sure what they have done or what their fate will be. Jacob pulls off his shirt, winds it, then tosses it on the small table where his dinner is neatly covered with a towel. He flaps on the bed and it creaks with his weight. Dacas chups and shifts her position, her eyes boring into him. He turns from her and meets the gaze of Arnold, his second to oldest son.

"You think me wutliss, boy?"

Before Dacas can cut in, Arnold responds firmly, "No, Daddy. How you fi wutliss when you an Mama wuk so hard." Jacob smiles, beckons Arnold to bring him his plate of food. He picks at the boiled banana and pumpkin with his fingers, then hands it to his sons. They are all suddenly awake and dive into the food with relish. Dacas scrambles out of bed and brings him the drink, sitting covered on the table. The ice has melted, so the top is watery, but he savours the rich milky taste of the sour-sop flavoured with lime. He smiles at Dacas and reaches for her hand. She stands silently in front of him, and he holds her hand while he drains the glass, and a new feeling, of having power, or at least of being in control, surges through him. Dacas smiles at him, takes the glass and puts it on the table, then climbs back into bed.

She turns to her sons: "Hurry up and eat, and wipe oonuh hand so ants don't bite oonuh tonight."

Jacob washes his face in the basin of water set aside for him, then takes the wash-rag and wipes his upper body before climbing into bed. Dacas places the baby in the corner and snuggles close to his back. He hears the strained breathing of his sons, and falls immediately asleep.

With morning comes the sun, along with a little hope. The rooster crows and as always Dacas manages to get out of bed without waking Jacob. Later, he sits on the step in front of his room and watches his children. He is about to scold them for being late, but remembers that it's Saturday. The baby, not yet a year, plays in the swept-dirt yard with her brothers. He smiles remembering how happy Dacas was that they finally had a girl, but how quick she was to point out to him that she loved their sons. Jacob closes his eyes at the sun, leans his head against the doorframe and dozes.

He recalls himself, like his children, dressed in khaki uniform, barefoot, walking four miles to school, clutching his broken slate and piece of lead-pencil, arriving just in time for the nine o'clock bell, but too tired and hungry to learn anything, his thoughts on the government lunch of powered milk and coco-bread.

Dacas was sixteen and Jacob almost eighteen when they met. Jacob was walking to his barracks room with a small bundle of cane on his head when she stopped him and begged him for a piece. He'd looked her up and down, and she had not quailed at his stare but met his eyes with her own bold assessment. So he had leant his small bundle of cane beside the fence, and fished for the sweetest piece which he peeled with his machete and handed to her. He'd expected her to say thanks and continue on her way, but she stood in front of him and declared, "Nobody go anywhere if it nuh sweet; me a go gi you back." She bit into the cane and juice ran down her chin and arm. Jacob noticed that her teeth were strong and even, as white as the whites of her eyes. He didn't see her again until the end of the crop season. He was heading towards the bar with some other cane-cutters, and she was sitting by the side of the road on a mound of cut stones with two other girls. They were eating cane, the juice leaving sticky white streaks on their chins and arms. That evening, as he left the bar, he saw her leaning against the fence. She called to him.

Dacas' mother always told her she was too bold for a girl child, but she didn't nag her or insist that she change. Instead, she left her, for the most part, to her own fate. Dacas didn't know what she wanted to do with her life, never entertained any such thoughts; she lived from one day to the next, eating cane and playing with her friends and the younger children, even after her mother told her it was time to be done with playing.

She had seen Jacob many times during the crop season when she went to live with her mother's sister on the estate. Her mother was tired of Dacas doing nothing but playing and wandering about, so sent her to her sister whom she hoped would have better luck teaching her child some womanly skills. But her sister had no luck, or maybe didn't try hard, so Dacas was left to wander and play with the other idle girls on the estate.

She often followed Jacob, though he didn't know it. But after that first time she stopped him for a piece of his cane, as a bet with her friends, she began to pursue him with a different interest in mind. A successful pursuit. When she found out she was pregnant she told him he had to go to her mother and ask for her, and that was how they got together.

Her voice pulls him into the present. He wipes the tears that have filled his eyes, threatening to overwhelm him. He picks up the baby to tidy her at Dacas' request. As he walks off with the baby, his hand ruffles his oldest son's hair. This is not the life he wants for them. Will they too have to end their schooling before sixth standard? Will they toil under the sun, day in, day out, with only a few coins to show for their effort? This is not what he wants for his children; they will have more.

Dacas calls them for their mid-morning breakfast of bread and butter and hot cocoa, and they gather around the small table in their small, dark room, and gulp the slim portion of food in silence, avoiding each other's eyes. Jacob senses that Dacas is embarrassed, ashamed to place such a meagre lot before hungry, growing children, and this realization makes him angry that he is unable to do more, even though his back is sore and his hands are calloused. If only he could to say to her, "Here is money. Go buy de children sardine or cheese fi have wid de bread." The children, through with their breakfast, run outside to join the other children, who are jumping and prancing all over the place, romping to ignore the hunger knocking at their stomachs. Jacob helps Dacas gather the cups and plates; their hands brush. Jacob looks at Dacas and her arms reach around his neck, stopping halfway in an awkward embrace. He holds her at her waist and massages her; she sniffles and he looks her square in the eyes.

"It won't always be like dis; betta gwane come; we gwane mek it." She half smiles, the reality of their existence making it hard for her to accept his optimism; the promise is too old, has been made too many times in the past.

Sampson's shouting for Jacob rescues them both, Jacob from witnessing Dacas' fading smile, and she from taking the strength away from his conviction.

Jacob takes his machete from behind the bed, dons his tattered hat and goes to join Sampson.

"So wha appen, man?" Sampson calls. "Today we gwane wuk for weself; today is fi we time." They walk for a mile in silence, then Sampson stops Jacob and pulls from his pocket a worn yellow piece of paper. "Ah wan share dis wid you," Sampson says, pulling Jacob close to him. "Is a poem a man give me a few years back." Sampson unfolds the paper with great care, and the voice that reads the words is a practised voice, full of passion, a voice that Jacob has not heard before.

CANE-CUTTERS

Sweat fertilizes soil
Machetes are hoisted
Machetes slash down
Sweetness plaited in stalks
Cane is tossed
Cane lands on a heap

Acres of bursting cane
Led astray by the breeze
Cane fields of fecundity
Like ebony-skin women whose breasts,
Hard with milk, seep freely,
Blending with cane juice

No faces
But eyes sunk into the earth
Bent backs and
Ragged handkerchiefs
Stained with sweat
Cling to heads
Their song appears monotonous
But to ears that listen
To the melody sung in the key of burden

Wagons loaded with cane
Lumber along narrow, dusty roads
Bees buzz, buzz, buzz around,
Suck at sweet succulents
Boy-child, being his own bold self,
Feeling the rod of manhood in his crotch
Hops wagon to steal sugar
Boy-child slips
Wheel gets hold of leg
Grinds flesh into the patterns of the dust

Bodies rise and bend again
Bowels are clamorous
Donkeys bearing load, bray, bray, bray
March unwillingly
Bleeding hearts paint a line of labour
Child hops, falls, leg gets kneaded
Cane stalks borne on their heads
Cane stalk, a stepchild hitched to their sides

Another wagon loaded
Another journey begun
Faces of drunken smiles
Become the pattern rolled into the earth
By wagons' wheels.

Jacob smiles and caresses the machete in his hand. There is
nothing he has to say to Sampson. Sampson sees the impact the
poem has on Jacob. Jacob doesn't understand a good many of the
words, but he feels the passion; he has been living that life. Jacob
takes the sheet from Sampson's hands, looks down at it. Looks at
Sampson, then looks at his hands and at his machete. He understands. There is no need to tell Sampson what happened to him
last night at the Revival meeting. Sampson already knows. Jacob
folds up the sheet and hands it back to Sampson and they walk on.

They reach the first leg of their walk, and Jacob sees the rest of
the men lolling by the canal. Sampson salutes them, then runs his
hand in the cool canal water, morass sprouting around its sides.
All the men, as if on signal, wet their rags and wipe their faces. It
will be another day that stings like tamarind switch on wet skin.
Jacob submerges his face like a dog lapping; he gargles, coughs up
and spits out the dryness pasted in his throat. The cane-cutters
stand silently by the canal. Efton walks over to join Jacob and
Sampson. A Land Rover speeds by; a pink hand waves; a trail of
dust lingers. No black hand reaches out in reciprocal salute.

As the dirt settles, Jacob begins the song that found him last
night when he left the bar. At first his lone voice mocks him in the
already fierce sun of the mid-morning, but soon Efton and
Sampson pick up the tune and strong baritone voices shape the

song as they head down the road, shut in on both sides by cane-fields. Their voices dare a chorus of triumph that floats in the wind.

They smell the sugar that sweetens their limeade, they smell the sugar that covers their sweet potato pudding, they taste the sugar that fires their rum, they taste the brown sugar that bustles their energy in the middle of the day, they feel the cool wet sugar juices of their women's mouths.

Theirs was not a plan, voiced and carefully worked out; theirs was an outburst fed by deep bowels of need, the vision they have for their children, the affirmation of their manhood and their right to more than the dregs. No more patience. Today their dance moves from the plains of the cane-fields; new steps will be added. Their stage will be the hills.

Jacob is the lead dancer. Efton at his heels. Sampson brings up the rear. Today they are heading for the houses of the Whites perched on the hill like sentries. Clad in faded khaki, edged with plaid or some other variegated rags, black to purple-coloured bodies prance around, creating new dance steps, steps which will be remembered for a long time to come.

Jacob's movements are strong, his motion firm.

He sees again Arnold's eyes in the dark of last night. This is for his son's future. In a lightning motion he splits through cane, flesh and bone. His left hand holds the disjointed stalk-limb, looks at it, shudders, before tossing it on the heap where others are piled.

Swish, swish, swish, machetes slice away. Swish, swish, swish, skin is ripped from body, flesh leaves bone, blood runs syrupy, sticking to hands.

Swish, swish, swish, the dance climaxes.

Jacob, Sampson and Efton move like a troupe of dancers.

Swish, swish, swish, a herd of buffaloes. Swish, swish, swish. Cane falls. Backras cower. Blood runs syrupy, spraying their lips, clothes, eyes. Jacob dances. All the cane-cutters dance, their machetes flying through the air, sure, directed, freedoming.

They are blackbirds flying home to rest, their black plumage dazzling in the sky.

Look homeward, cane-cutters, look homeward to rest.

Jacob's face wears a contorted smile.

The sun reaches the clouds.

Swish, swish, swish; the moon sings a lullaby.

Swish, swish.

Look homeward, cane-cutters, raise up your arms and reap what you sow.

Swish, swish.

The tired dance dies.

White houses on the hill are washed red, and only the shrieking birds punctuate the silence.

Bodies in a heap; flies buzz; John-crow circle. Look homeward, cane-cutters, homeward. Swish, swish.

Jacob examines the red-stained machetes. The canal water runneth over. Blood. Those who work will eat, swish. The workers will inherit the land, swish; look homeward, cane-cutters, swish; look homeward, swish.

A new day.

Swish.

TEACHMENT II:

"Judge a man by how he treats his family." That's another of Papa's sayings, and Papa always treated me like I was the first and last Julie Mango on the tree that everybody want.

Maybe because I didn't have a mama or papa that's why I live by myself. I like my own company best. I don't want any children. Suppose I go off and die or them father go foreign look work and die, then them end up just like me, well worse, alone because Papa dead now. No sir. I am just fine by myself. I don't have to answer to a soul but the Almighty, and that isn't for a long time to come. Still I welcome the new folks that move in the community.

After about ten years, as I say, folks start to move in this place like birds flying home to roost at night. Mostly groups of family, each building a house, some starting with one bedroom and expanding over the years, others move in even before the house complete. Nice houses going up about the place, painted pretty colours, sky-blue, lizard-green and hibiscus-yellow; people putting in gardens, bringing dogs, even goat and cows to graze in the empty bush-lots that still about the place.

I always had chickens that I raised, and since I have two lots, I had my garden where I grow callaloo, gungo peas and sorrel, so everyone know me as the egg and callaloo woman or in Christmas season as the sorrel and gungo lady. This way I come to know everybody and they know me. Since I grow up where everyone know everyone, I make it a point to find out who move in the area. If you don't know your neighbours, you could be living right next to a thief and not even know. So whenever I see a house going up,

I ask, and when the family move in, I bring them eggs, and red-ginger from my garden.

Edmond and his family move in right behind me. A nice loud family. His wife fat and laugh plenty. Edmond go to civil servant work every morning in white shirt. He is the reason I start to sell the *Gleaner*. I hear him complaining to his wife that she insist that they move to this bush, where he can't even get the *Gleaner* to read. So the next week, I take the bus to town and inquire how I could get to sell the *Gleaner*. A month later, I begin selling the paper to Edmond, every day, and so we get to talk.

For a long time he wasn't happy with his life. He put me in mind of a man who go to the beach in long pants to swim, then complain that him pants get wet. I ask him if he didn't know his wife voice loud before him marry her. Him say yes. I ask him, if she did laaffy-laaffy when him was courting her. Him smile and say yes. I ask him if he was quiet when him was a little boy. Him say no. I ask him if him ever know children quiet, except when them sick. Him say no. So I don't ask him anything else. Him stand up there in front of me scratching him head like him have lice. I tell you, sometimes smart people act like them don't have common sense.

Is which family you know that is perfect?

DE MYAL MAN
A Folktale Retold

Liming by *Good Feelings Bar*, Lionel sees Edmond approaching. "How yuh doing, man? Long time no see."

"Ah just passing; busy you know," Edmond replies, stopping beside Lionel.

"Is who you fooling, man? Everybody know you done put on Bermuda short and slippers. Married in yuh bone, man. It mashup yuh actions," Lionel teases, hitting his friend soundly on the shoulder.

"Come, lemme buy you a Red Stripe," Edmond says, turning inside the bar.

"Now yuh talking," Lionel grins, throwing his arm over his friend's shoulder.

The men enter the rum shop and Edmond buys two beers. Lionel spots an empty table in the corner furthest from the door. They hasten over before someone beats them to it and collapse in the chairs. Immediately, Lionel gulps down his beer, then glances around as if searching for someone. He nods to everyone who enters, hails several other men at tables, verbal sparring followed by ruckus laughter. Edmond nurses his beer, his eyes fixed on the table, apparently preoccupied.

"Wha do yuh, man?" Lionel asks, turning his attention to Edmond, but doesn't give him a chance to respond. "Yuh nursing yuh beer like woman? Drink up, me will buy de next round." He bangs the empty bottle on the wooden table. Edmond attempts to down his beer, but when he shakes it he realizes that it is still half full. Lionel sucks his teeth, and moves to the bar, loudly ribbing the bartender even before he is by the counter.

"Vince, you moving like starch in yuh hands. Wha happen, yuh wake up on de wrong side of de bed dis morning? Shake a leg, man!" Lionel waits his turn to be served, but keeps a running commentary going. "Come, come Vince, gimme two Stripes. Is not restaurant dis, man, so keep de juice flowing." Vince is accustomed to Lionel so ignores his comments. After a while, he pushes two beers towards Lionel, saying, "Mek sure yuh pocket can keep up wid yuh mouth."

"How you mean?" Lionel responds indignantly, taking the beers and turning from the counter. As he rejoins Edmond, he stops to observe the checker game going on in the middle of the room. He chuckles as he looks at the board: careless moves by the imminent loser; the game is almost over, the winner having retained all but two of his opponent's men. Lionel is humming, "Hill and gully ride o, hill and gully."

"Wait! Yuh still a nurse de beer?" he accuses Edmond even before he is seated. "Heavy load mus fall down pan yuh head, man." He quietly places the bottles on the table, and his face relaxes, the merriment wiped from his eyes and his jaws slack. He pulls his chair closer to Edmond and asks confidentially:

"So wha de story, man? Wha bring yuh to dis joint dis evening?"

Edmond is staring into the narrow mouth of the beer bottle as if searching for something that fell in. His body is held tightly like planks of board, stacked and tied together to be shipped. The many voices, clanking of bottles and glasses, banging of dominoes and checker pieces grate on Edmond's nerves. Lionel taps on the table, anxious for Edmond to confide in him, but he understands Edmond well enough. Edmond needs time to collect his thoughts before he speaks. Lionel twirls the beer bottle between his hands, waiting. When at last Edmond talks, his voice has the rushing flow of an undammed stream.

"Yuh know a love de wife and de three picknie dem and dem dogs, parrot and coop full of fowls, pigeons and rabbits. But wid all of dem around me kyan get any work done. Noise all de time. De picknie dem always playing wild, fighting and screaming; de TV always going, mostly watching itself; de dogs barking; de fowl dem clucking. Noise all de time. Me kyan think, me kyan get any work done." Edmond glances at Lionel to see if he is listening. Assured, he continues. "Ah tell yuh in confidence, man, most days a feel like a gwane go mad. De truth is, me need a new life; me need quiet." Edmond puts the beer to his mouth and drains it. As he places the empty bottle on the table, Lionel pushes the new bottle towards him. Edmond nods thanks, keeping his eyes focused on the table.

Lionel tilts back his chair, holding his beer in front of his spare-tire belly. He rocks in the chair, tilted precariously on its rear legs, and stares squarely at Edmond, his friend for more than ten years. They are very different. Lionel lives life to the fullest, relishing every moment, no matter how mundane. Edmond's life is tempered by his intense, sombre personality. He seems afraid to laugh or joke around. Lionel feels that his friend is unable to appreciate the very things he claims to love. He gazes at Edmond until their eyes meet, acknowledging each other. Edmond is the first to avert his eyes. Lionel decides the situation demands a parable.

"Well a have a story fi tell you, man." Lionel's voice, even and serious, penetrates Edmond's ear. "Yuh wan hear it?"

Edmond seems to consider the idea, shrugs his shoulders then nods his head.

"Alright. Ah so it go." Lionel positions the chair to rest against the wall on its rear legs; settles comfortably. He clears his throat, takes a swallow of the beer, belches, excuses himself, then begins.

"Not so long, but longish time, a man by de name of Obadiah was married and had three pretty, pretty picknies. Him wife not too bad in de looks department either and she talented bad. She was in choir; she play piano; she actress; she have professional job; she involve wid de picknie dem school; she jus in nuff-nuff tings. All time of de day, people call-call or drop by and laughta bruk out, and plenty-plenty chatting up in de place. Same wid Obadiah picknie dem; dem ave nuff-nuff friends who dem always invite fi play in dem yard; dem in an out de house; dem in and out de fridge; dem shout-shout and run-run thru de house. Dem jus nuff-nuff like dem moda. And to mek matters worst, one of dem dog was fool-fool; every little ting pass by de gate, even if leaf drop off tree, de dog would bark-bark, all day and night, and chase afta its own tail."

Lionel pauses to see if his friend is paying attention to the story. As he swallows a mouthful of beer, he is aware that, as usual, he has attracted an audience; several other drinkers have stopped their talking and have turned their chairs in Lionel's direction. When Lionel glances at Edmond, he notices perspiration has begun to form on his face, reposed in concentrated thoughtfulness. Lionel continues with the story.

"Now Obadiah did love him family bad, but dem was just de opposite of him. Whereas dem was loud and always had to be doing someting, Obadiah's greatest pleasure was to sit in a quiet spot and read and think. Him was always asking him wife why she always have fi run-run all ova de place all de time. Obadiah was a simple and private man who jus wanted peace, but no place him go in de house could him get peace, not even when him go fi ease himself. Always, one a de picknie dem would bang pan de door, bawling how dem wan pee-pee or dem need fi wash dem hand or get Band-Aid. No peace. Imagine that – a man can't find peace in his home. So naturally Obadiah get resentful and after a while him get frustrated and get well vex. Well, dis go on fah several years until Obadiah decide him can't tek no more.

"So one nite, after everybody fall asleep, Obadiah get up, get a glass of water, light a candle and sidown pan de floor an listen to him inner voice, trying fi figa out wha fi do bout de confusion dat was him life. De answer come to him quick-quick; him would go look up de myal man down de road. After all, Obadiah reasoned, de myal man, being a healer and in touch wid de ancestors, bound fi help him solve him problem widout causing him family too much pain.

"So de next evening when whole heap a people pile up in Obadiah living room, and him backyard full a picknie, some ah dem him neva see yet, and him couldn't even get a cool glass a wata cause de picknie dem just go-go in de fridge and drink off all de cool water, Obadiah pull on him cap and step quietly out de side gate. No one miss him, but Obadiah keep looking behind as if him expect someone to come running after him, demanding that him tek care of one or more of dem needs. But no one follow Obadiah, so after a while him settle widin himself, whistling as him walk de mile and half and go knock pan de myal man's door."

Edmond sits enraptured with Lionel's story. His elbows rest on the table like two columns that cradle his face. His brow is knitted and he chews on the inside of his bottom lip. *Like Lionel able to read me life?* Edmond pushes the thought from his mind, yet it remains like fibre threads of mango trapped between his teeth. *Obadiah sound like me twin*, he muses, but anxious to hear the outcome of Obadiah's journey, he urges Lionel on.

"So was de myal man home when Obadiah get there?" Edmond asks.

"Yuh listenin! Good," Lionel says seriously.

"But how you mean?" a chorus of men say almost in unison.

"Nuh boda wid you pantomime tonite, Lionel," shouts Vince, the bartender.

"De story a go on good, so lewwe pickup when Obadiah reach de myal man's house."

Lionel stretches, looks around at the men, some standing to the side of him, others seated, glasses and bottles held slackly in their hands, almost forgotten. Their attentiveness causes a smile to tickle his heart, but he is too humble to allow it to travel to his face. He studies Edmond's face briefly, then continues.

"De myal man did name Silence Reigns; him head did flat pan de top and de sides shape like avocado. Him did have a hawk nose, and him skin was purple-blue and shiny like every morning someone rub polish all ova him skin, den shine it wid coconut-brush. Obadiah push de myal man's gate and greet him wid plenty-plenty respect. Him apologize fah coming afta dinna bout business, but Obadiah said him was desperate and him just couldn't tek him life any more.

"Silence Reigns study Obadiah openly, him hands plaiting and unplaiting him braid as him did so. But while de myal man was studying Obadiah, Obadiah faget bout de myal man cause gradually him realize him was hearing what him hadn't heard in far too many years – de sound of serenity. Obadiah was hearing silence, and it sound sweet like guava cheese. Obadiah settle comfortably in de silence; it ease him stress; so him settle in de chair pan de myal man's veranda and a get ready fi fall asleep. Not a happier man dan Obadiah was dere at dat moment.

"De myal man recognize what a go on. Him figure out what

Obadiah did come beg him, but de myal man decide fi wait. Him mek Obadiah enjoy de peace and quiet a little while, den Silence Reigns seh to Obadiah, 'Wha boderin yuh, man? Speak yuh mind.'

"Instantly Obadiah felt self-conscious and awkward. Being a very careful man who liked to be fair and give all details, Obadiah start long story. Him tell de myal man how long him married, weh him meet him wife, when de first, second and third picknie did born and all de circumstance leading up to dem birth. Den Obadiah tell Silence Reigns what been happening in him job, and how him nuh have no time fi spend wid him wife cause she always busy-busy and she have nuff-nuff friends and how de picknie dem demanding and how none of dem like de same food, so him always have fi cook three or four different pot every evening, and how him can't even find a piece of a time fi practice him drums or write him poetry. On and on Obadiah chat, going on about horse dead and cow fat. By dis time star full up de sky and Silence Reigns realize if him no cut Obadiah short him could be out dere pan de veranda until dew fall pan him head and him catch cold and fall dead. So de myal man hold up him hand and stop Obadiah. 'So what you want me do bout yuh life? And mek it short.'

"Obadiah, being real sensitive, start to apologize fah going on fah two whole hours widout getting to de point. Him well embarrassed, especially since him member dat him and his wife quarrel cause she always complain dat him long-winded like kite string and neva get to de point. Anyway him catch himself going on again, and it did only tek Obadiah fifteen minutes to apologize. Finally, Obadiah seh to de myal man, 'Don't get me wrong. Ah love me family, but me can't tek de noise any more. Anything yuh tell me, me will do.'

"Silence Reigns' arthritis was acting up and him did anxious fi go inside, lock him door behind him, rub him joints wid some Tiger Balm and pull de cover up to him shoulder. But Obadiah was such a sincere man, de myal man didn't wan short-change him. So him tell Obadiah fi sit a while and he step off him veranda, go stand by de side of de house so him could tink about all dat Obadiah tell him, plus all de other tings dat Obadiah didn't know fi tell him. Afta contemplating on Obadiah's problem, de myal man come up wid a solution. Him climb back on de veranda and tell Obadiah fi go home directly and move de fowl coop wid all de fowl, pigeon and rabbit, and put it pan de back veranda near him bedroom window.

"Obadiah didn't know how dat was gwane solve him problem, but him know dat if yuh go seek advice den ignore it, no telling wha misery might befall yuh. So Obadiah walk home slowly. Once him reach in him yard, him strain him back and scratch up him hand pulling and hauling de coop pan de veranda. But yuh tink Obadiah get any sleep dat nite? De chicken dem act mad-mad like de damn dog or maybe dem did miss de roosta dat drop dead a week ago, cause is so-so cluck-clucking dem keep up all nite. Obadiah feel him was gwane go mad.

"Two days lata, wid cotton sticking out him ears, Obadiah march to de myal man's house, but as him approach de gate, Obadiah notice dat Silence Reigns rises from him chair and walk meet Obadiah a few yards from de veranda. Obadiah greet de myal man, who same time seh to him, 'Wah appen, de chicken dem not loud enough?' Obadiah extract de cotton blocking up him ears to better hear Silence Reigns. Him start to explain dat perhaps de myal man misunderstood his request, hastening to add dat him wasn't saying Silence Reigns wasn't competent – and once again Obadiah winding all de way round de river and crawling thru de bush before coming out on de oda side wid him story and explanation. Silence Reigns jus shake him head and ease de itch in him ears by makin a hollow-clicking sound deep in him throat. Eventually when Obadiah tek a pause, de myal man seize de opportunity and seh to him, 'A tell yuh what. Go by yuh neighbour and borrow him goats, and put all a dem pan yuh front veranda.' Before Obadiah could inquire how dat gwane solve him problem, Silence Reigns seh to him, 'Shut de gate behind yuh as yuh go.'

"Dismissed, Obadiah bowed, thanked de myal man, walked to his friend's house and collected two goats and six kids and tied them to the railing of his front veranda. As soon as Obadiah entered him house, de goats begin baa-baaing, and de chickens start fi cluck-clucking, and Obadiah picknie dem, who was playing pilla fight, commence to chant: 'Mosquito one, mosquito two, mosquito jump inna hot callallo, halfpenny rice, penny fish, bring back quatty change. . .' Meanwhile Obadiah's wife was in de living-room practising lines fah a play wid three oda actors and de blasted dog was by de gate bark-barking at de mosquitoes dat was buzz-buzzing. De crickets were also chirp-chirping and Obadiah, drowning in de noise-noise, was convinced him did mad fah true."

"Me know how Obadiah feel, for is same way me going mad at my house. Could be my house Obadiah live," Edmond burst out, interrupting Lionel, completely caught up in the drama of the story.

"But wait! Is when you turn storyteller? We not interested in fi yuh piece of life. Shut yuh mouth so Lionel can finish de story," shouts one of the drinkers in response to Edmond's outburst.

"Alrite, oonuh settle down if oonuh wan hear de rest of de story," Lionel cautions, cracking his knuckles. The men shift their weights, take sips of their beer or rum, yawn, stretch, then turn their full attention back to Lionel.

"Dat nite, poor Obadiah stuff him ears wid nuff cotton; wen dat didn't work, him tie-up him face wid towel like him have mumps, but still de noise pound in him head. Him didn't get any sleep and next morning him head feel as if it had been used for a drum and someone still pounding out a rhythm. But since Obadiah respect wisdom, him suffa through another day, den him go walking down de road in de direction of de myal man's house. Once dere, Obadiah stood by de gate thinking out wha him gwane seh to Silence Reigns. When him have it all together, Obadiah push de gate open and enter. Him had no trouble getting to de point. Obadiah tell de myal man dat everyting him recommend mek de noise worse and bring more confusion in him home. Further, Obadiah seh him hadn't slept in three days and him head feel like somebody was either trying to axe it open or beat on it like drum.

"Silence Reigns looked at Obadiah and smiled. Him tell Obadiah fi return de goats, and come back and report to him de next day. Obadiah rush home and return de goats to his neighbour. Although it still noisy, Obadiah instantly feel better. De next day when Obadiah visited de myal man, him was directed fi return de fowl coop to de backyard. Obadiah rush home and shove de fowl coop way back in de yard. Dat nite him get a good sleep. De next morning Obadiah woke up wid a start. Something was wrong. De house too quiet. Him could hear him picknie dem running back and forth and shouting at each other; his wife was singing in the kitchen and banging pots, yet de house seemed fairly quiet to Obadiah. He sat up in bed listening to de domestic sounds of his home, amazed. Fah de first time Obadiah heard de high and low chords, de riffs, de reggae and soca beat, de blues and jazz notes, music to him ears. Him find paper and pencil and a poem just flow out him head unto the paper.

"Quick-quick Obadiah get dressed and amble down de road to de myal man's house. Yuh should see him walk: hands in him pockets beating a rhythm on him thighs, head erect, eyes wide and seeing what's before him rather dan de ideas in him head, probably de first time in ten years. Obadiah nose was wide-open, sniffing at all de green fragrant earth smells, feeling especially good because of de nice-nice-piece him wife lay pan him last night. Obadiah was happy to be living de life him was living at last.

"When Obadiah reach Silence Reigns' gate, him notice it lock. Dog bark at him and him wonder weh dog come from cause him neva see any dere before. Him call out, 'Mista Silence, is me Obadiah.' While him wait fah de myal man, Obadiah hear de loud chattering of crickets, de rumble of a river somewhere close, all sorts of little sounds him neva memba hearing before. But before him could dwell too long on dat, Silence Reigns hail him from de veranda whe him stand, both hands holding up him pants. De myal man didn't seem too anxious to open de gate and let Obadiah in. (What Obadiah didn't know was dat de myal man was helping a widow of two years out wid her problem and him did leave her wid her baggy down and her dress bunch up round she waist pan him bed, and him didn't intend fah Obadiah wid him longwindedness fi get in de way of him administering a cure.)

But Silence Reigns didn't have to worry for Obadiah did have more pressing things pan him mind rather dan spend de whole evening explain himself. Yuh see, Obadiah did plan fi knock a few balls a cricket wid him picknie dem and help him wife wid her lines, so him hastily tank de myal man saying, 'A love me house; de noise is music to me ears,' and same time Obadiah turn round, hurrying home. Silence Reigns bust out wid one piece a laugh, reassured of him powers, but quickly him collect himself, and tun in him house rushing to de woman, spread pan him bed, waiting fah him guidance.

"And is so de story done."

Edmond is unable to move or say anything. He feels exposed, as if Lionel had gotten inside his head, inside his very life and made a tale of it. What was the bar full of men thinking and saying about him, he wonders.

Lionel tilts back his head with the beer to his lips and drains the bottle. He looks toward his friend Edmond, whose eyes seem shrouded, contemplative. Lionel allows the feet of his chair to fall to the ground, then he stands up, walks across the room to the counter. Men pat him on the back as he passes them. "Vince," Lionel says in a sombre tone, "Gi me two more Stripes fah de road." He reaches into his back pocket, but Vince protests:

"Dese on de house, Lionel. Is a good story, man. Real good story." Lionel thanks him and takes up the bottles, curling his fingers around the mouths. He whistles a light, wordless tune which floats up to the ceiling of the stuffy, smoked-filled rum shop as he makes his way back to the table where Edmond seems trapped in a dream. Lionel bangs down the bottles in front of Edmond who jumps, almost falling off the chair.

"Dese for de road," Lionel says.

Edmond reaches and takes one of the beers. He brings it to his mouth, but before he takes a sip, he raises and extends it to Lionel. They knock bottles together and Edmond says, "Here's to stories dat true more dan life itself." Then he flings back his head, and downs the beer in one continuous gulp. Edmond suddenly feels anxious to be home in the familiar noise and chaos that is his life.

TEACHMENT III:

"The Judgement you cast becomes dye."

Papa used to say to me, "Girlie," – that was his pet-name for me – "Speak only the truth and what you want cause every word has power. If you say you can't, you can't." And is a true thing Papa speak because whenever I get frustrated and pout out my lips and say I can't, no matter how hard I try, I just couldn't do whatever it was that I was working on. But if I say I can and I was determined, it might be difficult, but I always succeeded.

I telling you this to make a point about this young man who I help born. His name is Devon, and although I shouldn't speak ill about people, I just don't think some women should have children. Devon's mother was such a woman. Devon father leave her for another woman when she was four months pregnant, and ever since then, well before the boy born, she would say, "Is bad picknie a having; you see how him mek me feet swell." Or "Is really bad picknie this, him won't mek me sleep at night; is like him tek me stomach fi stadium." Her water-bag break right in front of me gate. I help her on the veranda, and shout to someone to call for taxi to take her to hospital. But taxi take so long, she lay down right on my veranda to have the baby, with me on my knees, the dish cloth I use to wipe the callaloo off my hands, the same cloth me use to wrap up the baby. I never see a thing like that. Me deliver baby! Then she come to me and say me have to be the bad-picknie godmother. You ever hear such a thing?

But my point is this, that poor Devon didn't have a chance, because not once did I ever hear his mother say a kind word about him. In fact, before he was two years old, everyone in the community call him Bad-Boy just like his mother and ever since then, whatever goes wrong is Devon blame. If other boys pick mango off people tree, even if Devon didn't pick any, but he was close by, then he got the blame.

So, as I say, his mother, Matilda, always ready to complain to everyone how Devon do this and Devon do that and how him bad can't done. One day I ask her why she name him Bad-Boy. She open her eyes wide and look at me like I said something stupid. I say, "Matilda, from the day the boy born, even before, the only thing you say about him is that him is bad. In fact he used to think his name was bad, until I told him it was Devon. So how can he be anything else?"

She look at me all indignant. "Is why you blaming me for having a bad picknie?" she cry. "The Lord knows I try to beat the badness out of him."

I look at her and I say, "Maybe you beat the badness into him."

She cut her eyes and kiss her teeth and walk away and don't talk to me till this day. You just can't say anything to some people. I was just trying to make her see that she should give the boy a chance, try to love him instead of telling him how bad he is.

I know that if you keep throwing words at people then it bound to catch and mark them, just like dye.

Devon is me godson, and I would always tell him that he was good and handsome, but the whole community took cue from his mother and call him Bad-Boy. Now he left the community and I don't know how he's doing. I hope he remembers all those times I rescued him from his mother's strap and told him, he was a good boy, and that I loved him.

BAD-BOY

At seventeen, when he felt an uncontrollable urge to thump down his mother and just cuss a whole heap of blood-claat in her face, and then mash up the place, instead him stuff up the four shirts he owned, along with the two good pants, a jeans, a few tee-shirts, one cap, one rasta tam, deodorant, his hunting knife, and four green guavas, and left his mother's house, pausing to cough up a blob of phlegm which he spat right in front of the gate. Then he gave the house the middle finger and rambled to the crossroads where he caught a bus going to Kingston, but not before going to kiss his godmother goodbye. She gave him two fritters that she had wrapped and saved for him.

"Later, Mama," he said to her before he left to board the bus. He did not tell her that she would probably not see him again, well at least not for a while. As the minibus took off, he glanced back and held up his palm, thumb across the hand, and waved to her.

"Is so life go," he muttered as the bus gained speed and the breeze blew onto his face from the window by his seat directly behind the bus-driver. "Is only me godmother and me little sister Audrey ever nice to me," he concluded, settling more comfortably.

Devon could not remember a time when his mother ever held him gently or kissed him affectionately, or spoke to him with kindness. He had lived with her loathsome anger all his life, and had taken enough. His earliest memory of her hatred went back to when he was not yet three years old. She was sitting on a bench outside eating something – what he cannot remember – but he knew he walked over and asked her for some, and she opened her palm and slapped him so hard across his face he fell back, his mouth bleeding. She got up saying, "You like you damn father, want to take de very food out me mouth then leave me. Get up off the ground and go wash out you mouth." She had gone into the kitchen and left him there, his tears like acid on his cheeks.

Another time, when he turned five years old and she took him to school, she told his teacher he was a bad-boy, lazy and stupid and only understood licks, so she was to hit him if he acted the fool. His teacher took his mother at her word and if other kids talked, he got licks; if he couldn't write his letters, he got licks; he got so much licks from the teacher he thought licks was one of the lessons he had to learn. No matter how hard he tried to please his mother and stay out of her way, he couldn't remember a week that she didn't beat him for one thing or another: wetting the bed, getting up too slowly to get dressed for school, not making her coffee strong enough (he had to make it for her every morning once he turned six years old), losing a button on his school shirt, breaking the point of his pencil while he did his homework, not getting up early on Saturday morning to do his chores, not answering his mother the first time she called him because he didn't hear, or answering with attitude, as she claimed, and for sulking when she said he could not play marbles with the other boys after he'd completed all his chores. Above all, he got beat and cursed at because he looked like his father, because he behave just like his father (even though he never met his father), because he was worthless like his father, and because he wanted to take advantage of her like his no good father. Period. His body was a map of the beatings that he suffered at the hands of his mother, of his teachers and some of the children in the neighbourhood, who took their cue from his mother.

Once, when he was washing the dishes and broke a glass, his mother used the cord from the iron and whipped him across his legs with it until there were big welts. He was eight years old. The next day at school his teacher asked him what happened to his legs. He told her that his mother beat him and she said he must deserve it because he was a real bad-boy; his mother had warned her. Before the day was out, his teacher gave him six hard slaps in his palms with the ruler because he couldn't remember his times-tables, and she told him, "You are a bad-boy and a dunce too."

His palms were swollen when he went home, and he knew he couldn't let his mother see them or she would beat him again, accuse him of being bad at school and not paying attention to his teacher. But because his palms hurt, that evening he took so long washing the dishes his mother said, "Yu is nothing but a bad, lazy boy," and she refused to give him any food. For three days she didn't give him any food, until he fainted coming home from school, and a few of the children ran and called his godmother. She had them carry him to her veranda and fed him bun and cheese and chocolate milk. When he told his godmother that his mother hadn't fed him in three days, she went to his mother and told her she was being wicked.

When he was nine, a group of boys his age took to teasing him after school, taunting him, "Bad-Boy, Mad-boy, beaten stick, stupid stick." They pelted stones at his feet each day for almost two weeks as he ran home as fast as he could. Then one day they waylaid and encircled him. With sweat blinding his eyes, and fear pushing out his heart, he had struck out wildly and blindly at the four boys, bursting one's lip, scraping the skin of another, ripping the shirt of a third, and bucking the fourth so hard that he got a coco on his forehead, the size of guinep. Of course the boys all went crying to their respective mothers – without telling them what they had done to Devon. Mothers and sons congregated at his gate when his mother came home from work, parading their sons' wounds and demanding retribution. Even though he was bruised and battered his mother refused to listen to him. Every time he opened his mouth to explain, she boxed him right in front of the other boys, and berated him. "God knows me try wid dis boy. Me know him bad from even before him born. Him is Satan's son, is Satan mus father him." Then she told each of the boys to come up one by one and punch him as hard as they could. After they left, she told him to take a shower and when he was naked and the water was running over him, she came into the bathroom with a strap and beat him so hard that for almost two weeks his entire body ached and the welt marks were visible. When his teacher saw the welts and asked him what happened and he told her, she again said he must have deserved it. It was only his godmother who listened to and believed him, daily taking him into her room, and applying warm liniment on his body, then held him tenderly to her bosom, and told him that he was not Satan's child; he was good, Godsent and loved. She made him warm Milo, which he loved, with crackers and jam. As his godmother walked him home, she told him that his mother didn't hate him, despite what she said, but that she was full of bitterness and disappointment about how her own life had turned out.

It was at this point in his life that Devon decided to do exactly what he pleased, because regardless of what he did or didn't do, he was blamed. So the third week after the beating and his ambush by the boys, he cut school and ran home early. He went into the kitchen where his mother kept her machete, took it and ran back to the path that the boys took home from school. When they appeared he jumped from out the bushes and brandished the machete over his head. He could feel his heart pushing way up in his throat, but still he stood and shouted.

"Anybody pelt me with stone again, or lie pan me, ah go chop them up like mince meat and chop up them mother too. Yes me is mad boy and me don't care who dead here today."

It was as if time stopped. Devon heard his own heart and the heartbeats of the other boys. All of their faces glistened with sweat, and because he was afraid his fear might push him to chop one of them, he shrieked at the top of his lungs and chased them. That was the last time anyone in the community messed with him and, eventually, he and those boys became friends of a sort.

At school he stopped trying, and even before the teacher called on him, he would go and stand in the dunce corner, taking the dunce cap from her table and putting it on. He even pulled his right ear with his left hand and gripped his left leg with his right hand, a contortion the teacher would order those few children to perform she deemed really dunce. After a while it became a joke and the children would snicker when Devon got up on his own accord to go in the dunce corner and the teacher would order him out of the classroom. But an interesting shift began to occur because of his daring – the other children began to help him with his spelling and to figure out the arithmetic problems and even to

61

share their lunch with him because his mother frequently denied him food. They managed to teach him what the teachers were never able to teach, so he stopped being mean to them and became quite popular, in an odd kind of way.

Life at home did not improve, except, left to take care of his baby sister most of the time, he discovered what happiness could mean. She loved to follow him around and would often hug and kiss him; he in turn liked bouncing her on his lap and tickling her until they both laughed themselves silly. She didn't seem to have a father either, and Devon wondered if her father was his father, but he noticed that his mother never accused her of being worthless like her father or called her stupid, although she sometimes beat her, but never like she did him. He loved Audrey because whenever their mother beat him, she would cry with him, and would always go to him and hug him and say, "Audrey love DevDev, Audrey love Dev," and pat his arm or leg or back as she whispered to him. As she got older, he could always rely on her to sneak him food when his mother refused to feed him.

Then, as he got more defiant, his mother not only refused to feed him, but sometimes would shut him out of the house at nights too. And when, out of pride or shame or both, he did not feel like taking refuge with his godmother, he prowled around and found someone's veranda to sleep on; a few times he even slept in a dog's kennel, the dogs growling and sniffing at him. What had led up to the last time his mother put him out, three months ago, was crystal clear in his mind. He had spent the entire day cutting and raking grass for a woman and was very hungry. At the end of the day the woman told him she didn't have any money to pay him, but thanked him, and told him to climb one of her coconut trees and cut as many coconuts as he wanted and sell them for payment. Devon was tired and vex because the woman didn't even have a cold glass of water to give him, claiming that her fridge wasn't working, so he headed home expecting to get the customary Saturday beef-soup. But the moment he walked through the gate, even before he washed his hands and face, he felt his mother's words like kerosene thrown on burning coals.

"From the day you born, you bad same way. Just wutliss.

62

Badness must be in your blood. Don't come ask me for no soup. You drop out of school. You standing all day on the corner as if you holding up fence just like your other no-good friends. All of oonuh must be waiting to rob someone of their hard earn money. Is only God know why I let you stay in me house, but me not feeding you today. Why I have to ask you to rake up the yard, to sweep off the veranda? You is nothing but badness. Ah rather feed the dog than you." And she poured out the rest of the soup from the pot into the dog's bowl. The truth was Devon had gotten up early while she was still asleep and had swept off the veranda, raked up the backyard and put the leaves in a pile intending to collect them in a drum and burn them when he returned. He looked out the window and saw that the dogs and fowls had scattered some of the leaves and the wind had probably blown away others, but it was still evident to anyone who looked that the yard had been swept. Hurt again by his mother's meanness, he cursed under his breath as he slunk away.

Hearing this, she had shouted after him: "You not sleeping here tonight, with yuh impertinence. Is who you kissing you teeth at? Don't let me catch you put you foot through that gate tonight. You just like you worthless father. No good. I don't know why I just don't wash me hands of you."

He went to his godmother who fed him, and allowed him to bathe at her house. When his mother left for the store, he went by his house, but his little sister, under instructions from their mother, refused to let him in, terrified of the beating she would get if she did. However, he persuaded her to pass him clean pants and a shirt. She gave him a mint from her pocket, and smiled at him. He went round to his friend's house who brightened up his day by offering to pay his entrance fee to the dance, and buy him a drink, in exchange for help in painting two rooms in a lady's house.

They arrived at the dance early and Devon, with a hot bottle of Guinness in his hand, stood near the door, pressed up against the wall where he could survey all the girls as they came in. He was trying to get in the mood, and for a while stood with his eyes closed, rocking to the rhythm of the music as it relaxed his body. As a hush fell over the dance, Devon opened his eyes to witness the entrance of Rude-Man. He was sporting a floral-design navy-blue shirt which was open to his waist; underneath was a white tank-top; jeans with razor-sharp creases hugged his body, and around his neck hung two thick gold chains. He came with a bag of girls who were dressed in skimpy, batty-rider outfits – real dance-hall queens. Devon could feel the air being sucked in by this entrance. Although Rude-Man was only five-eight, no taller than Devon, he looked tall to the youth. He walked with cool confidence, teeth flashing two gold-caps, and smelled as if he bathed in cologne. Devon had never seen him before but was certain Rude-Man was loaded, and hoped there wasn't going to be any tangling tonight. Devon just wanted to chill and watch the girls, and maybe even feel brave enough to ask one to dance, and rub-up on her and get a hard-on, and then go and ease himself off in the back, by the toilet before he went home. He didn't feel like having to dodge a bullet and run for his life that night.

Rude-Man and his posse took up post a few yards from Devon – who knew better than to look directly at him or the five girls draping him like doily on the arms of a sofa. Devon couldn't help but smile, wondering why any man would want to take up all that trouble at one time. It was hard enough talking to one girl and getting her to pay attention, much less five. He had seen porno flicks with men in bed with several girls, but didn't believe it happened in real life. He hadn't slept with any girl yet, well he didn't count the woman whose yard he had raked for $50 who had pulled him into her kitchen, pushed him against the wall, taken out his buddy and squeezed it until it got hard, then shoved it between her legs, forcing it up inside her and grunting. All the while, eyes wide with terror, he'd been praying that her husband wouldn't come home unexpectedly. The man didn't like him, and everyone in the community knew he was crazy and jealous. If he found him like that, stuck up in his wife, he'd chop him up. Devon was ashamed that this was really only his first sexual experience. He hadn't liked the woman, even before she asked him to come inside on the pretence of helping her move something, only to rob his virginity. It had hurt like hell, and he wanted to cry out but pride and fear kept him quiet. Of course, everyone, including the girls he tried to talk to, believed he had slept with many girls. Even a few of his friends, like ragamuffin Derrick who'd taken him to the dance, believed he'd slept with plenty of girls, but he hadn't. He wanted to. He'd tried many times, and got close. Well, a few girls allowed him to finger them, to touch their breasts, even to tongue-kiss them, but he was never able to persuade any of them to go all the way. Sometimes he looked at them, like these girls with Rude-Man, their breasts firm and high, dancing in men's face, their behinds tight and swishing, their legs, naked and plump, and he felt like thumping them, just like he wanted to punch down his mother when she went on about him being no good.

"Ah hate de bitch," the words escaped his mouth, without him even realizing it until he felt Rude-Man's eyes on him.

"Is who yu ah talk bout, spar?" Rude-Man asked, stepping away from the girls, a little edge in his voice, his right hand patting his pocket.

Devon's mother stayed in his head. He wanted to box her. No matter where he went, she followed him, causing him trouble. He glanced at Rude-Man, legs trembling and he blurted out, "Is me and me moda fight and she just inna a me head; won't give me peace."

Rude-Man looked Devon up and down and could tell from his cheap clothes and worn sneakers that he was harmless. He was prepared to be generous.

"Man, yu shouldn't hate yu moda. Is she give yu life, good or bad. Seen!"

Devon nodded. Of course it was a sin to hate his mother, and so perhaps she was right and he was nothing but badness. And in truth he didn't hate her all the time, but sometimes he wanted to kill her with his own two hands. But he was feeling alone and sad, so he continued to babble.

"But it look like she hate me from de day I born. She act like is me left her instead of me wutliss fada." Devon sucked his teeth long and slow, fighting way tears. "She hate me like rass-claat," he said, downing the Guinness to try to kill the feelings taking over him. To his surprise, Rude-Man walked over, put his arms around his shoulder and introduced himself.

"Chill little brethren. Is party we deh. Everyone call me Rude-Man. Me ladies thirsty and hungry, what say yu tek care of them

65

for me. Yu think yu can handle that?" Devon nodded, not sure he knew what he was agreeing to.

"So what's yu name, spar?" Rude-Man asked.

Taking his cue from Rude-Man, Devon squared his shoulders and said, "Everyone call me Bad-Boy. Seen!"

Rude-Man scanned Devon and smiled. "That name well suit yu. I can see yu is a really Bad-Boy. No so it go! Irie! Rude-Man and Bad-Boy should make a move. Seen!"

"Seen!" Devon intoned as they knocked knuckles together.

Devon scored that night as Rude-Man's runner. Rude-Man gave him $2000 to buy him a Heineken and his five girls rum-punch and food – jerk-chicken, curried goat and stew fish. Devon got to keep the change at the end of the night and he had a stew-fish and two Heineken himself, and got to treat his ragamuffin friend too. At the end of the night he had $200 in his pocket and Rude-Man told him that when he was ready for action to come and check him out at Slipen Road.

"Everyone know me dere, man. Just show up and ask anyone where Rude-Man live. Yu carn miss I, man. Seen! That's my joint. Seen!"

Devon smiled broadly. He could not have imagined having such a good time. Plenty food and drinks, and even two of Rude-Man girls to rub-up on, though he didn't get to brace either of them against the wall and grind them like he would have liked. He knew how men were about their women, and he had no intention of angering Rude-Man.

That was over a month ago, and as Devon climbed out of the bus at Half-Way Tree, he wondered if Rude-Man would remember him, and if his offer still stood. He wasn't sure, though, that he wanted to get mixed up in any serious crime. Police were killing people right and left, and everybody seemed to have guns. Devon had never handled a gun, and didn't want to have to be dodging and running every day. He just wanted a place to sleep, nice clothes to wear and regular meals. He didn't want to die or have to go to prison. Every day the papers showed the photos of one or more criminals gunned down by the police or killed by another criminal, or locked up in prison. Devon got off the bus with a heavy heart, slung his bag over his shoulder and went to sit in the park. He only had $350 and that wouldn't go very far. He sat and watched the hour hand of the clock in the square go round three times. He was aware of street hustlers checking him out, a few had even approached him, but he just looked at them hard, fingered the hunting knife in his pocket and kept quiet. Around him horns blared, street-vendors cried out their wares, tyres screeched. A nonstop, frantic pace all around. Sweat dripped from Devon. He was hungry.

He wiped the sweat and tears from his face, and hoped that no one had noticed. He hated how he cried about everything. He just wanted to live and not have his mother and everyone else call him Bad-Boy. He stood and looked around. He had nowhere to sleep. He couldn't spend any of the little money he had on food. He walked over to the fountain and drank water until he could hear it slopping in his stomach. He wasn't going to go back to his mother's house, but he didn't know where to go. He wasn't sure what Rude-Man was into, but he knew from that night at the dance that he carried a gun. Rude-Man had even told Devon that he would get him one. He didn't like the idea of carrying a gun and running from the law, but what alternative did he have?

He left the park and crossed the street, not sure where he was heading. He bumped into a woman struggling with several bags, and said, "Beg, excuse," and moved to walk around her. She called after him.

"Young man, yu can help me wid me bags? I gwane catch de bus round de corner der, yu can help me?" People were pushing and walking fast around them. Devon looked at the woman who reminded him of his godmother, and agreed to help her.

"Is where yu say yu going?" he asked, reaching for her bags.

"Just round de corner fi catch de bus down Molynes Road."

Devon took four of her six bags. They were very heavy. Pushing through the crowd, he turned around and asked the woman, "Is rock-stone yu have in here?"

Darting across the street to avoid traffic, Devon got the woman settled at the bus-stop with all her bags. She thanked him, and as he walked away, she reached for his hands, and pressed something into his palm. He glanced at it and realized it was money. He flashed her a big smile. Now he could get himself something to eat. He headed for the patty store. The woman had given him $30, enough to buy a patty and coco-bread. Although he was tempted to buy himself a box-orange juice to drink, he resisted, telling himself he would go back to the park when he was through eating and drink more water to wash it down.

For over two weeks, Devon hung out around Half-Way Tree, sleeping in the park and elsewhere in the vicinity. He befriended two of the homeless boys who stationed themselves at Trafalgar Square and earned a meagre keep by washing car windshields. He hated how the drivers, especially the stochious ones – he knew they had money from their cars and how they dressed – would often dismiss him with a wave of their hands, without even looking at him, as if he was less than paper litter sailing in the breeze. So he scouted the supermarkets, and watched for women who didn't have cars and were heading for the bus-stop. Their gratitude and generosity allowed him to survive those two weeks, eating well. But Devon was not cut out for street life. He wanted a place to lay his head at night, and a place to bathe and wash his face in the morning. He tried to keep himself clean – if he could find a pipe with running water and the opportunity to wipe himself off. Still he was not prepared to return home. He wondered if his mother missed him, and had been inquiring about him. He doubted this.

He didn't think he could get a good job because he had started cutting school by 5th class and just barely made it to 3rd form. He was getting desperate, could smell himself. One time he approached a woman to see if he could help her with her bags, and she looked at him, sniffed and said, "Is you smell bad so? Me can't have you carry me groceries, when you smell so bad. You must go and wash youself."

That decided Devon that he had to seek other means to earn a living and find a place to live. Beside, someone had stolen his bag with his clothes, including his knife, so all he had was what he wore, and the soles of his sneakers were paper-thin.

Youth-Man, who sold the evening paper and was friend to the street boys who cleaned windshields, had been observing Devon from the beginning, measuring him up to see if he could trust him. When Devon slumped on the ground beside his newspaper stand, he asked: "So wha yu sayin, Bad-Boy? Life a ride yu or yu a ride life?"

Devon looked up at Youth-Man and realized that he had on a clean shirt and looked and smelled clean.

"So how yu always clean, star?" he asked. Youth-Man merely chuckled, before he dashed off to sell a newspaper to a passenger hanging out of a car window. When Youth-Man returned to his post he sniffed at Devon.

"Yu smellin renck fi true. So yu tired of de street life? Yu ready fi mek a move?"

"Yes, I," Devon replied, springing to his feet, hope surging in his chest.

After Youth-Man sold all his papers, he told Devon he could get him a job unloading trucks with the opportunity to make a little extra on the side. He invited Devon home to eat with him, and promised that he would take him to see the man he worked for later that night. Devon followed Youth-Man, not sure where he was taking him or what to expect. He was on edge, but he didn't want to ask a whole lot of question in case Youth-Man changed his mind.

After walking about two miles, cutting through alleys and narrow streets, Youth-Man pulled open a zinc gate and stepped into a yard with several shacks. A group of men and boys were clustered around a low table playing dominos, a lantern their only light. They hailed Youth-Man and observed Bad-Boy.

"Yard," Youth-Man said, walking over to the men, "Ah want oonuh fi meet a new brethren pan de scene, Bad-Boy. Him gwane hang around and shelter wid oonuh."

When Bad-Boy approached he realized that they were not men, most looked to be his age, a few even younger.

Gesturing with his chin, Youth-Man indicated, "Is right dere de man can get a shut-eye. Back dere is de shower. Is only one and is nuff a we use it, and de toilet back dere too. Is every man fah himself, seen. A gwane lend yu a shirt and pants so yu can bathe and clean fi meet de boss man. Yu can wash wha yu a wear and hang it up fi dry."

Youth-Man gave Devon soap and showed him where the

shower was. Devon was so happy to take a shower that he forgot how long he was in there until he heard someone banging on the door.

"Look like yu want use up all de water. Look like yu think this is fi yu own private shower. Get de blood-claat out so me can wash de grime off me skin."

Immediately Devon turned off the faucet, and grabbed the clothes he had washed, but realised he didn't have a towel or anything to dry himself off. He stepped out to face a bulky man, who shoved him out the way and entered the shower without looking back. Devon stumbled but managed to brace himself from falling. Youth-Man hadn't given him the loaner clothes yet, and he didn't want to put on his wet clothes. For a moment Devon didn't know what to do. Should he holler for Youth-Man, or should he just put on his wet clothes? As he stood there feeling foolish, he heard Youth-Man calling him, asking if he was ready for the clothes. Quickly Devon replied and dressed himself in the clothes that Youth-Man brought him.

Introduced to Youth-Man's woman and two small children, Devon thanked the girl, who looked to be no more than sixteen, for allowing him to share their meal. She was the colour of slender dried bamboo vines and just as thin. Devon could not imagine how she could be mother to two small children. He hadn't guessed that Youth-Man, who was only twenty years old, was a father. They lived in one room that was jammed with a double bed, a dresser, a table with four chairs, a small two-burner gas stove and several boxes, stacked one on top of the other. Devon was so surprised by this revelation of Youth-Man's family that he ate without tasting the food. He didn't know where it was safe to allow his eyes to fall. He wanted to look at Youth-Man's woman, Evelyn, but was afraid if he stared Youth-Man might think he wanted her and put him out. And though he wanted to take in all that was in their room, he didn't want them to think that he envied them their stuff and was planning to rob them, so he kept his eyes on his plate and gobbled down the food. Youth-Man ate slowly, all the while rocking the older of the two children. The baby nursed while they ate.

Devon was glad when Youth-Man was finally done, and put

the infant on the bed, touched his woman on her shoulder and said, "See yu lata, baby. Ah gwane tek Bad-Boy here to de boss man and hook him up with some work. Seen!"

After walking for a long time, cutting through many alleyways and unlit streets, Devon and Youth-Man emerged on Molynes Road and entered a bar, where a tired-looking, half-clad girl danced on a matchbox of a stage, and men sat around with watered-down drinks, talking and looking bored. Youth-Man approached one of the men and whispered in his ear. The man got up and they stepped outside the bar. Devon didn't know if he should follow them, so he stood just inside the door and watched the girl on stage, with her arse up in the air, turned towards the men, her palms on the floor as she wiggled and grunted. Devon wanted to look but watching her made his stomach churn. Although he couldn't see her face, he didn't think she wanted to be up there, wiggling like that, her arse outdoor, trying to excite men who seemed so indifferent. He glanced away, just when Youth-Man called him, and stepped out of the bar.

Devon got the job unloading trucks, with the implicit instruction that he was expected to stash some of the cargo that would be delivered to the boss man to be resold later. He would get a cut of whatever was sold. Uneasy – he could not help remembering his godmother telling him that stealing was a sin – but desperate, Devon was surprised at how easily he settled into the routine. The first thing he bought himself when he got paid was a towel and a pair of sneakers. He also gave Evelyn some money for the food she had been feeding him. Now that he had a job, Youth-Man told him that he had to get his own food as Evelyn was not going to be cooking for him any more. Devon figured he would buy box-food like the rest of the boys with whom he shared a room, all of them, except for two brothers who shared a single mattress, sleeping on the hard floor with just a few old clothes for bedding. Devon longed for a bed, and decided he would save towards that, and then try to get his own place.

Two months later he was caught stealing from the cargo, but before the police arrived, he managed to escape, taking off, but losing one of his new sneakers in the process. That night when he crept home, after making sure no police were waylaying him,

Youth-Man told him he couldn't help him any more and he had to find a new place to stay. He was right back where he started, except now the law was probably looking for him. He didn't know where to hide and ended up back at the same bar where he had met the boss man, bought himself a drink and watched the same, tired-looking girl wiggle her arse. A rainy night, only one other man was in there.

Wiggling-Batty (this was the girl's stage name) had seen Devon come in. She could tell from that first night Youth-Man brought him to the bar that he was green. As she wiggled her arse, she watched him through her parted legs and decided he would be her next stopgap. The last two men she had taken home had beaten her, stolen all her money and then left, even though she cooked and washed for them and bought them clothes. She didn't really like men, but one, even a green one like this boy, was a necessity where she lived. He looked kind, yet she surmised that he could defend himself. What did she have to lose? When the music stopped, Wiggling-Batty walked over and asked Devon if he wanted a lap-dance. At first he didn't know what she meant, but when he understood, he simply nodded, not sure if he could say no to her request.

She straddled him, and up close he saw that she was much older than he had thought; she looked thirty, with eyes like a dog he had seen hit by a truck. Worried about being caught, about not having a job and needing to find a place to live, Devon's mind drifted. The woman continued to gyrate, one arm draped around his neck, the other pressed against his shoulder for balance; she panted close to his ears. Devon's buddy grew hard and Wiggling-Batty's hand moved to the front of his pants. He pulled her to him and kissed her. She responded eagerly, gyrating in his lap. Just as he began fumbling with her bra, the bartender shouted: "None a dat in here. Oonuh have to go outside with dat."

Instantly the woman stopped and pulled Devon to his feet. She giggled, then whispered in his ear. "If yu have money, ah don't live far. Rain gwane fall tonight. I could tek care of yu, mek yu feel real-real good." This she said pressing her body into his, and giggling. Devon could see that her eyes were tired and joyless. She didn't believe what she was saying, but he didn't care. He wanted to do it in a bed, not standing up against a wall, wondering if the woman's husband was going to come in and chop him up.

"Whe yu man?" Devon inquired.

"Is me alone live. Yu think me would tek yu home if me did have man."

"Is pan de floor yu sleep or yu have bed?"

"How yu mean if me have bed? Is whe yu think me come from? All dese questions, you must have money." She scrutinized Devon. "Is a $100 it gwane cost you for some sweet-sweet loving."

Devon nodded and the woman went into the back, pulled on jeans and a shirt, took off her horse-tail wig, revealing cornrows, and put her arm through Devon's.

"Come, let we go before rain start. Ah gwane treat yu real good tonight. Just wait and see."

Devon allowed himself to be led, not paying attention to where she was taking him.

Her room was dark and musty, but she had a double bed with a nice sheet on it. She offered him a beer from a small fridge, then began to undress. Once she was naked, Devon could tell from the stretch marks on her breasts and stomach that she had children.

"How many picknie yu have?" he asked her.

"Three, dem inna de country wid me moda."

He was feeling nervous. He was no longer hard – he didn't really want to sleep with her.

"So how often yu see dem?"

"Yu asking question like yu is inspector of police. Ah thought yu did want to fuck."

Devon didn't know what else to say, so when she flapped on the bed and said, all seductive, "Come nuh!" he walked over and began to kiss her. Soon he was hard again. She unbuttoned his pants waist, hauled them off, then pulled him on top of her. He knew what to do, had seen it done in lots of porno movies. He felt for his penis and tried to find the entrance between her legs.

She giggled and chided: "What a-way yu anxious. Is not race horse yu riding at Caymanas Park yu know."

But by then the ache in his buddy crawled into his stomach and he pushed it in her hard, and rode like his life depended on it. Just

73

as quickly he collapsed, feeling as if he had run twenty miles. She pushed him off and stood up.

"Ah see you is a sprinter and not a long-distance man. Well sleep. Maybe next time yu will try for de 400 yard dash instead of de 100 yards."

Devon snored, curling up like a baby. He woke to the sound of rain hitting the roof and felt her next to him. He didn't know her name, he didn't know where he was, didn't know how or where he was going to find work, he didn't know how he felt or how he was supposed to feel. The very first time with the woman who paid him to rake her yard, it had hurt. He didn't know that it could hurt like that. He had thought only girls who were virgins hurt and bled like that, but he hurt and bled as he broke the foreskin of his uncircumcised penis. When the woman saw him bleeding and realized that he was a virgin, she had laughed then pushed him away saying he had ruined her dress with his blood.

As Devon lay there, listening to the rain and trying to make out the pattern of the ceiling, Wiggling-Batty woke and whispered: "Ah won't charge yu if yu hold me."

Devon didn't quite know how to hold her, but she pulled his arms and wrapped them around her, pressing her back into his body. She didn't like being alone and would do almost anything to keep a man even though she did not like most of the men she met. But Devon, she felt, was different. Maybe he would stay with her for a year, or longer even.

When next he woke, the sun was forcing its way through the window and Wiggling-Batty was sitting, smoking. Without looking at him she said: "A nice man like yu don't have woman or place fi stay."

"Mek yu tink ah don't have woman?"

"So why yu here wid me?"

"Maybe ah like yu?"

"Yu want live wid me and be me man?"

Devon glanced around at her room. It was clean though musty. She even had a small TV. He didn't have a job or a place to stay, and Youth-Man had made it clear he couldn't continue to stay in the communal room with the other youth. He looked at her and felt no desire. He needed to pee.

"Whe de toilet?"

"Just out dis door to yu left."

Devon rolled out of bed, looking around for his pants. She tossed them to him and he pulled them on and went in search of the toilet. There he decided to stay with her. When he came back, she gave him a towel and he showered.

The woman wasn't in the room when he returned and he felt anxious just as he did when he was at home and his mother was due to return from work. As he got older, he often left the house before she arrived, only returning to sleep. He felt embarrassed, too, because he couldn't remember the woman's name, and he knew he hadn't performed well last night. As he was falling off to sleep, he'd heard her chups in frustration, but hadn't cared how she felt. He didn't want to have to look at her, but now he was going to be her man because she'd asked and he needed a place to sleep and someone to look after him. She had spread the bed, so he sat on the edge, looking around for his clothes. Maybe she'd hidden them like his mother sometimes did when she didn't want him to leave the house while she was away at work or doing some chore.

Devon was fifteen the last time his mother hid his clothes. He had been forced to stay inside all day, only able to peer out through the window. Even after she came home and he begged her for his clothes, she had refused, so he backed her up in the kitchen where she was cooking, his face so close to hers he could easily have kissed her, and for the first time he accused her to her face.

"Mek you so wicked! Mek yu hate me so? Yu know ah could kill you and God would fagive me." She read the rage in his eyes and did not berate him as was her way. She tried to sidestep him, but he kept close to her, his fist clutching the front of her dress. "You know ah could thump the blood-claat life out of you. You know I hate you more dan you hate me." He wanted to hurt her, but knew if he raised his hand against her, he wouldn't stop until she stopped breathing. His head pounded as loudly as his heart, and he didn't see as she felt for the machete that she kept by the kitchen sink, until he felt it against his back.

"Ah want yu to rass hit me today and see if ah don't chop you up."

Mother and son. Their eyes mirrored their mutual loathing. They were at a place of no return. Devon raised his hand, and he felt the blade of the machete slice his skin. He pulled back his arm and struck forcefully, but the sweat on his mother's face caused his fist to merely graze her cheek and smash into the wall. His knuckles hurt and bled. She stepped round him, with the machete raised.

"Ah should just chop you up and kill you. You did bad from the day you born. You is no good just like you wutliss father. Is only the Lord saving you this evening." She quickly left the kitchen and walked to her bedroom where he heard the door slam. Devon stood with his knuckles and back bleeding and didn't know what to do. He had hit his mother. Who would protect him? He had transgressed, sinned, committed a crime for which there was no forgiveness. His mother was right – he was a bad boy. Devon stood in the kitchen in his briefs while the meat on the stove burned, while the dogs yapped, while the mosquitoes buzzed, while night wrapped her darkness around his pain.

At some point either he or his mother or someone must have come and turned off the stove and cleaned up because Devon woke at dawn with his bed stained with blood. When he opened the door of his room, his clothes were in a pile on the floor, several shirts shredded. But his mother never hid his clothes after that, and was less verbally abusive. They kept out of each other's way, but up until he left, he felt they were on the verge of murdering each other, dancing around the inevitable.

"Ah wash you clothes them."

He sprang from the bed. His body was covered with sweat.

"You look like you see duppy," the woman said. "Ah hope you no sick. Me no want no sick man as fi me man," she pouted.

Devon forced himself to be calm. He was not in his mother's room; she was nowhere near; she was only a memory that kept visiting him. Feeling as if he'd been caught on the toilet, Devon looked at the woman and spoke harshly.

"So what you expect me fi do while me clothes dry, stay lock up in here? Is picknie you tek me for?"

"Mek you acting like someone bite you. Whe de rest of you clothes? Me will go collect them for you."

Devon grew calm with the realization that his other pants and shirts probably had been stolen already. Beside which, even if they were not, he was warned not to go back to Youth-Man's yard until things cooled down. Perhaps it was best that he didn't have clothes and had to stay inside.

"You have other name beside Wiggling-Batty?" he asked, not looking at her.

She smiled, her lips parting slightly to reveal white but uneven teeth. Then she turned her head to the side, almost resting it against her shoulder. "Me name is Cynthia Green, but down at de club dem call me Wiggling-Batty because me know how to shake this," and she slapped her behind loudly.

While Devon lay in bed and watched TV, Cynthia went and bought him a pair of pants and a shirt. She told him she didn't mind buying him things, but she expected him to leave something on her dresser weekly because she had three children and her mother to support. She worked as a go-go dancer four nights a week, and during the day worked as a lunch-worker in a government office downtown. She told Devon she wanted a man to keep others off her back, but she was not going to put up with another man abusing her, so if he was a woman hitter, he should leave then and spare them both the grief. Devon said he understood, then he asked her if she knew where he could find work. She told him she could set him up to sell jerk on the road; this way he didn't have to work for anyone. When he said he didn't know how to cook, she laughed and said, "No problem. I a good teacher."

Devon wanted to lay low for at least two weeks, but Cynthia said she checked around and no one was looking for him. She got him the grill and set him up on the Boulevard. The first two weeks, Devon did not fare well. There were several other jerk stands, and they were regulars. Besides, Devon was somewhat timid, not sure he knew the ropes, even though Cynthia had given him the rundown and seasoned the chicken for him daily. Although he tried to mask it by putting forth a rough exterior, Devon was intimidated by Cynthia. She was wiry and hard. In time their lovemaking grew more satisfying as she guided and directed him how to please her and he wasn't so anxious. But Devon did not really enjoy making love to her. Always, when he rolled off her, he hoped it was someone else, who he wasn't sure, but someone else, softer, rounder – someone who didn't expect him to run off and leave her as soon as he got his footing. This was exactly Devon's intention, so every time she accused him of planning to abandon her, he hated her a little more for knowing the truth. Though she whispered in his ears how much she loved him, her eyes told him she didn't really believe it; he suspected she said it because it made her feel good. Devon felt cowardly for pretending that he would be the man who would stay with her, even though in his head he had already left that first night she took him home.

Then things turned around for him. He was looking longingly at the queues of people at two of his competitors' jerk stands, waiting for the chicken to be done, while he had chicken that he was keeping warm. Life was unfair. But suddenly two cars screeched to a stop in front of his stand.

The male passenger in the front of the first car rolled down his window and asked, "How de jerk? It good?"

"Yes, I," Devon responded, spotting the gold rings flashing on the man's finger. "De best jerk on de Boulevard."

"Ah hope you telling de truth, rasta, cause I well hungry. Fix I up nuh."

Devon hastily fixed the man a jerk with two Johnny-cakes. The man got out the car, wolfed down a piece, smacked his lips and nodded his head.

"So what de man a say?" came a voice from the back of the car that sounded familiar. Once the window was rolled down, Devon recognized Rude-Man in the back. He was with two women. One of the women's breasts were hanging free from her opened blouse. "So de jerk good?" Rude-Man asked. The man who was still wolfing down the food paused only to nod.

"Hook us up," Rude-Man said as he disengaged himself from the woman with exposed breasts, and climbed out. Rude-Man stood by the man still tearing into the chicken, who looked at him and said, "Chow! What a way you smell like pussy," and spat out a chicken bone.

Rude-Man sniffed at his hands. "Ah so pussy strong fi true," and he called the other woman sitting in the back of the car to bring him a towel. She sighed loudly before getting out. Devon couldn't take his eyes off her. Even though the light was dim, he could see that she was beautiful, her skin smooth and even, her hair shiny, cut short, framing her face. Devon instantly got an erection, and was glad the jerk grill blocked him from the waist down. Disappointed that Rude-Man had not recognized him, Devon tried to concentrate and prepare the food quickly, but he couldn't help but glance at the woman Rude-Man called Marge.

She had the firm body of a sprinter, and when she moved into the light, her eyes were clear and bright like his little sister's, who always hugged him when their mother wasn't looking and told him, "Me love you Dev-Dev, me love you."

It had been several months since he left home and although he often thought about his little sister, he had not sent anything for her. Tears sprang to his eyes at the same moment Rude-Man walked up to his stand. Devon held his breath, hung his head, concentrated on preparing the food and sniffled. He could feel Rude-Man scrutinizing him.

"Is whe I-man know de brethren from?" Rude-Man asked, an edge in his voice.

Devon, as if pulling a shade closed, blocked the memory of his little sister, but not before making a mental promise to write and send her money. Then he looked directly at Rude-Man.

"Irie, Rude-Man. Yes, I, you know I-man. Me fix you up about six months ago at Lime Valley, the club at Central Village. The man is looking boss as usual."

"Blood-claat! I know I know the youth. Rude-Man never forget a face. Seen. So wha you a gwane wid?" Rude-Man smiled widely. "I-man didn't know de youth know how fi jerk. Pass up the food, mek me see if you is any good."

Devon grinned and handed Rude-Man his food. Marge came and stood by Rude-Man, then leaned on his shoulder as he took a bite of the chicken. Devon's heart sank. He had hoped that she was just in the car and not one of Rude-Man's women. Without meaning to, Devon sucked his teeth as he continued to prepare the rest of the food.

"So why mek you kiss you teeth?" Marge asked Devon as

Rude-Man turned to the woman in the car whose breasts were now concealed in her white frilly blouse.

"Is what you having, miss?" Devon asked, without looking at her. He realized he was angry at her for being one of Rude-Man's women, off limits to him.

"Me not sure me want food from anyone who kiss them teeth like them vex, and can't look on me when them ask question."

"Sorry, miss," he said contritely, but still not raising his head.

"If you hold up you head you will see what everyone say, that I'm very easy on the eyes."

Devon did as he was told, and handed her an extra piece of jerk chicken. She took it from him and smiled.

"Marge, come and get in the car and stop running you mouth," Rude-Man called. He walked over to Devon again. "De jerk well irie. You can cook anything else?"

"Yes, I," Devon lied.

"So how comes the man haven't check I? You forget where I live?"

"No, I. But ah just trying to make a little dunnies fah I self."

"Well I-man can help you mek money not dunnies, I. Seen?"

Devon nodded and waited for Rude-Man to say more. "So what de man dream?" Rude-Man asked, catching him off guard. Quickly Devon tried to figure out what Rude-Man was asking. What dream was he talking about? He hadn't dreamt or remembered any of his dreams for a long time, but he knew this was not what Rude-Man was asking him.

Devon scratched his head. His stomach was in knots, his hair felt as tight on his scalp as if he had it in cornrows. He could feel the fear and tears bubbling up inside. He was in school again and the teacher was asking him a question and he didn't know the answer and he knew she was going to hit him, call him a dunce or fool-fool. Devon turned the chicken on the grill, concentrated on his hands, and told himself to toughen-up, to act like a man.

"What a way de man a think deep?" Rude-Man intoned.

Devon stuttered, "Well, well, dream is a big thing…"

"We have to roll, Rude-Man," said the man who had gotten out the passenger seat and whose name Devon never caught. He knew from his demeanour that he was Rude-Man's bodyguard or main man. He noted too that the driver never got out of the car or turned off the engine, even though they had been there for well over fifteen minutes. Rude-Man stepped behind the grill to come closer to Devon. They were almost the same height. He spoke softly to him.

"You know de man could be I-man brother. You look just like me little brother who died five years ago. Ah think that's why me spirit tek to you. So listen here, Bad-Boy," Rude-Man whispered, "me know you fraid fi get into anything too hot and I-man can't say I blame you. So here is what me gwane do fah you. You jerk smoking. I just open a little private spot up town. Legit, for the uptown people. A little place on Constant Spring Road. Some nice go-go dancers, a little gambling and food. You know them uptown man walk with them hungry belly. Me cousin used to cook, but she get sick and says she want go back to country so her mother can look after her. Is deh we just a come from. So I-man need a good cook like tonight. What say you cook fah I-man? Yuh get fi see lots of classy girls, nice body, no stretch mark or cut-up pan dem foot, young, prime, ready to be pluck like a nice juicy mango."

Devon's mind immediately went to Marge, wondering what she looked like in a bikini costume? Did she go topless like Cynthia? Did she dance on men's laps? Did she take men home, too, for extra money? Devon felt like someone was bowling cricket balls inside his head. He wanted to see Marge again. He couldn't stand making love to Cynthia any more. He couldn't help being rough and quick with her, feeling as if what they were doing was fighting, trying to bruise out their disdain for each other. When he fucked her he felt cruel, wanting to hurt her for wanting him, even though he didn't want her. He was using her, and although he had often heard men and youths brag about using women, he hated how he felt every time she made him realize that for him she was only a safe place to stay – and he was not yet able to leave her. Although he'd had the jerk stall for almost three months and it was doing okay, he had not saved. He had bought clothes and shoes, and given Cynthia the money she asked for. Truth was, he was no better off than that night she took him in. Devon felt as if he was locked inside a cage by yet another woman. And like his mother, Cynthia had the upper hand.

"So what de man a say?" Rude-Man tapped his shoulder.

"If I man make de move, I will need a place fi stay." Devon was surprised at the ease with which the words came from his mouth.

"Seen. Everything could work out well. You could be a watchman too. There's a little apartment at de back of de establishment. It need fix up, but you could kotch there. Seen."

Devon nodded, already seeing himself gone from Cynthia. He would give her most of the money he made, buy a bag and pack his clothes in it, and leave while she was out working as a lunchworker. He would be gone, without a trace, before she returned.

"Give I de address, and I-man will come through tomorrow afternoon." Devon knocked knuckles with Rude-Man. He was tired of the bowing and scraping. He was tired of women controlling his life. Rude-Man had given him permission to dream, and he wanted out.

The night of Rude-Man's visit, Devon did the best he'd ever done on the Boulevard. Two people from Central Village stopped to get jerk and recognized him. One man said Devon's mother had been walking around telling people that he stole her money and left while she was at work. Devon told the man that his mother was a liar, that she wouldn't dare to come and accuse him to his face. He suspected that the man would tell his mother that he'd seen him, and feared his mother would come looking for him, just to trace him out about how bad-minded and worthless he was. He was glad that he wouldn't be on the Boulevard any more, but he would still write his sister and send her money.

Devon got home later than usual, and Cynthia was there, massaging her feet, complaining they hurt and were swollen. Devon looked at her then turned away.

"So how it went tonight?" she asked.

"Why every night you have fi question I like you is police? How you expect it fi go? Me is a big man, and ah don't need you fi question me like you is my moda. A tired, so don't bother me blood-claat to rass." Devon's voice bounced off the wall, surprising even himself. Cynthia mumbled under her breath. Devon stared at her hard.

"Ah not up to you mouth tonight or ah gwane have to knock out you teeth," he said, pulling off his shirt and getting his toothbrush and towel and heading to the bathroom. He spent a long time in there, just sitting on the toilet, thinking, not wanting to face Cynthia. He hoped she would be asleep when he returned, but she was not and the naked light in the centre of the room blared harshly. He snapped it off, and slumped down on the bed with a sigh. He could hear Cynthia breathing hard beside him, but he closed his ears, and pictured Marge.

Look how me a go get meself killed, eh? Devon thought, resigned to pursue Marge, even if she was one of Rude-Man's women. He soon fell asleep, not even aware that Cynthia was wide awake, cautious and alert, the memory of her previous man's fist on her body, prominent in her mind.

Devon woke to find Cynthia still in bed. He glanced over at her, then went to the bathroom without saying anything to her. When he returned to the room, she was sitting up in bed.

"Devon, ah not feeling well. Me feet dem swell up bad, and me chest paining me. Ah have gas."

"So what you want me fi do about that?" he asked, annoyed that of all days to be sick, she chose this one. Then he told himself it didn't matter. He was going. He didn't need to take his clothes, or he could come back and get them another day. He wasn't sure how she might react if he told her he was leaving; he didn't want a confrontation. He gathered himself and softened. She had been good to him, demanded little. Had helped him to set up the jerk stand. Showed him how to season it. He had watched her cook on Sundays and had learned a lot. She had a sweet hand, and whenever she cooked he had seconds.

"Just stay in bed," he said, turning to her, "Ah will make you some mint tea and bring you bread." Devon went into the tiny kitchen and made her mint tea, which he sweetened with condensed milk as she liked it, sliced her two pieces of bread and brought it to her.

"You so good to me, Bad-Boy," Cynthia said, taking the tray and caressing the back of his hand.

"So you want me to call and tell them you not coming to work?" he asked, moving just out of her reach. She looked at him as if she was seeing him for the first time, then nodded.

"You have any paper and envelope?" he asked.

"No, is who you going write? You mother."

"No, me little sister. Me think about her last night."

"Me neva know you have sister. What she name?"

"Audrey. Me gwane write her and send her little money."

Cynthia looked at Devon more closely, wondering if he had another woman who he was claiming was his little sister. She wanted to ask, but remembering his anger of the previous evening, held her tongue. If he had another woman, she would know soon enough.

Devon left to call her job and told her he had an errand to run. He was gone for close to two hours, and when he returned he had a shoulder bag slung over his shoulder. She was dozing but woke when he entered the room. The soles of her feet were itching her. Where was he going, she wondered?

Devon took the envelope and paper out the bag and sat at the table and began writing.

"Is Audrey you writing?" she asked.

He nodded his head.

"So how old you say she is?"

"She gwane turn eleven on her next birthday. She must grow big now."

From the ease and manner in which he spoke, Cynthia felt satisfied that Devon was indeed writing his sister. She turned over on her side and dozed. When she woke, Devon was dressed nicely, the bag slung over his shoulder looking heavy. He tapped the sealed letter against his left thumb. He looked guilty.

"You wake up. See some food on de table there for you. Ah gwane post de letter to me little sister, then a gwane check this man about a runnings. Irie. Feel better," and before Cynthia could respond, sleep still clouding her eyes, Devon was out the door, running down the steps, and stepping swiftly out the gate, allowing it to bang shut behind him.

He decided to splurge and take a taxi rather than the two buses that would be required. He arrived at the address about four o'clock and found the gate to the premises locked. He knocked at the gate and a uniformed guard approached lazily.

"Is who you and wha you want?" he asked.

"Rude-Man, ah expect I," Devon replied.

"Man come here all de time saying how Rude-Man ah expect dem and Rude-Man never see dem from de day him born. You have name?"

Devon felt annoyed by the guard's attitude and was tempted to curse him out, but knew that would not get him anywhere.

"I look like man-come-here to you? I is Bad-Boy, so open de blasted gate."

The guard looked closely at Devon; his nostrils flared, but reluctantly he opened the gate. As Devon stepped through, he said, "I is de guard here and me can't just let anyone who come knockin walk through de place. Is me responsible for de safety around here."

"Seen." Devon relaxed, having learned long ago not to antagonize a potential ally.

Rude-Man was not there, but had left instructions for Devon, including what to cook. Devon read the list and muttered, "Blouse-claat!" He'd not expected to have to make so many different dishes daily. All the while the guard had been observing him.

"You gwane need help. I can see that. Me know a woman who don't live far. She just have baby, but her big girl keep de baby when she come home from school. She real cool and cook sweet. She need a little work evenin time, close to home. If you want, me can call her for you, and you can tell Rude-Man is your assistant."

Devon knew he couldn't pull it off on his own. He wasn't sure if he wanted the guard to know he needed help, but if he messed up, then Rude-Man might throw him out, and he was not going back to Cynthia. Devon walked around the kitchen trying to look as if he knew what he was doing. The place was dirty and needed to be cleaned before he could begin preparing any food.

"So what you name?" he turned to the guard.

"Just call me Guardy. Dat's what everybody call me. Me been working fah Mister Rude-Man long years now. We go back a long ways."

"Alright, Guardy, call de woman. But she better be good. She need fi clean this place before I-man can cook. Seen." Devon said this with a scowl on his face, hoping the guard saw that he was tough, and not someone to be messed with.

"No problem, mon, Sista Dee is good people, a hard-working Christian woman. Rude-Man must know that you was going to bring your assistant."

Devon suspected that Sista Dee was probably Guardy's woman or baby-mother or someone he was interested in. He smiled and went to put his things in the apartment in the back, and realized that he and Rude-Man hadn't talked about pay, but he'd assumed it would be more than he'd been making.

That first night Devon saw Rude-Man only briefly and he worked harder than he had ever worked. Sista Dee proved to be a life-saver and well knew how to season meats. Devon watched her closely to learn from her – while telling her she was putting too much of this and too much of that in the food.

The music blasted and the only time he saw any girls that night was when the club closed and they came in the kitchen to get food before leaving for the night. He didn't see Marge, and didn't think the girls were that hot, but they all looked his age, or younger.

There was only a mattress on a broken-down bed-frame in the apartment, but still Devon was happy. This was his first time living alone, not having to answer to anyone. He spent the next week cleaning up the apartment, and when Guardy informed him that there were several half-empty cans of paint left over from painting the club, Devon decided to ask Rude-Man if he could have the paint for his apartment. Learning the run of the place, working out the quantity of food to cook each night and having to take on the shopping for food without Sista Dee's help on weekends when there was a larger crowd kept Devon so busy the only time he left the premises was to shop. Each time, he hoped he would not run into anyone who knew him when he was living with Cynthia or from Central Village to tell his mother that they had seen him. He had written to his godmother to tell her that he was well, sent her some money and thanked her for always telling him that he wouldn't live with his mother forever. Back then, he hadn't believed her, but for three weeks now he had been living on his own.

Just when he had given up on seeing Marge, assuming that she was Rude-Man's personal and private girl so didn't strip at the club, she showed up one Friday night in a short jeans skirt, blue halter top and her nails painted metallic blue. She breezed into the kitchen as if carried on waves, her voice high and loud and demanding.

"You have any food yet? I hungry."

She had not looked at him. Devon felt his mouth go dry. He wanted to respond with something smart, but couldn't think of the words. Sista Dee replied for him.

"You have to ask Cook here. Is him in charge."

"Is me in charge when Rude-Man not here, so just bring me something to eat," Marge said, tossing her head as she walked out of the kitchen. Sista Dee looked at Devon to respond, but he merely stopped what he was doing and made Marge a big plate. Satisfied that she had lots to choose from, he handed the plate to Sista Dee to take to her, without either of them exchanging a word. It just wasn't fair, Devon thought. Rude-Man had been kind to him, but Rude-Man didn't deserve Marge. One or another of the go-go dancers were always going down on him, and on more than one occasion Devon saw or heard him fucking one or more of the girls before they left at night. He slammed the covers down on the food containers and mumbled under his breath. Before things got busy, Marge stuck her head through the kitchen door and said, "Thanks, the food well good." She flashed them a smile and was gone before Devon could get enough of her. Throughout the night, he took every opportunity to spy on her, and was relieved that she was the hostess and not one of the strippers. As much as he wanted to see her naked, he didn't want it to be with other men gaping at her.

Devon had not seen or had much to do with Rude-Man since working at the *Easy Does It Club*, and he was relieved about that. As much as he admired him, Devon was clear about the path he did not want to take. He liked nice clothes, but beyond that he didn't really have an intense desire for fancy things. He allowed himself to dream of one day owning a car and a house, but he was not willing to risk going to jail, or being a wanted criminal to achieve these things. He found he was by nature content with simple things. He enjoyed cooking and learned more and more from Sista Dee, whom he considered a friend, although for quite some time he shared almost nothing about his life with her. Sista Dee had started to tell him about her three children, and her pride in them, especially her oldest daughter who, in addition to being a good student, cared for the baby and the other child while she worked. It was the affectionate way that she spoke about her children that most struck Devon, so that after a while he found himself, almost daily, asking her about them. She appreciated his interest and would eagerly relate various stories, and no matter if she related something unfavourable that they did, she always ended with how much she loved them, how proud she was of them, and how much they made her life worth living. Devon wished that Sista Dee could have been his mother; wished that his own mother could have thought of him this way, even just once. Sometimes when he and Sista Dee talked, he would complain how the onions or garlic made his eyes tear. Sista Dee would look at him and shake her head and say, "Onion mek me cry too," even if the onions had long been peeled and cut. She liked Devon, and although he hadn't told her anything about his life or family, except about his little sister Audrey, she felt he was on the run or had something, some sadness, he was hiding. She also saw how intently he watched the dancers when he got a chance, so one afternoon as they prepared food she asked: "You have woman, Devon?"

Although he had introduced himself to her as Bad-Boy, and everyone else at the club called him that, Sista Dee never did. At first she called him Cook, then she asked him if he had another name, and thereafter she always called him Devon or Cook. Devon was scaling fish to fry when she asked and he paused and looked at her. He had learned that she was indeed Guardy's woman and her baby was his, although they did not live together. Apparently Guardy had a wife and grown children, and was twenty years older than Sista Dee, whom he met at his church. She did not speak about the father of her two older children, except to say that she got an occasional letter from him in America, and though he sent money for the children, he clearly did not understand how expensive it was to live in Jamaica, pay school-fees and buy books, much less shoes, clothes and food.

Because Devon didn't answer, Sista Dee said, "I don't mean

to fast in you business, but I was just wondering, because you is such a nice young man. If me did have an older daughter, or me was younger, you would be a nice young man to have."

The skin on Devon's face tightened and if he could have seen himself, he would have noticed that despite its deep, earth-brownness, it had changed to burnt-out clay. He smiled.

"Me is nice young man? Sista Dee, me no think you know what you a talk bout."

"Me is a good judge of people and me know that you is a nice young man."

Devon went back to scaling the fish, and the mood was broken when, before he could respond to Sista Dee, a delivery van arrived, and he had to stop to check the supplies.

While Devon's feelings about Marge were no less intense, he saw little of her because she only came in on Fridays and Saturdays when he was busiest. She seldom came in the kitchen and, if she did, it was just to give orders or get something. But each time she was there, he observed her keenly, taking note of what she wore, how she moved, and the ease with which she moved among the regular male customers. One night he stepped out into his customary spot, in the hallway near the bathrooms, from where he could see the girls gyrate and dance, to witness Rude-Man corner and warn a man who had been pulling on Marge's hand. "Don't touch she; she off limits." Devon felt his stomach drop. Even though he knew that he was no match for Rude-Man and had always really known that Marge was off-limits to him, hearing Rude-Man spell it out still felt like a blow. Besides, he reasoned, she hardly looked at him, and compared to Rude-Man, what could he offer her?

Devon's motivation waned. He had wanted to fix up his place, but after concluding that Marge was out of his reach, he stopped doing anything. He had bought a new bed and a table with four chairs, but otherwise his place was empty. There was an old TV in the club that Rude-Man said he could have, and when Devon wasn't working or shopping, he watched TV or talked with Guardy, who spent a great deal of time at the club, away from his home and close to Sista Dee.

"So what happen, Bad-Boy?" Guardy began one Monday

when the club was closed and he and Devon sat on boxes outside near the kitchen door, drinking beers. "De man is batty-man or what? Me no see you with no woman."

Devon sprang up, defensive.

"Is who you a call batty-man? Me look funny to you?"

"Easy, easy, Bad-Boy; me neva say you *was* batty-man, me just ask."

Devon kicked at the box on which he had been sitting, took another swallow of his beer, sat back down, and allowed his head to fall between his legs.

"Sometime I-man want a woman so bad my buddy hurt." He cradled his face in his hands, elbows hunched on his knees. Guardy was like the father Devon never had. He felt comfortable with him, and they often talked during the day when no one else was around. "Me no lucky like Rude-Man. That man rass lucky. Look how much woman him have. Him must fuck all the girls in this club, plus him bring others who a hang all over him. Is him rass lucky. If me did have such a sweet girl like Marge, me would a neva look at other woman. Me swear to God." Devon wiped his face with his hands.

"Me did know Rude-Man since him was boy. Me and him father was good friends, and same way Rude-Man have girls, is de same way him father did have women. Is women mek him father dead. Dem wear him out. Him catch nastiness from one of dem women a foreign and get sick and dead, bout fifteen years ago when Rude-Man was still in school. Me tell Rude-Man fi tek it easy. Is time him settle down. Me glad him open dis club and stop some of de stuff him was into. Him no bad like him show yu, yu know, but yu know how it go. If yu no act tough, man want fi manhandle yu and tek whe what yu work for, so Rude-Man have fi act tough fi keep what him have." Guardy paused and downed his third hot Red Stripe.

Devon thought about what Guardy had said, knowing that he spoke the truth, but still he wished that Rude-Man would treat Marge with more respect.

The wind rustled the leaves on the trees, the zooming of cars occasionally interrupting the quiet in the yard where they sat. For a while both Devon and Guardy seemed absorbed by the ordinariness of the day – a doctor bird hovering over a red hibiscus, lizards scurrying, the conversations of pedestrians walking close by on the street, the shadows cast by the sun, the mundane rhythms of the day. When one of the beer bottles rolled over, clanking, Devon picked it up and said to Guardy: "Why a nice woman like Marge want to be with Rude-Man and all him other women dem? She pretty can't done. She could have any man she want."

"Is how you mean?" Guardy sounded defensive. "Rude-Man a send her to CAST fi study accounting. Is her mother used to be cook. You tek her mother' place. Marge is a sweet little girl. Don't let her toughness fool you. Rude-Man and her mother is first cousin, and him promise her fi tek care of Marge; dat's why Marge only come here on weekend and why Rude-Man so protective. Miss Roselyn – dat's her mother – warn Rude-Man dat she will chop him up if him mek any man ruin her one girl-picknie. Rude-Man have fi watch her and mek sure she do well in school. Little Marge live with Rude-Man and him main woman who is de mother of him three children," Guardy explained, stretching out his legs.

Devon shook his head from side to side, trying to unscramble what he had heard.

"So wait! What you saying to me? Marge is not Rude-Man's woman."

"Is deaf, you deaf or what? How you could think that sweet little girl is her cousin's woman? Shame on you," Guardy said, rising in response to a knock on the gate.

Devon was stupefied. He sat there as he heard Guardy greet Runners, Rude-Man's main driver, and open the gate to let him in.

As the information sank into Devon's consciousness, he wondered how he could get Marge to give him the time of day. Would Rude-Man object to him pursuing his cousin? If she was going to school to study accounting, would she be interested in him, a mere cook? Maybe she already had a boyfriend. Maybe she wanted a man like her cousin who had a car and money to blow. Devon felt as if his head was full of marbles. Why would anyone want him? He was a no-good bad boy. That's what his mother always said. But Sista Dee who was kind, as kind as his godmother, said he was a nice young man. Women always wanted nice young men. He didn't plan to work for Rude-Man all his life. He was saving his money. On Sista's Dee suggestion he had gone and opened a bank account. He wanted to have his own little restaurant one day. Maybe Marge would be impressed with that, if he mentioned it to her.

"Me just have to forward meself and be a man; let her know me like her," Devon said aloud, before he noticed the shadow. It didn't look like Guardy, so he looked up and there before him was Marge.

"Is who you talking to, yourself?" she asked, standing over him.

Devon glanced up at her, and the soft, gentleness of her face free of make-up clipped his tongue.

Devon went limp.

TEACHMENT IV:

"Judgement comes to the old; no man can escape if he has squandered his life."

Papa had written this in his book, and whenever I did something he felt I shouldn't do, he didn't beat me, but had me sit and get his book, then he told me to copy this sentence down. Sometimes I had to write it twenty times, sometimes a hundred times depending on how upset he was with me. Even now if I close my eyes I can see the sentence written in bold print in Papa's book. In it he wrote down all the important dates: births, christenings, marriages, deaths, the first day I walked, the first word I said and all kinds of things. I still have Papa's book on my dresser in my room. Since he died I have been writing down important dates, like our Independence day, August 6, 1962. That was a really grand day; it was the day Jamaica became a big person.

So why I telling you all of this? Well the morning of the day I met Padee and directed him to his daughter's house, I had picked up Papa's book, and for some strange reason, I got a piece of paper and wrote that sentence and I put it on the centre table in my living room.

The community had been changing, and now all kinds of professional people like teachers and nurses and civil servants had started to build houses and move here. Mostly they didn't live on my street, just two streets over where the houses were larger and many of them had a carport and a car to put there too. Padee's daughter was a really nice-nice lady with polite children. She had just moved there, not a year yet when he first came to visit her. He would come yearly, and each time he would stop to talk to me.

Now I am not a woman to go foolish for a man, but he is a man who could make most women go foolish. He was dark like black-pepper grains, and his skin was shiny like someone polished it. But it is his mouth that could let a woman lose herself. He had the widest smile that make his entire face light up with pretty white teeth. I tell you that man could laugh and talk all kinds of things nice so, make you just want to be foolish.

Over the years we became friends, and sometimes he would come and have dinner with me. He could certainly make me laugh, but he never seemed settled, so I laughed along with him, but kept my heart locked behind closed door. Each year I watched him get older and wondered whose heart he was stealing.

Still he was my friend. When him come visit his daughter, he would get up early morning and keep me company while me sell at the crossroads. Afternoons he would accompany me home and follow behind me like ant trailing after crumbs. Then he would leave come evening and go eat with his daughter and his grand-children. He loved his grandchildren. And he was proud-proud of his daughter. That Padee was a storyteller. He could tell you a story until tears run down you face like waterfall, and the next minute he telling you a story that make you laugh so hard you fall off the chair, your stomach in stitches. Padee is a man I could have loved, yes, but I was always too sensible for love.

SUN'S SON

Only a handful of men have the good fortune to be Sun's son, Padee is one of these rare breeds.

Fire shouts from his eyes, spilling on you as onto a canvas on which an artist has splattered his passion. His face appears like a sun that dances tirelessly, bouncing up and down. His walk is like lightning darting through a velvety-black sky. Everything about him beckons women to run their fingers over his arms, trace the full, arching lines of his eyebrows, caress his shoulders, press their bodies into his and laugh so close to his face they drink-in his breath, feeling as if they are being undressed in the most delicate, indecent, yet natural way. Ebullience gives voice to their deepest feelings. They are satiated just by the proximity of his body to theirs.

Padee is a man women can't help but touch.

He causes private places to throb and itch.

But even the sun gets tired sometimes, and longs for sleep.

On a not particularly distinguished afternoon, Padee sits leaning against the wall of the grey, weather-beaten wooden tenement where he has a room that no one visits, and muses over his life, chuckling quite often at the memories. For a few seconds he wonders if he had led a foolish life. No. He is proud and happy about the carefree life he has led. Even now at seventy-five, without a penny to his name, no woman in his life for the first time, and no visits from his twenty children, thirty odd grandchildren and many, many great grandchildren, Padee refuses to even entertain the possibility that he might have wasted his life. No! Absolutely not. He's had lots of fun, some of the best women, repeatedly proved his manhood by all the children he fathered. No one could ever claim that he got any "jacket" because all of his children bore a keen resemblance to him. The first thing one saw on meeting his children were their strong white teeth which, like his, were always open to inspection because laughter filled their lives and crinkled lines were permanent around the corners of their mouths and eyes. His children were successful; not one was a thief or whore. His daughters were his pride: two nurses, three teachers, four secretaries, a librarian, a store owner, and two housewives; he has every right to be proud.

Padee nods on his stool. He's glad the rainy season has passed and the earth is once again dry and sure under his feet. Although he's still spunky, his knees sometimes wobble and when the earth is wet, he fears slipping, even when he proceeds gingerly. He was a man accustomed to moving about. Lately, however, since arthritis invaded his knees, Padee is forced to pass the greater part of the day sitting out in the sun, allowing the heat to warm his body while he reflects on his life. Padee doesn't enjoy journeying to the past, but for the last several months, whenever he sat quietly, he found himself travelling that path. The memories steal on him and hold him captive, especially now that his buddies, Sam and Justin, rarely come to visit him.

Friends since childhood, like Padee, Sam and Justin still consider themselves dashing. Often, the three old men would saunter to James Street and pass the day in the dilapidated bar run by Blind-Joe, a distant cousin of Padee's. They would share a half pint of white rum between them, drinking it slowly without water or ice. The small quantity of rum that Padee now consumes is directly related to his all too frequent bare pockets. He remembers the many nights that he drank a pint of rum and was still able to work the next day.

"Yes sah. Dem days me was in me prime!" Padee often says, to no one in particular.

Sun wraps Padee in his shadow and stirs him.

Padee slowly boosts himself off the stool and makes his way to the pit-toilet outhouse. When he opens the door, a swarm of flies greets him and he spits as the stench assails his nostrils. This is a signal that it's again time for him to visit one of his children so he can eat well, sleep in a comfortable bed, and not have to confront his latrine daily. Padee doesn't have to live like he does, but he's stubborn. Some say he cuts off his nose to spite his face. He could be at home with Josephine, his wife of over thirty years, the only woman he married, but he blames her for ruining his life, and has not yet arrived at forgiveness. But his thoughts refuse to linger on Josephine, choosing instead more recent hurts.

His last visit to his oldest daughter, Mazie, was painful. She was angry and accused him of giving her away. Padee had laughed at her outburst. What nonsense. She was his favourite child; she looked like him and her mother, Charmaine, the true love of his life. Padee remembers sadly his break-up with Charmaine; her moving away from their village, leaving the three girls they had made in passionate love behind with her mother. He had felt lost, incapable of looking after his daughters alone, but not wanting them to be raised by Charmaine's mother. That was why he quickly moved in with Josephine, who eventually insisted that he marry her. He didn't feel he could refuse her since she took good care of his daughters. Then his brother, who was a civil servant married to a teacher and living in a fashionable area in Kingston, wrote asking Padee to allow him and his wife to raise one of his many children since they were childless. Padee recognized the opportunity, and though he thought of Mazie as his "little Charmaine", he knew his brother could provide her with a better future. He wanted her to have all the opportunities he, a sixth-standard dropout, could not to give her. But he never articulated these feelings to her, and though she became a nurse through the generosity of his brother – who sent her to university, paid for piano and dancing lessons and bought her fancy dresses – she was angry with Padee and accused him of not having loved her. Why had he given her away to his brother? Padee had smiled at her accusation, but his heart felt as if someone had driven a nail in it. He laughed, not because he was amused, but because laughter was the only antidote to pain, and laughter had kept him alive countless times. He'd laughed again when Mazie, the child he loved most, told him she owed him nothing and he should not expect anything from her, especially since she was recently divorced and had four children to support. Padee laughed and the muscles around his heart tightened. She called him worthless, and laughter squeezed tears from his eyes and his chest pained.

Padee does not understand Mazie's resentment or her bitterness. She has more than most of his other children; she is a success. What does the past matter? Why should it matter who provided for her? She had received the best because of his foresight. But Padee is willing to forgive Mazie her unkindness. Her children, his grandchildren, love him and are always happy when he visits and they listen eagerly to his tales. Although Mazie often appears cross with him, she feeds him well, and has her helper make him his favourite chicken-foot soup almost every day when he visits her.

She should thank me, Padee reflects. *People just don't appreciate their good fortune.* With that thought, he closes the memory. It is then he decides to visit Mazie and enjoy the clean comfort of her house.

Padee goes to get his toothbrush and a change of clothes.

Sun is directly overhead, fooling around like a juggler juggling limes. As Padee steps out into the lane, Sun taps him on his head, but he walks unfalteringly, hoping to mooch a ride and reach his daughter's house before dusk.

Sun follows Padee like a younger brother tagging along with an older brother. Padee's head itches from the sweat which gathers under the felt hat cocked at a dangerous angle on his head. He is poor and alone, but his spirit is not broken. Never that. As long as he breathes and a smile still forms on his face, he can make small dreams come true.

But it is getting more difficult to get women to do more than listen to him with that look in their eyes which says, "Papadee, Papadee, I'd have liked to have known you when you were in your prime; you heart-breaker; you rascal; you sweet dandy." He wishes that young women would want more from him than to bury him before he is dead. If they would just allow him to take their hands in his, play with their palms, smell their sweat from sitting under Sun's vigilance; if only they would acknowledge that he still has the right to look knowingly and longingly as he watches them walk, their full thighs and generous behinds making him sweat more than Sun did. He wants young women to listen to him and agree that his being alive is important; that he, a man, has the right to desire to have them, even though he is old. Age has not quieted his desire; it has given it more focus. Women still make him tremble. A few weeks ago when Inez, the new barmaid at Blind-Joe's shop, almost fell, Padee had caught her, pulling her onto his lap. Feeling her there, the sweet joy of his youth flooded him so that he didn't hear his friend Sam cautioning him to take his hand off the young woman. Padee had wanted to release her, but his need wouldn't let him; he held her firm in his lap, her heat arousing him. She felt good on his lap, even though his knees ached. He wanted her to sit there forever. It was not because he disrespected her that his hands travelled to her knees and were creeping under her skirt. He just wanted to feel the smooth brownness of her skin, to rest his head against her milk-filled breasts, to smell her, drink her in. But she wouldn't indulge him. She tried to get up, but he held her firmly; she broke free from him and vituperated him for being a poor-ass old man who couldn't do anything for her in any form, be it in bed or at the grocery store. Padee quivered at her tirade, then became disgusted. These days, women seemed more preoccupied with what a man had in his pocket than what he had in his pants. Why was it always about food for their children or clothes for themselves?

"Damn! Where de joy? You know what ah saying, man?" Padee had said to his friends. "Me hand have its own mind, not like seh me can tell it no fi wan feel-up oman."

When Padee was a young man and in between women, many days he went without food. Hunger was part of the desire he wore on his face that made women want to pull him to their bosoms. Passionate, loving him all night and through a rainy day, not stopping – not even to eat – women were the very definition of sweetness.

Padee leaves the memories behind and walks on, Sun still trailing. He crosses the street, walking beyond the bus stop where a small group of people are waiting for transportation. There are more people waiting than he had anticipated. Getting a ride will be all the more difficult and the few coins that jingle in his pocket are not sufficient for the bus fare. Padee surveys the group and quickly spots a sprucy-looking young woman, wearing an orange and yellow dress that stops above her knees, her hips jutting out to the street, confident and free. Padee is sure she will get a ride so he approaches; he will stand a better chance of getting picked up if he strikes up a conversation with her. He knows himself. He knows other men and he remembers his escapades when he used to drive from Montego Bay to Kingston. Almost a hundred miles; quite long enough for a man to score with a female passenger. A woman made allowance for a man who gave her a free ride, transportation being a luxury. Padee knows this from experience. He reflects on when he used to drive, first the market truck from his village, then a bus, then a taxi service between Montego Bay and Ocho Rios.

"Dem time me had nuff gal," Padee mumbles to himself. But driving caused him to lose Charmaine, Mazie's mother, his first love.

Sun is romping wildly.

Padee wipes his sweaty head with an old brown-stained handkerchief, pushes his hand deeper into his pockets, hoping to come up with some hidden riches. Nothing. Still he proceeds, smiling at the young woman in the perfectly fitting orange-yellow dress who is gliding over to the coconut man. Padee sees the vendor drink in the woman, dangling his shiny machete in front of his cart full of jelly coconuts. Padee surmises from the small pile of trash by the cart that business has been slow all morning. Encouraged by his observation, Padee's smile widens and his eyes dance.

"Brodaman," Padee opens the bantering, "You jelly coconut dem a sweat. Lemme tell you bout dis fada ah mine known as Massah Sun." The coconut man offers Padee a crate from under his cart; Padee seats himself comfortably and the tale about Sun at noonday unfolds.

"Sun, as you know, is a picknie made in de heat of love. Some seh dat's why him so intense. Spoil and lef fi roam bout de place all day, Sun grew bold and him foot dem wanda nuff-nuff place. Him hardly see him parents cause even dough dem ave picknie, dem still lovey-dovey, always a sneak off to rudeness one anoda. You can well imagine how de big people action sometimes vex Sun. Nuh picknie wan see dem *mama and papa hug-up-hug-up all de time. So Sun jealous. All him did wan is little attention every once in a while."*

Padee pauses and fans himself with his felt hat. The coconut vendor is leisurely husking and stacking coconuts in the cool part of his cart. Padee clears his dry throat and looks around to make sure the woman in the orange dress is still waiting for a ride. He rests his hat on his knees and continues with the tale.

"As de story goes, one day shortly afta Sun tun thirteen, him wanda far-far and him stumble ova tree and stump him big toe bad-bad. Pain shoot through him body; him squeeze him eyes shut and roar like a lion. Well Sun breath was suh hot, him scorch him cheeks and blisters rise up round him mouth. Is frighten, him frighten den. But den him curious fi see wha would happen if him bawl out again. So Sun go all de way down in him belly and bellow as loud as him could."

Padee mops the sweat beading his forehead and neck. The coconut vendor hands him a coconut with a wide opening from which to drink, and signals for him to hold on with the story, as he runs over to a car, handing the extended hand two coconuts and pocketing the money. He sticks the machete in a coconut, then pulls a crate close to Padee. Juice spills on Padee's shirt, but it is so sweet and cool that he doesn't pause until the last drop drains into his mouth. He holds out the coconut to the vendor, who takes it into his palm and splits it down the middle in one swift, clean movement. Padee places his hat back on his head, takes the jelly and spoon fashioned from the husk into his lap and savours the soft, fleshy white meat. When he's done, he throws the husk on the pile. That's when he notices that the woman in orange has moved beside the coconut cart and is surveying him as well as the vendor, mischief in her eyes. Padee smiles at her and continues the story.

"Sun's mama and papa were by de river bank mekin love when dem hear dem son shriek. Same time dem felt de intensity of him rays. Many of de small plants and animals near Sun withered and die instantly. Sun papa rush ova to whe him stood hollerin and tell him fi stop him damn foolishness. But dat day Sun discova dat him was a man who could either impregnate de world around him and produce splendid growth, or him could inflict it, mekin it dry like drought. Sun was a little youth so him didn't know how to measure him manhood. Him

desire fi experience him new powa did well strong. So Sun bleed de earth fah days until him mother step in. She watch him and realize nutten him do outta real badness; little attention him want, so she decide how fi handle him.

"Every day come noon time, Sun mama call him to her and she teach him how to use him power widout bunnin and scorchin up all de earth. She tell him dat de earth is him stage. Sun nuh really know wha she ah talk about, but him glad fah de attention. So eva since dat day and even today, from dat time way back in de ages, at noon time, Sun and him mama wanda de earth slowly, talkin and swappin wisdom. Sun, him always dress-up at noon time and him cheeks puff-out unda de keen attention of him mama. And dat's why him no longa scorch de earth all de time. Sun and him mama a walk still right now."

Padee ends his story. The woman in the orange dress and the coconut vendor squint and, guarding their eyes with one hand, they stare into the noonday sky, as if hoping to see Sun and his mother strolling about. Padee observes them and chuckles. The heat has pasted his shirt to his back, and the woollen pants that one of his daughters in England sent him itch in the oppressive heat. Padee extends his creaking knees and looks around, momentarily disappointed that there isn't a crowd listening to his story. But the coconut vendor carefully selects another coconut, splits open a mouth opening and, as he hands it to Padee, he says, "Dat irie; dat's a irie story."

This jelly coconut is sweeter than the first one and cool going down Padee's throat; liquid trickles from the corner of his mouth, but Padee drinks on allowing the juice to wet his shirt and kiss the earth, an acknowledgement to the spirits, the flesh of his past. Padee and the young coconut vendor smile at each other; both are Sun's sons; it is visible in their tall, panther walk, twinkling eyes, the smile always present on their faces, their willingness to roam and lay their hats wherever a flower blooms. Both men push back their hats and squint beyond the clouds to glance at Sun dressed in bold yellow, with orange flames splattering from his lips as he explains himself to his mother. Even there, sitting under the gigantic cotton tree, they feel the intensity of Sun. Their deep earth-coloured skins glow, their lips part so that their pearly white teeth glisten, and their manhood comes up full on them so that the younger man, the coconut vendor, openly massages his crotch while Padee mops his brow. Everywhere he turns he finds sons.

"So is done de story done like dat?" the sprucy woman in orange interjects. Padee's eyes rove her body, the coconut vendor wets his lips; both men's looks are loud with suggestions as they undress her garment by garment. She feels their eyes like lice on her body, pushes out her chest, throws back her head and laughs.

"Ahsah." She is familiar with the indiscretion of men, their one-track minds. It's a game she plays well.

"Well in some part of de world," Padee banters, feeling obliged to satisfy the woman, "people ave more sense dan to work or walk about come noon time; dem find shade and tek a nap..."

"Siesta," the woman interrupts.

"Same ting," Padee continues, wanting to hold her attention, live in the admiration of her eyes. "Sleeping time was establish out of respect fah Sun, but even here in Jamaica whe we nuh do such tings, when Sun hot like now, we always find shade fi rest and pay we respect to dis mighty fada. Sun is a dancin man, him love fi bruk-up and love-up. Whe'ever dere is celebration, Sun be dere: Crop-over, Revival meetin, Jonkonoo romp, Carnival. Him love good time and him moma nuff-nuff." Padee's voice spreads over the vendor and the woman like avocado pear on bulla cake.

"Sun fulla himself, sah," the woman declares, smiling at both of them. The men now focus their full attention back on her. The coconut vendor's assessing eyes begin at her thighs and slowly travel up, lingering at her waist, pausing at her neck, tripping at her lips. Padee's glance begins at the earlobes, stumbles over the neck and drools on the full mouth painted orange to match her dress and disappears behind her knees. The young woman feels their eyes loving and devouring her, and titters out as if she is being tickled and teased.

"A woman could be in big trouble wid brazen men like oonuh about," she says, leaning against the cart.

They all laugh, relaxed. The young woman is Sun's lover; they recognize each other.

"Coconut man, ah want three sweet jelly fi tek wid me to town."

103

The vendor smiles, nods at her, splits open a coconut jelly and hands it to her. Then he prepares four of his sweetest jelly coconuts. Draining the last of the liquid, she hands him the husk to pry open so she can get to the meat; her fingers touch his as he takes the shell.

"So is suh you sweet like de jelly," she flirts. It is not a question and he knows it. He accepts her invitation.

"Is find out you wan find out?"

The flirtation is open and honest. She pays him for the three jellies, he gives her a fourth, brata, a gift of appreciation, an indication of affection. She saunters off, down the road, waiting for a ride from a passing motorist, not a bus.

The coconut man turns to Padee, his voice soft like the young meat of the jellies he sells.

"So, Papa, whe yuh headin and Sun still naked?"

"Hopin fi spring a ride fi visit me daughta who live jus pass Central Village," Padee offers.

"Dat alrite. Tek dem three jelly fah her so she know dat yuh love her."

Padee thanks the coconut man, clutches the bag with the three coconuts and lumbers off to where the young woman is standing. He introduces himself to her and begins small talk. He knows with her he is guaranteed a ride.

The woman in orange is named Claudette; she lives in Kingston although she is from the outskirts of Montego Bay. She's been visiting her mother who's had a stroke, and has spent the night with an aunt who lives not far from the tenement yard in which Padee has parked himself. Several cars and a few buses stop, and conductors shout, "Town! Town! A town we a guh." But Claudette ignores them all, confident of a ride.

They stand in the ranking sun for almost an hour, then a shiny new cream Oxford Morris zooms by, then comes to a screeching halt several yards away. Claudette steps into the road, shades her eyes and looks at the car. She picks up the basket with the coconuts and the small bag with her clothes and begins moving slowly towards the car. Padee follows behind, thinking perhaps she knows the man in the car. He sweats, breathing hard, holding the bag of coconuts close to his chest. The car reverses towards them. Claudette walks up to the front passenger door and leans her body through the window. Padee is standing to her right and he recognizes the eagerness in the driver's eyes. It is clear that he doesn't know Claudette, but intends to change that.

"Is Kingston a going; you want a lift?" he says with a friendly smile.

"As long as is only ride you offerin," Claudette says flatly.

"Hop in," the driver says, staring into her eyes.

"Thank you; me fada travellin wid me." Claudette motions to Padee.

She indicates her bags, forcing the man to get out and open the trunk, then secure her in the passenger seat up front, but not before Padee is settled in the back seat behind her. Padee waves to the coconut vendor, grateful for the coconuts; he reclines in the seat, now really looking forward to seeing Mazie. The car pulls back onto the road and the cool wind sprays Padee's face; he feels himself drifting, being called by the women and children of his youth.

Sun never did learn how to control his power, and the sons he fathered are the same.

Padee loved women in every way and that was why he ended up fathering twenty children – at least those were the ones he knew of – with eight different women. He was certain all the children who bore his name were his and he took pride in them because they were, after all, a confirmation of his manliness which he wore like a badge of honour and an armour of protection. Women loved him and he loved them, and even though on a few occasions there were spats of jealousy and name-calling, he could always lay his hat at any of his women's doors without prior notice. He loved women for what they were: their strength to continue in spite of endless obstacles; their willingness to forgive; their ability to carry life. What above all drew him was their lack of need to daily confirm their womanhood. Women were complete unto themselves, Padee discovered early, and it was this that he loved and envied most about them, because he was never able to be completely open with them. When he slept with and loved them, it was this quality of completeness that he sought and tried to walk away with from the women he loved, but every time he thought he was close to capturing it, he was accused of some ruse.

His fondest memories are of Charmaine, his first woman. Then there was Josephine, the only woman he married and who'd been his anchor throughout most of his life and from whom he still received food and had his clothes washed, although they didn't speak to each other. But that was another story and his mind didn't want to visit that tale right then. He thought of Janet, the wildest, most daring, disregarding person he'd ever known in his life, his fifth alliance and mother of three of his sons. The others were not as spectacular. Liza and Carol lived next to each other, were lifelong friends and shared everything, including him, and had their two respective children a week and two days apart from each other. But after five years of go-between with the pair of them, Padee felt he was on display and that they were using him like they used everything else that passed through their lives – used as a point of discussion, to provoke laughter, make comparisons or grumble about the unfairness of life and women's lot. He'd decided to stop seeing them after they tied him up the morning of his marriage to Josephine, to try and prevent him from taking his vows. They didn't succeed. After his marriage to Josephine he had gotten involved with Beverley, who was ordinary like her name, except she could cook and had the most beautiful hands he had ever seen. Padee loved kissing her palms or sucking her fingers, which were as sweet as the food she happily cooked for him. But she got tired of his roving ways and found herself a husband. After Beverley, the other affairs, back to back, were with Rosalind and Elaine, two Christian women who professed weakness and obedience, but who, in fact, were quite manipulative and pretended Padee was Jesus to justify their craving for sex. He had the best rudeness with Rosalind after Sunday evening church. But after a time, all these women gave him up. He could always visit them and the children he had with them; they would feed him and even make him a place to sleep, but they all, in their different ways, stopped needing his love. They were unmoved by his pleas, although he tried, mistaking their kindness to mean more.

These were the major women in Padee's life: from farmers to clerks in stores to a typist and a nurse. They were scattered all over the island: the first two women in the parish of his birth, St James, one in Savanna La Mar, others in Mandeville, Port Maria, St Thomas and two in Kingston. He had other women, from time to time simultaneously, but he never made children with any of them, and they were not *his* women, so to speak. He slept with them, whenever he found them willing, but didn't believe a man could say a woman was his until he'd planted his seed in her womb and made children; then they were connected irrevocably. Support or marriage had nothing to do with that bond. Padee still considered all these women his, even though he hadn't seen some in years and probably would not recognize them. Others had married other men and had more children. He had never really supported any of his children, at least not consistently. If he had something when he went to visit, he would give it to them, but he never felt any obligation to provide for them. He was confident of their mother's ability to fend for them, to make a way. He didn't understand why some of his children despised him for not giving their mothers money. He fathered them; they ate; they went to school; they had life. He had to take care of himself, and that was not always easy.

These memories and thoughts whirl in Padee's mind, threatening to burst out as the car comes to a sudden stop. He's jostled awake by the feverish smell of bustling people near Spanish Town market: unemployed men leaning in front of rum bars from which music blares; shoeless street boys peddling the *Star* and its staple of scandalous gossip; men on bicycles, pushing carts, carrying loads; women with baskets, some walking briskly, others sauntering. Padee comes fully awake as the car comes to a standstill in the dense early evening traffic. He wipes the corner of his mouth, rubs his eyes clear and massages his crotch. This is his lucky day. Imagine! By saying he was her father, Claudette had secured him a ride; he isn't even crammed like sardines between others; he has the entire back seat of the Morris Oxford all to himself.

Padee yawns loudly. Claudette turns slightly, looks back at him, a big grin on her face. She teases, "You did well tired, Papadee. You drop a piece a snorin before we travel five miles."

The driver chuckles. Padee leans forward and pats her on the shoulder then returns to gaze out the window at the people hustling and hurrying about. Padee mourns his youth, he longs for it, the joy and speed and sweat of it. He wants it back, the squandered days; the times when he slept with three different women in a single day and was confident that he'd pleased them all; his strength to tally crates on foreign-bound ships; his love and friendship with other men just as strong, just as dashing, just as manly as he was. He lived life and life responded to him. When did it leave him? Why so soon? Padee couldn't imagine anything better than to be a man, a black man in Jamaica, where life was sweet yet hard. Daily a man had the opportunity to carve out his place, to scale fences, to make himself. He knew the truth of his manhood and had, on numerous occasions, confirmed his virility. Was it wrong to love women, to desire them?

The sound of Claudette and the driver talking pulls Padee back. The car makes its way carefully through Spanish Town, picking up speed on the Central Village Road.

Padee leans forward, "Drop me off by de big cotton tree, just before de police station."

"Whe you daughta live, Papadee?" Claudette asks.

"Ah thought you said him was yuh fada?" the driver asks.

"So wait, you is police man now?" Claudette turns sharply to the driver.

A moment of heavy silence, then Claudette chuckles and turns back to Padee to find out where his daughter lives. She tells the driver to drop Padee at his daughter's house, two miles off the main road, and says to him, "Ah just hope you not married, cause me nuh date married man."

"You can come a me yard, come check if you nuh believe me," the driver declares, turning off the main road.

Padee is dropped directly in front of Mazie's front gate behind which is a well-kept yard with flowers in bloom. Stretching his lanky legs from the car, Padee thanks the driver and squeezes Claudette's hand in appreciation. She shows him her teeth, and he sees the splendour of life in her eyes. Padee can smell her womanhood and wants to pull her close and lick the sweat from her face, but he restrains himself, settles for patting her hands, before turning into his daughter's gate. The dogs yelp and chase the car down the road. Mazie is still at work, but his grandchildren are home with the plump, friendly helper who immediately asks Padee if he is hungry and busily prepares him something to eat.

Sun is climbing down into the valley, his breath blowing pinkish-orange fumes into the sky. Sun's art captures your attention and you can't help but pause, momentarily mesmerized, unable to move.

Padee reclines in one of the rockers on Mazie's enclosed veranda. The helper brings him corn-beef sandwiches and lime-ade. His grandchildren have resumed their games; they glisten with sweat, romping with Sun, chasing their shadows, twirling in glee.

As Padee finishes wolfing down the two sandwiches, a cloud passes over him. He suddenly feels cold and shivers visibly. For several months now these feelings have been descending on him like a heavy blanket. He rises slowly from the chair, his knees creaking, and stands to his full six feet, squaring his shoulders, running his crooked fingers over his thinning, mostly salt sprinkled with pepper hair. He does not understand so cannot articulate the confrontation of self with self that he has been experiencing. These feelings began one afternoon as he sat alone in the tenement yard, feeling lonely and abandoned. Now he focuses on his grandchildren at play, not wanting to deal with his memories or feelings. He stands watching his grandchildren until his feet and lower back hurt, but Mazie is still not home. He settles again in the rocker, takes off his shoes and, closing his eyes, allows the pain room.

Disappointment. That was the feeling, disappointment. Padee does not envision the end of his life, yet he knows it is close. He wants bugles, parades of women, salutes to his manhood and outpourings of love from his many children. What had he done to deserve such a fate? He was once a farmer; he knew how to cultivate. Padee shakes his head and clasps his long, gnarled fingers. He remembers what he remembers. Laughter spreads on his face like a shutter being opened in the early morning, flooding a room with streams of light.

Sun had mastered the art of wandering, a charismatic, unapologetic womanizer, always preoccupied with himself. A man who loved women, his job was virility and sweet-talk. You loved and hated him all at once. His sons spent all their lives trying to walk in his shoes, but those shoes were too big for most men, or too tight. Padee's shoes pinched his bunions.

"Sun is still king." Padee's thoughts spill from his tongue as he sits rocking in one of the two rockers on Mazie's veranda, comforted by the thought that he will be cared for and fed. He sees Sun trotting off to another woman, a new sweetheart, camouflaging himself in dusk, his smile tame, one hand in his pocket, whistling as he walks, stopping to pick flowers and thinking about how he is going to take his new love into his arms and hide behind Moon and love her until they both are spent.

As they were from the same village, Padee had watched Charmaine grow up. As a young lad, he would often creep to the river, hide in the bushes and watch her and her friends bathe. Whenever he had the chance, he would brush against her, touching her breasts and behind. She frequently fought him for touching her, both of them rolling in the dirt, tearing off each other's clothes. He loved her peppery spirit, her cinnamon coloured skin, her soft, firm breasts, her small stature – which earned her the name Miss Tiny. Most of all, he loved her slender, long neck, which somehow seemed separate from the rest of her body, and made her appear taller than her four-foot seven-inch frame.

The first time Padee loved Charmaine was in the bush near the mouth of the river; he had ambushed her as she was walking to the river to wash. They were both sixteen. Although he was almost six foot then and strong, she had wrestled him off and knocked the wind out of him. But she didn't run off, instead sat studying him, eyes intense and serious. Once he had regained his composure, he had reached out for her, but she slapped at his hand and said, "Man nuh hold-down oman; man win oman heart." Then she had taken his hand and placed it on her stomach and he felt her heart beating through her navel. He openly watched her bathe that day and for the next two weeks. He brought her fruits, picked her wild flowers, dove into the river and showed off his skills. The third week, as she approached the mouth of the river, she beckoned to him and they made love. Padee discovered that Charmaine was ticklish when he kissed and caressed her neck. He enjoyed hearing her giggle whenever his tongue tasted its salty sweat. He knew from that first time they made love he would always love her, her fragrance and the taste of her neck. He would say to her then, "You is a river and me hands not big enough fi catch all of you." They stayed together for eight years and made three girls. He loved his daughters like he loved the woman who bore them, demanding as she was. Though they had arguments, especially when she insisted on going everywhere that he went, particularly in the evenings when other "decent" women and girls were home sewing or doing womanly things, he soon got used to the idea and rather enjoyed her company, even in the midst of his men friends because she didn't stick out. She played dominoes as well as any man, could knock back a rum and didn't make men feel like they had to censor their language in her presence, even though, out of respect for her, they did. Charmaine wore femininity like flowers wear colours, so many of Padee's friends envied him. He knew that they would try for a piece the first opportunity that availed itself, but he was confident of Charmaine's affection and fidelity.

The trouble started when he was hired as a truck driver, delivering bread and biscuits. He was often required to drive to Kingston, which sometimes meant being away for a few days. He had no intention of seeking women, but temptation was always stalking in some corner, ready to strike. She struck: a barmaid with an arse so fine, with lips stained glossy purple like starapple's skin. Padee just wanted to taste if her lips *were* like the sweet, milky juice of starapple. He sat drinking a beer after delivering bread and saw her giving him the eye; he tried to ignore her and concentrate on his beer, but the more the barmaid moved casually, swinging her hips, her hand always lingering on the shoulders of the men she served, the more Padee's desire rose and his manhood ran forward. He ordered another beer, even though he was not done with the one in his hand. As she approached, her skirt tight around her hips, her breasts small and round, Padee glanced out the corner of his eyes. Damn! She could walk, and she knew it, gliding and twirling all in one. She had him. He knew she had him. Padee surrendered. She was bold. She placed the beer in front of him, brushed the side of her body against his arm and rubbed her wet finger in his palm as she took the money from his hand. She was a dangerous woman. Yet even now he would give his left hand just to experience that moment over again.

Padee sent a message with a fellow driver to his boss and Charmaine, claiming that the truck had broken down. He stayed locked up with the barmaid for three whole days, returning home broke and weary. Well, sweet nanny goat run him belly. A week after his return, Padee's buddy hurt when he peed. Finally he went to the clinic and the nurse asked him what was wrong – in front of the whole clinic of people. He smiled and put his hand in front of his pants. She did not understand his gesture so asked more loudly. He whispered, "Me buddy hurt when me pee."

"Wha you do mek you buddy hurt?" the nurse inquired loudly, looking at him squarely, a quiet smile on her face. The clinic rang with laughter. Padee didn't know how to tell Charmaine, but the nurse said he had to as she needed treatment too.

Charmaine hit Padee on his head with a pot when he told her; she screamed that he was no good, then packed up her things and left, leaving their three young daughters with her mother as she headed for Runaway Bay to stay with an aunt. Charmaine never spoke to Padee after his infidelity, not even a year later when she married a farmer in Runaway Bay, or even years later when she had two sons, one after the other. She died when Mazie was nine, but Padee had long given up hope of them ever getting back together.

What Padee regrets now, after all those years when he had convinced himself that he had pushed Charmaine out of his mind, is that he never took the time to tell her before she died that he was ashamed of sleeping with the barmaid, or that he loved her, next only to his mother. But he was also angry with her for giving up her daughters, just because they were his.

Blinking, Padee opens his eyes, which are moist. The children are no longer playing in the yard. The breeze has waned; Padee's eyes follow a flock of black birds heading home, their splendid wings spread, their leader at the peak of the isosceles triangle that they formed. He thinks of flight, but to where, now that he is in the deep,

deep harvest of his life? All his life has been spent in flight with laughter his shadow. He has never probed the reasons why of anything; he was always moving in or out, gathering his few belongings and finding somewhere else to rest his head.

Sun is in hiding. Padee gets up slowly from the rocker and walks into the living/dining room where the table is neatly set. The helper offers him another glass of juice, and tells him to go and lie in his grandsons' room if he is tired. Padee shuffles into the room, plops down on a single bed near the window. He is surprised at the neatness, everything in place, doily on the dresser matching the curtains and bedspread. Josephine, the woman he moved in with two years to the day Charmaine left him, and whom he married ten years later, keeps a tidy house like this, he reflects, memory taking hold of him like a bitch carrying her puppy in her mouth.

After Padee lost the job delivering bread, he had gotten another one delivering furniture around Montego Bay. One Tuesday afternoon he had delivered a mahogany upright cabinet to Josephine's house. She lived alone as four months earlier her father had died, going the path of her mother who had preceded him two years earlier. Josephine was a light-skinned woman, the colour of yellow yam, fleshy, with strong legs and a bosom to sleep on. He admired her and told her so. She invited him to return on Saturday evening and sit with her on the veranda. He did and three months after Padee had delivered Josephine the cabinet, he and his three daughters, whom he took from their protesting grandmother, moved into Josephine's three-bedroom house. She was a quiet woman who took pleasure in combing his daughters' hair, making them pretty dresses and taking care of him. No matter what time he came home she always had his food neatly covered on the table waiting for him; the house was always clean with floral curtains and doilies everywhere; his clothes were always starched, pressed – including his underpants – and neatly folded in drawers. She never nagged him, although her silence was sometimes an anchor weighing him down.

Josephine wasn't a strong woman and had difficulty carrying a child to term; she lost four before she gave birth to Padee's first son. It was at that time that Padee's oldest brother (the civil servant, married to a teacher who was unable to have children) wrote asking Padee to allow him and his wife to raise one of his children and he decided that Mazie would be the beneficiary. The decision had been made in love, but the day Padee took Mazie to his brother and his wife all he said to her was, "Behave yuhself and listen to yuh uncle." Then he was gone, with only a quick hug and pat on her head.

Padee turns on his side and snores loudly and the story of his birth floats around inside his head.

Padee was born feet first, his slender long soles seeming as if they were feeling for solid ground on which to go wandering off. Padee was born hands second, fingers touching skin. Padee was born a child in a man's body and how his mother lived after the unreal ordeal of his birth was nobody's business. But she did, and when she moved his mouth to suckle him at her breast, he played with her nipples, licking as a cat rather than sucking. But after his difficult beginning, he never gave his mother any trouble, was always a comfort to her. They fell in love with each other from the very first, and Padee never stopped loving her, not even after she died when he was more than thirty. He had a premonition that day. He was due to drive to Kingston, but refused – and was fired. Padee's attitude was: easy come, easy go; he didn't allow trouble to mar his steps. He was determined to visit his mother as he had dreamt about her four times that week. On his way there, he'd stopped at the market to buy her favourite yam, St Vincent. When Padee entered the gate of his mother's yard, the dogs barked as if he was a stranger. He had to shoo them in a rough voice before hollering, "Mamaoh!" as he'd done ever since he was a boy. He waited but no familiar reply, "Papadeeoh!" invited him into the fold of his mother's arms. A new puppy jumped around his legs, and Padee used his left foot to push it out his path as he walked to the side of the little cottage where his mother often sat in the shade near the cat-o-nine-tail bush. There Padee found his mother bent over on the bench where she sat, her face in pain, her mouth ajar, the upper lip twisted to one side. Padee dropped the bag of yam, lifted his mother in his arms and took wide strides to carry her into the dark, cool house where the shutters were partially closed. He gently laid her on the bed and reached for the water jar on the bedside table. Miss Esmee opened her eyes, looked into her son's face and smiled. Her leathery hands, much like his, except wrinkled, reached up and caressed his face, then fell to her side. Padee bent and kissed his mother. They held each other's hands, silently waiting; one feeling the life fading out, the other receiving the life moving over for him. All was silent for a while. Padee's mother smiled up at him, then closed her eyes. In the same moment the old hound started howling. Miss Esmee clutched her son's hand. Padee's tears began to fall, first like dew shaken from a tree, then like stones pelting a roof. His body shook as he felt the warmth of his mother's hand turn to stiff coldness. His tears washed over her and he sat for many hours, his mother pressed against his chest. He would have sat like that forever if his aunt Ada, his mother's sister, had not come and found them. She had to get help to pry Padee away from his mother.

Six months after Miss Esmee had been buried, Padee was still mourning her. He made himself a prisoner in her room, daily eating roasted St Vincent yam that she loved and drinking cocoa that she used to harvest. He lost twenty pounds, abstained from women – for the first time since he was fifteen – and did no work. He did little beside cook, bathe himself and sit on the bench by the side of the house. He might well have continued in this way if his mother hadn't dreamed him. He might well have continued disregarding the women who visited him daily, bringing him all kinds of delicious dishes; ignored Josephine's pleas for him to come home, telling him that his children missed him; and continued shying away from his male friends who visited him, sitting around rude talking in the hope of enticing him out of his mourning. His mother's death made him feel extremely vulnerable. She was the first woman who had smiled at him, told him he was loved and special and that he was her man. She was his first and most passionate lover. She had given him himself as an investment. Some of the women who observed Padee grieving became jealous of his affection for his mother and hoped that he would be a tenth as dedicated to them as he was to her.

Miss Esmee decided enough was enough, so she dreamed

Padee one night, knocking him off her bed, pulling his arms as she often did when she had to wake him to get up for school, or to fetch water to fill up the drums. Padee hit the floor, coming wide awake, laughter spilling from his throat, startling the croaking lizard. He knew then that his "mamaoh" was back. He wanted to touch her, kiss her cheeks, but her eyes told him to stand back, sit quiet and listen. She talked to him until morning broke and Padee saw Sun peaking over the mountain, a rude boy hiding to watch his mother change her clothes. Padee had done that countless times, spying on Miss Esmee. He bursts out in laughter. His mother had caught him in the act.

Sun sprang from behind the mountain and sprinkled the zinc roof. Tiny diamonds fell onto the floor and Padee's mother told him to go outside and dance under the sun.

For the next three weeks after Miss Esmee had visited Padee and told him to get on with life, everywhere he walked, women smiled at him, mischief playing at the corner of their mouths and satisfaction oozing from their bodies.

Mazie's children greet her at the gate, each vying to be the first to kiss her. Almost in unison they tell her that their grandfather is here. Mazie finds her father asleep on her son's bed. He looks tired and weary, and in that moment she remembers their quarrel that last time he visited and regrets having been so harsh. But she can't help but believe that he doesn't love her, or why else would he have given her to his brother to raise? Mazie sits on the edge of the bed and gently shakes her father awake.

He rubs his eyes as if to clear them and says, "You look jus like yuh muma."

Mazie is taken aback. She doesn't know if looking like her mother is good or bad. She walks to the dining room and calls her children for dinner. Padee joins them and leads the grace. All throughout the meal, Padee jokes and teases his grandchildren. Mazie is all ears and eyes. Stuffed, they gather on the veranda. Mazie sits in the rocker beside her father. She wants to touch him, to talk to him, but she doesn't know where to begin. They rock in rhythm. Then Padee takes his daughter's hand in his rough but warm palms and pats it.

"Yuh pretty bad. Just like yuh muma, Charmaine. She was me first love," Padee whispers.

Mazie shivers. It is as if the moon speaks those words.

The day is gone and Madam Moon is only half-dressed, splendid in her golden-blue frock, her hair swept up on one side, the other side of her head half-hidden in the clouds. The evening is pale, not velvety black like Padee likes it, especially when he is at peace as he feels now, his stomach full and surrounded and bathed in the love of grandchildren and his daughter.

Time moves slowly, lethargic.

Padee steadies his rocker, his grandchildren at his feet. He begins the story.

"Sun's birth catch him mama by surprise. Oonuh wan hear how it go?"

The children nod their heads and clap their hands. Padee clears his throat.

"*One time, long, long, long time gwane, Madam Moon did live in de Ocean. De fact of de matter is, Moon and Ocean was one person in charge of life and death, food and drought, sorrow and joy. All anybody had was fi do is knock pan OceanMoon door and beg her wha dem need. Well yuh know how some people badminded. A few old nega get jealous, a few long-eye sumbody get angry, and a few grudgeful ones plot fi tek weh OceanMoon power.*"

Mazie's youngest, not yet four, crawls into her lap. She gently kisses her daughter on the forehead, cradling the child in her arms. The other children clap at mosquitoes. The light of a passing car temporarily blinds Padee before disappearing down the road. Padee leans forward, his hands grasping the sides of the rocker. The dog sallies on the veranda and creeps between the two boys. Seated at Padee's feet; they ruffle its fur.

"Go on wid de story, grandpa," the older girl, back resting against her mother's legs, encourages. Padee swallows and continues.

"*Yuh see, back in dem days, people call her OceanMoon or MoonOcean according to dem fancy; it neva boda her wha dem call her as long as dem show her respect. Well OceanMoon or MoonOcean did well powerful. Fire, a braggadocious little man who did live nearby, did well love OceanMoon. But every time him practice plenty speech and dress up and guh visit OceanMoon, she force overpowa him and him was nutten but a little beenie flame in OceanMoon's presence. Him was too weak and shy fi enamour she wid him love. Afta she shame-shame him plenty time, Fire join de conspiracy fi tek weh some a MoonOcean powa. But ebery plan him come up wid fail, cause before Fire can reach fi sit-down in OceanMoon livinroom, him powa would be smitten and him wouldn't ave nuh energy fi even declare him love. Finally, eaten up wid anger and feelin like OceanMoon mek fool of him, Fire go to a obeahman and pay him plenty-plenty money fi blend potion catch OceanMoon."*

"How did Fire know where to find the obeahman, Grandpa?" the oldest grandson asks Padee, as he stretches his cramped legs.

"Just listen and you will find out," his mother quiets him.

Padee's rocking is smooth and even; he picks up the story as if the interruption was a part of the plot.

"Obeahman consida Fire request fah a long time cause him didn't have no quarrel wid OceanMoon. In fact, him did fancy her himself, plus him draw nuff powa from she twinself. But Obeahman did greedy so him mek Fire convince him if he help him tame OceanMoon and de both a dem would benefit. And dat's why even today, de obeahman is not sumbady fi trust, cause long-long time gwane, him allowed Fire fi samfie him fi steal OceanMoon powa, but dat's anoda story.

"Anyway, Obeahman blend a potion fah Fire, and quick time, Fire saunter off fi visit OceanMoon. Now all a we know, unless is hurricane season, de ocean calm at night like blanket. Dat's cause she tired like we and need she beauty sleep tuh. So wha you tink Fire do? Him wait and strike at night time. Wen him hear OceanMoon snoring, Fire tiptoe like cat and spring dry foot pan her veranda. But Fire suh scared, him breathin hard, and before yuh know eh, him wake up OceanMoon. Fire scared bad cause Obeahman warn him nuh fi wake de great Madam. OceanMoon tun pan she side and open she eyes fi see wha disturb she sleep. Same time, Fire feelin him power wanin, open de bottle of potion Obeahman gave him and dash de whole a eh in OceanMoon eyes cause him couldn't stand de idea of her findin him powerless in she bedroom and laugh pan him, den flingin him out pan him backside.

"De potent bun OceanMoon eyes. It was just like acid nyamin away at skin. OceanMoon bawl out a painful scream dat echo all over de place, and in she haste to get up, OceanMoon roll ova. De sea rumble

and roll, great waves lash up against de shores and flood de land. In she agony, Ocean and Moon separate and de earth was dark fah two hundred and seventy-three days. Den one day de people heard so dreadful a scream dat dem dig hole and hide dem head. But afta a few hours de world quiet, except fah baby bawling, and bright-bright light light up de place. De people crawl out dem hidin and discova dat Ocean and Moon separate and a bawlin picknie, de image of Fire, was cradle in Moon arms. Same time de picknie chat and seh him name Sun, Fire picknie. But him bad can't done cause him did form in treachery. Fore you can seh, 'Who dat?' Sun scorch up de whole place. Moon had was to collar him and teach him manners.

"Ocean and Moon mourn dem partin, but wha dem could do but mek de best of ah bad situation. So dem decide, night time, when people sleepin, dem would visit each oda, and reflect each other joy and beauty. And if you doah believe me, go to de ocean when moon out and you will see dem a chat-chat and laugh. As fah Fire. Well, him was lef alone to him own misery, him powa curtail. But wheneva Fire get a chance, him blaze thru de heart, leavin a trail of pain and him own pent up desire in piles of ashes."

Long after Padee ends his tale, Mazie and her children sit in silence staring at the moon. They are spellbound; myriad thoughts rush through their heads. Mazie's arms are cramped where her youngest daughter Charmaine, named after her mother, lies asleep. Then the dog gets up, shakes himself, as if to say, "Me nuh impress," and ambles off the veranda.

"Grandpa, is true story dat?" Stanley asks. He's the younger of the two grandsons, named in Padee's honour, eyes dazzling even in the dim night light. Padee chuckles. His dinner has settled, but his mouth craves something. Mazie is still caught in the plot of the story. She finds the idea of it intriguing and beautiful, and so true, her mind flitting to the relationship between men and women. She doesn't want to get up and put the child to bed. She wants to go for a stroll, to stand in the open air, bend her neck way back and stare into the sky.

The older children seem to read her mind; they implore in chorus: "Mummie, we can go by de gate so we can see de moon betta?"

"Yes," Mazie smiles, rising with difficulty, the sleeping child in her arms. The three children race down the five steps leading from the veranda. Moon smiles down at them and they wave. The children cannot see the ocean from their yard, but Stanley, the younger boy, suddenly remembers the large conch shell in the living room, and shouts while still running, "Lewwe go hear de sea in mummie's shell!"

Racing, they push their ways inside the house. A fight ensues about who should put the shell to whose ears first. Padee intercedes, holding the shell to each ear. The children's faces light up as the splashing of waves yowls in their ears, a lament of longing. Little do they know it's the sound of their hearts. Soon bored of the novelty, they dash into the kitchen, turn on the stove, blow out the flame in anger and scold Fire for separating Ocean and Moon.

Mazie calms them and, not without loud protests, sends them to bed. After brushing their teeth, kissing their mother and grandfather and singing out goodnight, they try to imagine themselves in that time, way in the distant past. And when their heads rest on the pillows and their heavy lids cover their eyes, they dream of the time when Ocean and Moon were one, uniting the earth, ocean and sky.

Long after the children are asleep and their snoring rings through the house, Padee and Mazie sit on the veranda, sipping hot Milo and staring up at the moon. Finally Mazie turns to her father and, in a voice wounded with pain, says, "You never told me these story when I was a child."

To Padee's ear, his daughter's voice has the feel of bread weighed down by water. He has no words to erase Mazie's bitterness, so he pulls her hands in his, and the tears in her eyes are the same tears that blind him.

Padee stays three weeks with Mazie, the longest he has spent with her since she was an adult, and while he is there, she takes him to see four of his other children who live nearby. Padee marvels that they are all the spitting image of him, especially the girls, which explains, to his way of thinking, why they are all doing so well. Everyone knows that girl-children who resemble their fathers are blessed. They are all ebony hued, with black gums which contrast splendidly with their strong white teeth when they smile; they are all full of laughter and take great pleasure in life.

"Me life nuh wasted," Padee ruminates. He has fathered more laughter than most other men, loved more women than he can remember and just now feels bathed in love. For the first time, Padee and Mazie speak to each other as adults and he tells her things about her mother that no one has ever told her, things only he knows. He is contrite; he tells Mazie that he loves her, and how much he missed her after she went to live with her uncle. Mazie feels cheated but, not one to harbour grudges, forgives her father. "What's the point?" she thinks to herself. "Soon he will die and what will I do with my hurts then?" When Padee says it's time to leave as he has *other fences to mend*, Mazie, on impulse, invites him to live with her and his grandchildren. Padee declines, promising to visit more often. Mazie and her children drive him to the train station. Before boarding the train to return to Montego Bay, Padee takes Mazie into his arms and tells her that she is beautiful and that he always knew, with opportunity, she would be successful. Mazie understands that this is her father's way of asking for her forgiveness. She embraces him and whispers in his ear, "Ah glad you fathered me and loved my mother."

Long after the train pulls off, Padee dabs at his eyes. At the end of the long ride, he rises and tucks the tail of the new, royal blue shirt into new woollen pants, both are gifts from two of his sons whom he visited during his stay with Mazie. He glances at himself in the dusty window of the train, confident that he is still a dandy. Old, yes, but dashing with his felt hat slanted to one side. Padee steps off the train; his slight bow-leg gives his walk the suggestion of bounce and vigour. He pauses, looks around as if seeking someone to meet him, but of course there is no one. Still, the smile remains on Padee's face as he ambles from the station.

Sun isn't out today, trapped in the clouds, in the skirt of some woman.

Padee knows he has one last major load to get off his mind, but he feels hopeful. Mazie has accepted him as her father; she understands he is a father who tried to do right by his children, even if they don't understand his ways. Full with this feeling of tying up loose ends, he takes the road leading to his wife, Josephine.

He is unaware of the bustle about him as he walks.

For a minute, Sun peeks out, but quickly pulls back his head. Padee chortles at this father of his, forever playing games. His mind drifts to the past.

Four years after moving his three daughters into Josephine's house, Padee had gotten entangled with Liza and Carol. For three years he carried on with them, while living with Josephine. Throughout the seven years, Josephine had cared for him unselfishly and loved his daughters as if they were her own. The only time Padee recollects Josephine opposing him was when he decided to send Mazie to live with his brother. She told him there was no need to send her away, even calling on the neighbours to help her persuade Padee that it was wrong. After he sent Mazie away, Josephine didn't speak to him for a week. His other two daughters regarded her as their mother. It was when Josephine finally carried a child to term that she demanded Padee marry her, or else, she said, "You gwane ave to leave wid you womanizing ways, and you not takin any child wid you either." Padee realized she was serious so he agreed. A month after she gave him the ultimatum, the wedding was planned for a Saturday evening. Josephine made her own dress, as well as dresses for his daughters.

The Friday evening before the wedding, Padee decided to visit Liza and Carol, both of whom were pregnant again. The three of them had a good time and they convinced him to spend the night. He ended up sleeping with Liza whose house was next to Carol's. Early Saturday morning, as he was preparing to leave in good time to get to his wedding, Carol knocked on Liza's door and excused her outside. As Padee fumbled around for his shoes, Liza and Carol barged into the room and cornered him. Someone had just informed Carol that he was getting married – that very day. At first he denied it, then admitted it was true. He had not anticipated them getting so angry. They had always known he lived with Josephine, and that had not prevented him from visiting them and making children. However, marriage to Josephine suggested more commitment, a favourite; Liza and Carol were livid. Before Padee knew what was happening, they gagged him, pulled off all his clothes, except his underpants, tied him to a chair in Liza's bedroom, then took their children and left. Padee stayed a prisoner for three hours, until he managed to kick over the chair and roll to the window, crying out for help. A little boy who had come to steal tamarinds heard his shout. The boy crawled to the window and peeped in.

"Mek you tie up like dat, sah?" the boy asked in a whisper.

Padee laughed before answering. "Me wife so jealous she fraid someone steal me so she tie me up. But is church ah suppose to go. Ah promise de preacher to help him fix some church benches." Padee forced a chuckle. He could tell from the boy's frown that he was not sure what to do, but Padee knew what would force his hand. "If you leave me tie-up here, Sunday, when you mama go church, she won't have no bench fi sit pan," Padee stated matter-of-factly, then began whistling a tune. Convinced, the boy pushed open the window, crawled through and untied Padee. Once Padee was free, he dashed through the window and ran down the road in his underwear, praying he would not encounter Liza or Carol.

Luck as usual was on his side, and he was able to borrow high-water pants and a shirt from a man who lived nearby. Even so, Padee arrived at the church very late. Josephine, his daughters and over twenty other people were waiting, bottled up in the hot chapel. He couldn't find a smile to face Josephine with, but hadn't needed one, because she didn't look at him, not even when the preacher asked, "Do you take this man to be your lawful...?"

She had replied hotly, cutting off the pastor, "Yes, him is de cross me ave fi bear."

When they returned to their house, many more people than had been at the church congratulated Padee and Josephine. However, she still refused to speak to him, and when it was time to cut the cake, she shoved him aside and called his daughters to cut the cake with her. The eating and drinking had gone on late into the night, but Josephine ignored Padee. She did not speak a word to him for an entire month after their wedding, nor did they share a bed. After Liz and Carol had tied up Padee, they had gone to see Josephine and traced her out, cursing her loudly. Everyone said the marriage was a joke and wouldn't last. Indeed, with every new woman that Padee had outside, Josephine grew more silent, although she welcomed all his outside children into her home.

She gave birth to two sons, and a daughter, yellow and sickly. Her face aged with her unhappiness. She loved and hated Padee, but felt tied to him. An only child who'd cared for both of her parents until they died, Josephine had not had much love in her life and had not believed that she would find a man to marry or have children. The moment she had seen Padee she fell in love with him, with his zest for life, his laughter and even what she read as his refusal to be tied to any one person. She loved him, knowing that she would never be able to tame him, and she really didn't want to, envious as she was of his wandering spirit. Whenever he had needed her, she was there for him. But that changed.

Two years ago, Padee moved out of Josephine's house, the home where he had always found peace, a delicious meal and clean clothes. He never told her why he left. He remembers it clearly.

It was a musky Wednesday afternoon. Padee had arrived home and made his way quietly to the backyard. As he got to the side of the house he recognized Josephine's voice and the voice of her lifelong friend, May. He was about to call-out to them, when he heard May say, "Josie, memba de obeahwoman yuh go fi tie-up Padee. She dead yuh know. She did know her work. Me memba how Padee fall off de truck, almost bruk him back; how de accident mek him did afi keep him ass home fah almost two years. Damn dog. Is yuh husband, but me nuh know why yuh put up wid him. Fi him hood must lace wid honey." May paused, her voice like dry leaves underfoot. Then she added, conspiratorially, "Ebery dog ave him day and ebery puss him four o'clock, and is fi you day now cause me see de one Padee home ebery day dese last few years."

Padee was riveted to the ground. He stood sweating. Then after what seemed like an hour, he heard Josephine cough up phlegm and spit. And in a tone flat as bammi or cassava bread, she said, "Him home now, but him nuh ave no use. Padee mash-up afta whorin fah most ah de seventy-three years of him life." Padee could not move from the spot where he stood glued, sweat sucking his shirt into his skin. The sound of the fishman pushing his cart up the street was what unglued him. By the time the man shouted for the second time, "Fishee! Fishee! Fresh fish!" Padee's feet found wings and by the time he got to his cousin, Blind-Joe, and collapsed onto a bar-stool, he was out of breath, sweat dripping from his body as if he'd been caught in heavy rain.

Padee could not bring himself to tell Joe or his friend Sam, who was also there, what he had just heard. But after knocking back two shots of rum, Padee begged Sam to go to Josephine and demand his clothes as he was not going to live with her any more. Padee could not be talked out of his decision, so Blind-Joe got him a room in one of the tenement houses he owned, where Padee has been living ever since – two years, three weeks and four days.

Josephine tried several times to convince Padee to move back home, even visiting the yard where he had his room, hoping to learn why he moved out. But Padee refused to talk to her, locking himself up in his room whenever she came. After a few months Josephine gave up, but she still sent him food with one of the girls who was apprenticed to her. Padee never ate anything she sent. A boy, who before Padee moved into the yard was frail, fattened up nicely.

Padee puts aside his memories, like a handkerchief tucked into a pocket. He has no more use for bitterness. What Josephine did was wrong, but perhaps he deserved what happened.

The house is just ahead.

Sun closes its eyes tight and turns on his stomach.

Every dog has its day and today is Padee's. He chuckles.

Padee steps sprightly into Josephine's yard where, over the years, with his help, she has built two cottages in the rear which she rents. This, along with her sewing, puts food on the table and contributes towards the children's education – including Liza's and Carol's four.

Quietness reigns.

The yard is swept clean and Padee notes the lines on the loose brown soil left by the broom and he smells the arid heat and dust that rises. Padee stands by the gate surveying the yard, seeing it as if for the first time. Forty odd years he has lived here, on and off, but today he surveys the whole place registering all the details: the fowl-coop tucked to the far right side of the yard; the splendid blackie mango tree laden with fruits; the hedge of gungo-peas that tries to shield the coop from full view; the shrub of red and yellow hibiscus near the gate; the crotons that enclose the yard as far as the eyes can see; the lime tree, like a little soldier in front of the two cottages; the old tamarind tree, trunk twisted and hollow in places; the old basins in the middle of the garden; tomatoes growing near the veranda; splintered pieces of boards, piles of discarded zinc sheets, scraps of bicycles and other items that throughout the years he has shoved under the house, which Josephine has asked him many times to discard. The quietness frightens Padee. No clothes flap on the line; no dogs bark; no lizards dart; no voices divulge lifelong secrets.

Fear runs down Padee's spine; he doesn't recognize the quiet. He stands waiting for a child to run out to greet him, for Josephine to stand in the doorway, her hand shielding her eyes, looking like a satisfied cow, asking him if he is hungry. Too quiet. No laughter to swallow his thoughts. The peeling paint on the house accuses him. Yellow is not the colour he remembers it being. Where did time go? All the laughter? Children bickering? Where is Josephine seeing to his food, pleading with him to stay home just this once? Sickly Josephine. Contented Josephine. Josephine who always opens her legs for him, but who never seems to get any pleasure. Fat Josephine. Josephine who cared for all his stray children. Josephine who was cursed and even beaten by other women for him. Good Josephine whom he loves but never liked because he senses that she doesn't like herself. Josephine always there. Forgiving Josephine. Clean Josephine. Sewing Josephine. Josephine with a big heart, but only a little place for herself. Josephine who is reluctant to demand anything for herself, who silently put up with his love for other women, with his drinking, his domino playing, his wandering, his need to be free. Where is Josephine?

Padee looks at the ashy grey sky, and clutches his head remembering the pain, too many years ago to still be aching. Anger jumps on his back like a rooster riding a fowl: he was in the prime of his life when he fell off the truck. No one could explain his accident, but Josephine knew; she had obeahed him. His mother had said as much, but Padee had laughed, dismissing her. He didn't want

126

to judge or malice anyone, or he too would be subjected to the same rules.

Pain shoots through Padee's head. He slowly climbs the stairs leading to the veranda, clutching the bannister. Once there, he drops himself on the nearest chair and hollers at the top of his voice, "Josie! Josie! A fagive yuh."

All at once sound bleeds from everywhere: dogs bark, a radio blares from the next house, a woman sings at the top of her voice, out of tune; water drips in a basin or bucket; leaves rustle in the cool evening breeze; crickets chirp. Noise tries to swallow the pain and vexation beating steel-pan in Padee's head. Then he hears voices approaching, that of Josephine and probably one of her apprentices.

He presses both hands to his temple and shouts, unnecessarily, as the figure appears at the door, "Josie! Josie!"

"Papadee," Josephine says, pulling a scarf over her head, greeting him as if they rose together this morning. "Yuh hungry? Food cova pan de table." She steps onto the veranda, regarding him, her eyes dull.

"A eatin out yah," Padee says flatly, tapping the arms of the chair and beginning a steady rocking. Josephine calls to one of her apprentices to bring food on a tray. When the girl comes with the food, Padee glances at her, recognizing something familiar, but he cannot identify who she looks like. The girls seems about sixteen and her virgin breasts test the seams of her tight blouse.

Padee thinks to himself, "Me nuh know dis child, so why her spirit draw me to her." Of course, who she is doesn't matter, Padee thinks to himself; she will stay until she learns how to sew then move on and Josephine will get another girl, continuing the endless cycle, all the while complaining that she isn't going to take in any more apprentices. Then a mother will come and implore her to teach her child a trade, and Josephine will agree, taking the girl into her home, treating her as her own child, guiding her daily, telling her her fingers are stiff as a piece of board, her head dense, and she has no eye for a piece of cloth, or how to cut and piece it; she's no use to anyone. Until finally, the girl, like all the others, can make a dress or blouse without a pattern, although none are ever as efficient and creative as Josephine with a piece of cloth. The girl smiles shyly as she places Padee's dinner on the side table beside his chair, her eyes slightly downcast as she mumbles good evening.

Padee no longer looks at the girl; his eyes are now steady on Josephine who stands off to the side, regarding Padee. Her expression says, "Me nuh give up pan yuh yet, neva." Padee feels her thoughts like a large stone tied to his foot while he tries to stay afloat. He is home to stay. He reads this knowledge in Josephine's unguarded eyes in which flecks of pain shimmer, her light brown irises fevered. Even though she has stopped pleading with him to move back home and live like a decent man with his wife rather than in the one-room shack he has been holed-up in for two years, Padee can tell from Josephine's posture that she has not given up on him, never will. He suddenly feels comforted by that thought. He lifts the doily off the food and finds mackerel-run-down, boiled bananas, yam and corn-meal dumpling swimming in lots of onions and oil just as he likes it. He smiles up at Josephine, nods his head approvingly before he tastes the food. However, his head still throbs and he has no appetite. He re-covers the food and pushes the table back to the side. As Padee's thoughts linger on Josephine, he feels an overwhelming emptiness. He doesn't know her, has not spent the time.

Silence hangs in the air like an overripe breadfruit. Josephine walks deliberately towards Padee; he grabs her hand and is surprised at the warmth; her hands are warm and large, almost as large as his, like his mother's he realizes for the first time. He feels Josephine's life pulsing strong and in that moment knows that she will outlive him. He feels just under the surface of her palm a youth he never saw in her. Josephine was nine years his junior, only eighteen when he brought her his three girls. Most of her life she has taken care of others, including her father who left her the house when he died, and money in the bank, most of which she depleted when Padee was laid up on his back for over two years. Josephine sits in the rocker next to Padee, and as he glances at her, a realization washes over him: he has never felt youth or vitality in Josephine until now. Josephine was always safe, an anchor, someone who could be counted on; he has never had to consider her feelings. Padee is ashamed of his thoughts.

Josephine rocks, her chair moving in its own rhythm. Padee slows his rocking, trying to match her rhythm, but it eludes him. He concedes and focuses on the creaking of their chairs and the singing of the sewing machines inside, familiar music.

Padee is a patient man and knows that Josephine is always uncomfortable with his silence. Tonight he is determined to speak with her. When she speaks, her voice is unfamiliar, yet intimate, like the sound of the stream that ran through Padee's mother's property where, as a boy, he often went to sit, watching and listening to the crystal water glide over pebbles.

"Stanley Wilson," Josephine utters, calling him by his name long in disuse, "Mek you so badminded? Two year now every day me cova up dinna lef fah you, cause me nuh ave no one fi bring eh, like me send yuh breakfast and lunch, but yuh no come eat eh. Every marnin de dog get eh. Mek yuh mus still worry me heart in me old age. Yuh no tink me put up wid enough? Three weeks now me send Patsy fi go find out if you dead. De people in de old stinkin yard whe yuh park yuself seh dem no see you gwane three weeks. Mek yuh suh badminded? Good ting all yuh picknie dem know me and always stop by. De one Jeffery who is de spittin image ah you, and who dem seh is you sameself repeat – him already ave four picknie fi three gal – stop by tell me how him see yuh at Mazie. And yuh know Mazie nuh call me. She still vex wid me; she still tink is me neva did wan her, mek yuh gi her to yuh breda, but me nuh ave nutten but love fah Mazie. But yuh, Padee, is plenty years me ah nurse me hate fah yuh, but hear me well, today me ah belch out all of yuh bad-ways and dis bitch of a life yuh come lay down at me door off me chest." Concluding, Josephine hollers for someone to bring her a hassock to rest her feet. Another girl, not the one who brought his food, comes with the hassock. Josephine rests her feet, pulls up her dress, revealing swollen knees. As the girl turns back inside the house, Josephine says to her retreating form, "Chile, boil me some mint tea and sweeten it wid condensed milk so me can belch dis gas off me chest."

"Yes, Grandma Josie," the child replies, before disappearing. Padee does not recognize this girl either. Josephine shakes her head and laughs. She sighs, rubbing her palms on her thighs.

"Is one a yuh granpicknie dat. Liza oldest daughta picknie."

Josephine cannot see or read the furrow on Padee's brows, but his fidgeting in the chair informs her that he's uneasy. Josephine sniggers, taking time before answering Padee's unasked question; she senses that he wants to know about her and Liza.

"Me and Liza write each oda, and when she come in town she visit me. We fagive each oda fah me wedding day long time."

The girl brings Josephine tea, and before she can escape, Josephine says to her, "Hole up yuh head and say goodnight to yuh grandpa."

Even in the semidarkness, Padee can see that the girl does not look his way. He senses anger in her gesture, the way she holds herself rigid, as if she has some grudge against him. Padee has an unexplainable need to plead with her.

"Me neva do yuh nutten; me nuh even know yuh." But his appeal is useless. *Why doesn't he know her?* some part deep in his being inquires. The girl disappears. Padee shrugs off the feeling as Josephine's voice pulls him.

"Liza was raisin de picknie. Is de older son yuh ave wid her chile, but him and de moda gone ah town fi try get work. Liza not doing so well so she beg me keep her and learn her sewin."

"Yuh is a good oman, Josie," Padee offers.

"Is jus now you know dat?" she replies, a faraway tone in her voice. Padee offers no response. He can't remember once thanking Josephine for caring for his children, for keeping their home together, for being always there. He doesn't know the words with which to thank her, so he says what has been most pressing on his mind since he left the train station and made his way home.

"A fagive yuh, Josie, fah obeahing me," Padee spits out, not looking at her.

"Me fagive meself fah dat long time now," Josephine says, taking the cup and sipping tea. Padee is stunned by her response. He always believed that Josephine needed his approval and love, but here she is, informing otherwise. He coughs, feeling as if a hard piece of coconut meat is caught in his throat.

Time is old.

Sun is mawga.

Padee shivers, but still he has to ask.

"Mek yuh do eh?"

Josephine doesn't answer him right away. He feels himself holding his breath. The air is suddenly thin. He needs Josephine to talk to him, he needs to know, has to know.

"Why yuh do eh, Josie?" It comes out as a whisper, a plea. Padee turns in the chair.

"Yuh did guh too far, when wid yuh drunken self, yuh fall down and tek advantage of Miss Hilda gal down de road. Didn't matta dat she was pan de street a catch man; she was sixteen, just little younga dan Mazie. Yuh did out-order." Josephine pauses, sips her mint tea. Her tone is even, even banal, but a bitter taste creeps into Padee's mouth. It tastes like coarse salt. He hauls off the chair, limps to the edge of the veranda and spits in the hibiscus shrub just off the side of the veranda. As he sits back in the chair, he presses his legs on the board slabs to still the trembling.

"Ah didn't touch Hilda gal picknie, Josie. As God is me witness," Padee declares.

"Since when God ah defend yuh?" Josephine dismisses him. "Nuh boda swear an brin down judgement pan me head; too late fi defend you actions now." Josephine puts the tea on the table beside her and rubs her knees. Padee pulls his rocker to face her, pushing the hassock out the way. He reaches for her feet, and places her heavy legs on his lap. He begins to massage her soles and lower leg, feeling the stiffness of his fingers.

"Yuh haven't done dat in a long-long time," Josephine pronounces, adjusting her bottom on the chair and positioning her feet more comfortably in Padee's lap.

She is remembering the first time she saw Padee when he came to deliver the cabinet, the same cabinet that is in her dining room. She had gazed at him from head to toe and suddenly felt hot and embarrassed. She hoped he did not read her desire, but in that moment Josephine had known she would love him and he would be her heartache. Padee hadn't disappointed her. She hadn't imagined then, forty-seven years ago, that Padee would test her in every way, but he hadn't broken her. He could never do that. Her awareness is like the opening of a flower, the colour of which is so surprising. Josephine smiles. Her life is not wasted. She lived the only way she knew how, but now she is discovering new doors, new colours, new fragrances. She turns her eyes on Padee.

"Ah know yuh didn't rape Hilda's daughta, but yuh did guh to her room; yuh did tink it fah a moment. Anyting else, I was willing to forgive! All yuh women and stray picknie, even dat one Janet who attack me at de market and tear off me blouse, but Hilda picknie was de same age as Mazie." Rancour sounds in Josephine's voice. She sits forward, and pulls one of her legs from his lap. Padee's fingers are like glue around Josephine's ankle.

"De obeahwoman say yuh buddy would drop off, but yuh fall off de truck instead. Good! Yuh brute!" Josephine utters with deep satisfaction, as if it was yesterday when she and her friend May visited the obeah woman carrying Padee's pants wrapped in a brown paper bag.

He swallows, his Adam's apple doing a drunken dance in his throat.

Now is the time to regret the doings of the past, to remember things not voiced, to shed blood for crimes committed in darkness, to repent for deeds he should never have thought, much less done. It is time to clean the slate and receive salvation. Padee swallows, his saliva bitter medicine on his tongue.

Sun is wrapped in some woman's skirt, but is restless in his lust. The night is fully visible, like a cloth draped in front of Padee's eyes.

The zig-zag singing of a sewing-machine is still audible; music blares from somewhere down the street; crickets chirp and mosquitoes buzz, sucking at blood. Padee has to clear his name.

"Me neva do eh, Josie, me neva touch Hilda picknie. Me neva even did tink eh, not really; me did drunk and she seh she gwane tek me home. Me neva know whe me did dey, when me wake up. Is lie she did lie cause she breed and neva know who was de fada and she fraid Hilda throw she out." Padee rushes, gasping for breath.

"Save yuh breath. De past kyaan mek up. Hilda done tell me lang time dat de picknie seh she lie pan yuh."

Padee sighs, his shoulders relax; he remembers Josephine's legs on his lap; his fingers begin to massage, relieving their mutual ache.

Josephine lifts her pained legs from Padee's lap. She feels

neither shame nor remorse and anger is too ordinary. Bitterness never stays on Josephine's tongue too long, nor does she ponder on what she feels she can't change. She did what she needed to do.

"Ah goin to bed," she says, rising loudly, stripping both of them of the ghosts of the past. Padee feels disoriented.

Memories are an uncontained fire ravishing the forest.

"Me comin," Padee replies absent-mindedly.

"Lock de door wen yuh come in," Josephine commands. Padee nods and continues rocking. By the time he enters their bedroom Josephine is under the covers, although not asleep. Padee sits on the edge of the bed, his back to her. As he pulls off his shoes, he feels the gas break free from his chest and he belches loudly. He is too tired to take off his clothes, so he slumps on the bed. He rolls on his side, reaches over and pats Josephine on her arm, saying, "Yuh is de best ting dat happen to me, Josie, de best."

She does not respond, merely turns over on her side, away from him. Padee hears her snoring as sleep claims him.

In the middle of the night, in his seventy-fifth year, Padee smiles at the earth for the last time.

For the next four days, Josephine sends telegrams all over the island, to Canada, England, the USA, the Caymans and Panama where Padee's children and grandchildren are spread out. He is held in the morgue for ten days so all can be notified, and those who have the means can fly home for the funeral. At the nine-night, the day before the funeral, people are still arriving, and large numbers, mostly relatives, spill all over Josephine's house, into the yard, and out the gate. Stories and rum mingle and sisters and brothers greet each other for the first time in years, cousins meet, nieces and nephews are introduced, addresses are exchanged, details are filled in, birthdates are compared, and old enemies – six of the women who had vied for Padee's attention and love – embrace.

Laughter falls like a rain storm.

POSTSCRIPT

They shot a policeman, a constable, three times, once in the head and twice in the chest. Mazie hears this on the radio as she drives, accompanied by her two sisters (her mother's children) to dress their dead father for burial. Their oldest brother, Jeffery, a soldier, the spitting image of their father, and building a similar reputation, will bring the casket with two other brothers, one of whom Mazie hardly knows. As they enter the morgue to dress the dead, they sense their father's presence. Mazie, wearing a sea-blue hobble dress, enters the morgue first, followed by the middle sister, just returned from England, wearing a green dress, and the youngest of the three, just the night before arrived from America, wearing a brown skirt and a white blouse. The morgue, a narrow, dimly lit rectangular room, has an examination table in the centre, opposite the freezer. The walls are a dingy yellow, in need of paint. No windows; a place one quickly passes through. The porter pulls open the freezer packed with bodies, horizontally stacked like beef, mutton, pork, or whatever meats one finds stored in freezers. The porter reads off the names on the shelves loudly, looks towards the sisters after reading Stanley Wilson. They nod at him. He pulls out one of the shelves.

"Dis is oonuh body," he says motioning to them with his hand. "Rite on top of him is de constable dem shot. Oonuh did hear bout it on de news? Dem nuh find out who do it yet."

Mazie walks over to the shelf and her eyes are pulled by the face of the policeman, a red nega with freckles, wearing a plaid blue shirt bursting at the stomach; blood is smeared all over his pot belly, which tells stories of Friday night binges at the bars, and fatty foods swallowed in a hurry. Then Mazie sees no more, only her father, Padee, who seems to be smiling at her. No fear or surprise is written on his face. Mazie shakes her head. Her father's life wasn't easy; he had too many women, many more children than he could provide for adequately, but that was how he chose to live his life, so now at his death she tries not to pass any judgement, happy that they had come together and accepted each other before he died.

He knew he was going to die, Mazie is certain.

Padee was a laughing man just as she is a laughing woman, just like her sisters beside her and all the other brothers and sisters she has become acquainted with these last few days. Laughing people, fathered in laughter, Padee's children.

The three sisters talk and laugh as they sponge down their father, skin discoloured and mushroom textured. The sons arrive and together they dress him in a white shirt and pinstripe suit, sent by the daughter in Canada who couldn't come. Josephine had sewn all the pockets closed. Padee's children's voices compete with scattered memories about the father, most of them never saw enough of him, never knew him well. All they have are the pieces of stories their respective mothers told them, the few stories he told them. Their voices are loud and full of life as they dress their father without tears or long, sad faces.

As they place the body in the coffin, their voices join, piecing together the different versions of stories about Sun that Padee had told them on different occasions. Their bodies wrack with laughter and tears stream down their cheeks. The porter enters and asks, "Is party oonuh come to party or fi bury oonuh dead." They burst out laughing, and the man looks at them oddly, before exiting the morgue, giving their grief space.

The church is a box crammed with stuff, the heat stifling. Josephine is red-eyed. Wails and blowing of noses drown out the organ. Mazie looks around and wonders if there is a face among the crowd who is a sister or brother not yet identified.

Sun, which was brilliant when they left the morgue, has gone to sleep, or so it seems.

Finally the brief service is over, not a word reaching Mazie's brain. They march out the church behind the coffin. A woman rushes forward and throws herself on the coffin. Everyone looks at her puzzled. No one knows her identity; whispers rustle through the crowd.

The coffin is raised into the army Land Rover that Jeffery, the soldier, has borrowed without permission. As they make their way to the interior of St James to bury Padee beside his mother, clouds grow black and smokey. By the time they turn off the main road, just after the White Witch of Rosehall's house and enter the village that is lined with people, thunder reverberates and a wind begins to rumble and stir.

Mazie's car is second behind the Land Rover, crammed with her four children, sister from England and two cousins, the children doubling on laps. All the other vehicles are equally packed, including the Land Rover in which is squeezed the coffin and four sons, pallbearers. They make haste, trying to beat the rain. The unpaved, gravel, windy country road is not agreeable to speed; potholes slow their pace and the precipice to the left cautions care.

Suddenly the Land Rover drops in a pothole and the coffin, which extends from the opened rear door, slides dangerously back and forth, hands quickly grasping it. Mazie laughs, certain that the coffin will fall and poor Padee will curse his children for being no good, but no such thing happens.

At last they arrive at the entrance of the grave site, fifty yards beyond, not accessible to cars, only donkeys, mules, and feet. Throngs of people dressed in black, white, purple, and some a combination of all three, form an impenetrable line to the graveyard.

As the sons carrying the coffin move between the line of people, the wet soil tests their balance. It rained heavily last night.

It begins to drizzle as the coffin is moved forward slowly. Just about everyone reaches out to touch it, giving Padee a final pat, sending him home, asking him to return to them in times of need and moments when laughter is the only antidote for their pain.

The rain changes from a drizzle to a steady downpour; the mourners surge forward, trekking up the hill, through the field of St Vincent yam where Padee will be buried. Rain falls steadily, but unexpectedly Sun smiles boldly through the clouds.

People make haste, pushing against the pallbearers, one of whom stumbles, falls and the coffin lunges downward. Josephine thinks she hears Padee chuckling, and others, including Mazie who is close to the coffin, hear him too. An old woman remarks loudly, "Papadee is a devilish duppy, jus like when him was alive."

Laughter rings throughout the gathering. Another woman offers, "All him plenty oman dem betta wear black baggy or dem in nuff trouble when him come visit dem." The pallbearers recover their balance and the procession continues.

Shoes are muddy and mud splashes, smearing clothes.

"Padee a guh sidown near Massa God right hand," declares a woman in the rear.

"True indeed," rejoins another.

"See how it a rain steady and Mista Sun jus a shine and grin all ova himself," a man offers.

Humming refocuses the mourners. Children splash in the mud. The preacher attempts to manoeuvre his way up the hillside without soiling his shoes, but with no luck. The community of grievers turn and watch him approaching, some speculating about his ability to remain clean, others chuckling, a few impatient, wanting to get out of the rain. Finally, a lady standing near the grave, identified as Padee's grandniece, her hands clasped on her head, shouts, "De pasta betta mek haste and climb dis beeny hill and come bless Papadee quick. Him nuh see how de sky face mek up mean and me have young baby ah yard. Me no wan rain soak me, mek me catch cold, drop dead like Papadee."

Outburst of laughter, grumble of agreement. A stocky man goes to help the preacher; just as they both are about to clamber over the final grading, two other men reach out their hands to pull them up and all four slide and roll down the hill. Laughter abounds, echoing to the sky. Even Padee joins in, knocking his knees in delight. Josephine wipes at the drizzle that beads her face. There are no tears here, yet it is evident that Padee is loved, was loved, but joy breeds love, and death is not a reason for tears, especially when the living was good and the person led a joy-filled, carefree life as did Padee.

Thunder claps and rolls. The preacher brushes off his muddy suit. Hands cover mouths, but splutters can be heard. The preacher hurriedly recites, "De Lawd is my shepherd, I shall not want."

"Amen!" voices shout in response.

"He maketh me to lie down in green pastures," he continues.

"Praises!" voices rejoin.

"He restoreth my soul."

Thunder drowns out his voice and rain bleeds in buckets on the people who open out their arms to receive the blessing. The preacher wipes his water-blurred glasses and gives up under the torrential rain.

"Go on wid de prayer," a man's voice shouts above de rain.

"Yeah though I walk through the valley of death, I fear no evil." Thunder and lightning completely obliterate the rest of the twenty-third psalm. The amens are loud and plenty. Wreaths are thrown into the grave as the coffin is hurriedly lowered, wet soil thumping on the coffin even before the preacher mumbles, "Ashes to ashes, dust to dust."

Spades and muddy hands toss red, wet soil, filling in the grave.

Everyone is soaked, but merriment flows as people gingerly make their way down the hill, praising and rejoicing, their voices in song, the women doing little jigs, bumping hips together, arms around each other's waists, dancing to send Padee home. Some of the older men, Sam and Justin, Padee's lifelong friends, stand around, looking foolish, not seeming to feel the raindrops that are the size of marbles.

Just as Mazie, her sister, cousins and children pile into her car, soaked to the bones, the rain stops and the sun comes out, brilliantly, golden yellow, virile, dancing in the sky.

Mazie declares, "Padee bad, sah," slamming her car door shut.

They make their way carefully, and the rain begins again. The Land Rover leads the way. Mazie glances to her right shoulder, and smells Padee. Her head feels as if it swells and floats from her body; goosebumps cover her arm. Then the smell dissipates. Mazie clutches the steering wheel and peers through the foggy windshield. It's as if they are all holding their breath, waiting for something to happen. They turn onto the main road, leaving the village of their birth and their father's land behind. In unison they sigh, relieved, burst out laughing.

The rain is playing storms again. An explosive sound interrupts their laughter. Mazie's car swerves as a tyre goes flat on the rear left side. She blows her horn and pulls off to the side of the road. Shortly, the Land Rover reverses, coming to a screeching stop a few yards in front of Mazie's car. Jeffery disembarks in the rain, and mumbles under his breath when Mazie indicates the flat tyre. He kisses his teeth and goes back to the Land Rover. They wait. The rain is steady. After about fifteen minutes in the oppressive vehicles, all the pallbearers pile out the Land Rover, raise Mazie's car, one of them working frantically to change the tyre. Finally the spare is on, and the son who is now the father shouts through the partially cracked window at Mazie, "Tell yuh fada fi behave himself and mek we reach home safe."

The rain stops.

Sun shines, welcoming them home.

TEACHMENT V:

"No matter where you go, judgement will seek you out."

This is not one of Papa's sayings; this is my own, learned from experience.

When Sheldon come back here, long after his grandmother died, when I, too, was so old all I could do was just walk in my garden, and wave to people as they pass by my house, I almost didn't recognize him. I knew him when he was a boy living with his grandmother, who was my good friend. That boy had brains can't done. His grandmother used to say that Sheldon brighter than Christmas tree.

By then the community had changed. More people living here than I could afford to give eggs to, besides, each year I was keeping less chickens; just too much work. But I still grow callaloo and sell *Gleaner*, except now folks have to come by my gate and buy it. Knees too old to walk to the crossroads. Beside, there are so many cars and buses and trucks, everyone driving mad like them don't have sense. With all the hustle and bustle everywhere, it's best that an old woman like me stay put. I just don't get out too much these days, never thought the world would move this fast, TV and microwave and cell phone. What next, eh? What next?

Now I have this young woman living with me. She claims that she is my third cousin on my father's mother's side. She was trying to explain how we related and I got a headache. I told her don't bother, but she can stay a while. Well is three years now that young lady staying with me and it look like she don't plan to leave. Look how I avoid children my entire life, and one come find me in my old age. How she find me, I don't even know, but most times I don't mind her company. She is a neat girl, and pretty too.

After a while, all the old stray boys that never linger at my gate before start coming around asking me if I need help. Is fool them think I fool. As if I don't know when baby smell milk and start to cry. But I chase all of them away and tell them I ain't having any of their tail-wagging around me, and they best clear off and go somewhere else. The girl mother send her here to study, to make something of herself, not to grow belly. I just chase the whole lot of them whenever I see them lingering, skinning them teeth in my face as if I blind.

I tell you, I just can't keep up with all the goings-on and comings. Nowadays people jumping on plane as if they jumping on bus, going to America, Canada, Germany, even Amsterdam. I found out that is where my mama went and got cold and died. I found a letter in Papa's book. As old as I was, I just cried for my mama. I sure wished I knew her.

But back to Sheldon. I remembered visiting Sheldon's grand-mother, sitting with her and listening to her read one of his letters and cry. She really loved that boy. I often wondered how he made out in foreign. Seemed like he forgot about his granny in the end. Seemed like he forgot that judgment tracks all of us.

TRYING WORDS

The words galloped out of his mouth and landed like corpses at his feet. His temples throbbed. He quickly glanced around to see if anyone had witnessed his dilemma. This had never happened in public before. A woman to the right of his peripheral vision, wearing thick lenses and hair pulled back tight, caught his eye. She gave him a sheepish smile and, only bending her fingers to pat her palm, waved to him. Did she see the words, *Beguile*, *Amuse* and *Agitate*, leap to their death? And if so, was she going to report him? As these thoughts went through Sheldon Jerome Bowen's mind, while he glanced at the dead words at his feet, he decided to turn around and face the woman, but she had gone, as quickly as a mosquito. Angry at the lack of protocol, at this complete exposure, he decided to step over the words and leave them right there. Let them bury their melodramatic selves, he grumbled, as he made his way out the store and into the street. The cool air greeted him, and he felt the sweat drip from his forehead and realized that his shirt, especially under the armpits, was pasted to his body. Damn blasted words, he sputtered, almost colliding with a woman, who glared at him before scampering out of his way.

Forgetting his plans to shop, he hastily made his way to the bus stop, trying to erase all ideas from his head. Ever since his fight with the verbs, they have been attacking him. He knew the nouns were the instigators, but of course they denied everything. The verbs would surely be awaiting him, once they found out that three of their associates had died. He knew it was futile to try and convince them that he had nothing to do with their members' deaths. He could almost see them gathered, strident and persistent as ever, not caring if anyone else overheard. The bus pulled up, and he stepped back to allow two elders to get off. Just as he was about to step into the bus, a group of nouns whizzed by his cheeks and buzzed in his ears.

"You saw them, didn't you?" he turned to the bus driver, who looked at him with a blank stare, except for his knitted brow. "They are instigators," he insisted, showing his bus pass.

"Man, if you drunk, you can't get on my bus," the bus-driver eyeballed him.

Dr. Bowen heard the nouns, *Content* and *Ancestors*, chortling in his ear and decided to ignore the bus-driver and find a seat at the back. Because of the blasted verbs he had been given administrative leave, and now the nouns were trying to make him appear drunk or mad. He didn't know what he'd ever done to make them hate him so. He was becoming a recluse, afraid to go out or speak to anyone, in case a word decided to debate with him, or worse, jump to its death so he could be blamed. Dr. Bowen walked to the back of the bus, his head bowed, eyes to his feet, jacket hanging from his dwindling frame and found a seat at the very back by a window. It just isn't fair, he thought as he slumped into the seat and the bus stammered off.

He refused to look at anyone on the bus because, if he did and something about them provoked a thought, then the words would collide in his head, he would start to speak in tongues, and get thrown off the bus, like the last time, when he had to walk home five miles in the pouring rain, only to be greeted at his door by a chorus of words, taunting him. He cracked open the window and allowed himself to look out. The gentle breeze calmed him, melted away his agitation, and soothed the throbbing in his head. If only he was a little boy again, living with his grandmother in Jamaica. He recalled riding the bus with her from the market, sitting in the back, both of them munching on the treats she always bought for them. Distracted by his childhood memory, Dr. Bowen's mind was like a freshly polished mahogany table, and his face, fully relaxed, was handsome.

"You're enjoying the breeze, aren't you?"

He hadn't noticed that the bus had stopped, nor that the same woman with thick lenses now sat beside him, but the moment, she spoke, he felt her shoulder pressed against his and his skin goosebumped. Suddenly he was afraid, and something told him not to look at her. Perhaps it was the nouns, disguising themselves as a woman. They had tried to trap him before, although never camouflaged as a human. Normally he didn't have any problem with them, except lately some had become traitors and were working undercover for the verbs, trying to implicate him, tricking him to confess crimes he didn't commit. He continued to look out the window and pretended he hadn't heard her. He could feel her leaning closer to him and trembling.

"Professor, listen." Her voice was crackly in his ear, like a poor long-distance telephone connection. "I am no longer the person you wanted me to be. I saw *Beguile* and *Amuse* jump to their deaths from your mouth and *Forget* and *Run* did the same thing a few days ago. I have been trying to catch up…"

"Get away from me, get away from me," he hollered, springing up, sweat instantly glistening on his face and spreading over his body. "You're an agitator! I do not know who you are. You can't fool me." He hopped over her as if she was contagious, almost falling on the man in the seat in front of him, who shoved him to the floor, with a dismissive, "Fool, what's wrong with you!"

"They're trying to trick me, get me to confess to crimes I didn't commit," Dr. Bowen offered to the passengers who were looking at him as if he had lost more than one of his marbles.

"I'm not that person any more," the woman who had been sitting beside him hollered. "You have no business treating me like I am one of them. I tried to follow the program you outlined for me, but I kept getting lost, unable to find myself."

"Keep her away from me," Dr. Bowen continued to sputter, as the woman rose from her seat, his hands raised as if to ward off blows to his body. The bus came to a screeching halt. He tried to stand up, but each effort only made him slip and stumble. He felt as if his muscles were conspiring against him too. Then the bus grew quiet and he heard feet walking towards him, and the passengers parted. He imagined this is how it must have been when the Red Sea parted for Moses; this is how he had hoped words would part for him, but instead he looked up at the bulky frame of the bus-driver. The woman stepped forward, and touched the bus-driver's hand.

"He doesn't know who I am either. He thinks I'm one of them. How could he not recognize me? I was one of his most diligent students. I saw how it happened. It wasn't his fault."

"Ma'am, I don't care whose fault it was; you all can't be making confusion on my bus." The driver's words were slow and deliberate. "Now you have two choices as I see it. First," and the bus-driver looked deliberately at the woman, whose fingers still rested lightly on his arm, "you best remove your hand and step off my bus and maintain some dignity, or I will lift you off myself. Now which will it be?" he asked, pointing to the back door. The woman looked around her, and could not find a sympathetic pair of eyes, so she squared her shoulders and stepped off the bus, protesting, "No wonder they are killing themselves; he refuses to heed the truth."

"You did the right thing," Dr. Bowen said to the bus-driver as he rose to his feet.

"I know I did," the driver replied. "But you getting off, too. I knew from the moment you got on you would be trouble. Now get!"

Dr. Bowen managed to hoist himself up, and cowered off the bus, feeling whipped and wronged again.

Once off the bus, he looked around, but the woman was nowhere to be seen. Nonetheless, he felt her sting as sore as a mosquito bite.

In less than an hour he made it home by staying off the main streets and hugging the buildings when he had to pass by someone.

His relief was great when he turned into the yard where the grass and weeds had overtaken the walkway and were working their way to the front steps and door. Inside, all the drapes and blinds were drawn. For some time he'd shied from turning on any lights, as that would just be an invitation to the nouns. They had taken over his sanctuary; they had caused him to be banished from his only place of refuge, his office in the beloved university where he had taught successfully for the last thirty years; they had also helped to isolate him from the few associates he had. Even more devastating was their invasion of his home so that, quite literally, he had to hide out from them, sitting in a tub of water to keep them at bay. He had tried to smoke them out, but had set the

145

house on fire. The fireman told him he should seek counselling. He had sneaked into a Catholic church in the middle of the day and filled a gallon bottle with water from the font and had tried to drown them, but that only made them more furious. Now they were all over his house, except for in the bathroom, the only place where he felt free from them. He wasn't sure why the bathroom was off limits to them, or why they feared water, but on these two small points he had the upper hand.

Although hunger gnawed at his stomach, he knew that if he ventured into the kitchen they would be there, perched on the knives, sprawled in the pots, meeting on the plates, waylaying him on the rim of a cup or glass, eager to condemn him for deaths he did not cause. He tiptoed across the living room in the darkness, stubbing his toe on a stack of books he had been intending to read and, ignoring the pain, gingerly made his way to the bathroom down the darkened hall. He could hear the nouns singing out of tune, "Come we go down, Come we go down to Linstead Market." He wanted to shout at them to shut up, tell them what awful singers they were, and that he was very, very far from Linstead Market, had not graced it for over seventeen years since his grandmother died, but he was hoping to get some sleep, and if they knew he was home, they would be relentless, singing dirges throughout the night.

What abominable hooligans they are, he thought.

At the bathroom door he held his breath as the singing quieted, then he pushed open the door with force, and sprang in, shouting over his shoulder, "This is my house damn it." Slamming the door behind him, he turned on the cold faucet, shouting at the top of his lungs, "You dirty, nasty words. I will drown you yet." Instantly there was quiet and he sighed, too weary to enjoy his small victory.

He stripped down and got in the tub and, as always, the fatigue peeled from his body like the skin of a guava. He let his body relax and for a moment forgot his quarrel with words. He felt normal, as he did as a boy, taking his ritual Saturday herbal bath in his grandmother's house, who sang loudly in the kitchen as she prepared the ingredients for the pastries that she would rise to bake before dawn on Monday to sell from her little stall at Crossroads.

146

Sheldon Jerome Bowen loved living with his grandmother because she was never cross with him. No matter what he did, she never sucked her teeth in vexation or told him to "just clear out from me sight," as his mother did. His mother would punch him whenever he did something that made her angry, or when she was upset with his father. His father was often stone silent, moving about the house like a shadow. What Sheldon Jerome liked best about living with his grandmother (she always called him by both names, although she often shortened it by calling him SJ), was his soothing Saturday evening baths, made from a concoction of various leaves and herbs she purchased from the small obeah stores tucked in a corner downtown, near Parade Square. Bath was always followed by a light supper that would often include fresh pineapple. But even better than his Saturday bath was Monday morning, which he always recalled as an endless dream – waking to the aroma of sugar and spices infusing the house, and knowing full well that in his lunch box would be a variety of little cakes, made especially for him. His mouth watered from the memory, and he sat up in the tub, and reached over to the shelf he had installed in the bathroom for cans of food for those times when the words were especially aggressive. He grasped the can of pineapple and smiled. He had not known until he was almost fifteen that pineapple and other fruits could be canned, accustomed as he was, living with his grandmother, to eat all fruits and food fresh. But when at fifteen, on June 3, 1957, he joined his parents who had relocated about five years earlier, to Canada, and his father took him to the supermarket, he could not reconcile the pictures of the fruit contained in the can with the fruits he knew. Befuddled, Sheldon Jerome didn't eat for almost a week, until his mother called his grandmother in Jamaica and told her to tell him to eat before he starved to death or the authorities would arrest her for neglect. Sheldon Jerome could still hear his grandmother's words, her voice soft, but firm.

"Don't mind. You mama and papa can't help but give you false food. Is foreign you is now. Eat it for Granny so you don't get sick. Eat it and pretend like it fresh-fresh and I just peel it for you." When he got off the phone, his mother gave him slices of pineapple that were perfectly even, round slices, without a trace of moles (as his grandmother called the dots that patterned all pineapples). Sheldon Jerome had bitten at the edges gingerly, tasting what he suspected were traces from the metal can. He forced himself to eat it, although it tasted very little like the pineapple he loved. Over time, he grew to like the taste, and now, without foods that he could eat directly from cans, he would probably starve because of the conspiracy of words to do away with him.

Dr. Bowen reclined further into the tub and ate the entire can of pineapple cubes, then dozed, but not for long as he jerked awake when he heard the verbs banging on the door and shouting, "Murderer! Murderer!" He turned on the faucets to drown them out, but they kept up their strident accusation, until he filled the empty pineapple can with water and tossed it under the door. He couldn't help but laugh when he heard their hasty retreat. As always, his happiness was short lived, as the nouns started their mournful songs. He decided enough was enough and that it was time to face his accusers. He unplugged, stepped out the tub and pulled on his robe over his wet body. Armed with two bottles of water, just in case the darned words tried to get physical – he could put up with obstreperous behaviour, he could put up with shouting and unfounded accusations, but he would not countenance being physically attacked. The memory was still raw, almost twenty-seven years later, of being beaten by three young white men one night when he took the wrong exit off the freeway in Utah and decided that he wanted a beer before finding his way back to his hotel. Once he had stepped out of his rented car, he could tell they were tipsy, and he tried to stay clear of them, but one of them almost tripped, and instinctively he reached out to help the drunk man regain his balance. All Dr. Bowen remembers after that was feeling their fists and boots connecting to his body. It was in a daze, while in the hospital, that the first word, *Kindness* jumped to its death from his mouth. But then he was so consumed by pain, he didn't give it much thought. Ever since, he avoided physical pain at all costs.

Dr. Bowen flung open the bathroom door and bellowed, "This is my house and I am declaring peace." An adjective fizzed by him. That was so uncalled for. He knew adjectives were colleagues with nouns, but normally they were cheerful and without guile. He just didn't understand what had caused words, which he was very fond of, to turn against him like that. He'd had enough.

He squared his shoulders and even though his body trembled, he blew out a full breath and marched into the living room, where the words had been sitting-in for the last three months, barring his entrance. As he stepped on the blue Persian rug, he almost lost his resolve. They had made a mess of things: the rug was covered with crumbs and grime, his prized leather sofa was ripped in places, cushions were on the floor, books, gutted and mangled, were strewn all over. Tears sprang to Dr. Bowen's eyes, but he blinked them in. He would never give them the satisfaction of seeing him cry. They were assembled everywhere, like an army on alert. Why had he not gathered a similar army? Who would come to his defence? He had no friends. *Friend* was a word he killed long, long ago, when he was only nine years old and still in Jamaica.

When he was a boy, living with his grandmother, a group of children from the neighbourhood took to taunting him each day as he walked home from school, chanting as they trailed him, "Cry-Cry Baby, Moonshine darling, take off your shoes and run on home." They used sticks to beat near his feet and force him to run. By the time he got to his grandmother's gate, he was in tears and all the other children had disappeared. The first few times, his grandmother took him onto her lap, wiped his tears with her large, warm palms, and pressed him to her bosom.

"Hush, don't mind, is jealous dem jealous dat me love you more dan all de world." Then she would tickle him until he laughed, and then take him into the kitchen for a sugar-bun and a cold glass of cherry or guava juice.

After the fifth time, however, she didn't wait for him to come through the gate and run and hide his head in the folds of her skirt. Instead, she met him outside.

"Don't come in here wid you long face. Defend youself. Same way dem hurl words at you, you dash some back at them. Use words to pelt dem, so dem leave you alone."

She refused him entrance, took his book-bag, then sent him

running after the children who had been chasing him. SJ ran after them, and words he didn't know he knew spilled from his mouth. Even grown-ups stopped in their tracks. Still he ran, flinging words at the backs of the retreating children until he was exhausted and they had all taken refuge inside their respective homes.

That was the last time they bothered him; it was also the beginning of his public speaking. People came to his granny and asked her to let him speak because he was so eloquent and used big words, such as *erudite*, *mollycoddle* and *casuistry*, the meaning of which they didn't even know. Each word had a specific smell and taste and he knew them, not by their meaning, but by their action. He didn't study the dictionary, yet he knew words, and daily more words came into his head and leapt from his tongue, amazing and astounding everyone, most of all himself. Every evening after school several people would gather in his grandmother's yard and listen to him read the *Daily Gleaner*. As SJ's confidence grew and he saw the pleased and pleasing approval in his grandmother's eyes, he began to comment on the news after he read it. Soon, more and more people came for him to read letters from relatives abroad, or even documents from the government about their land. SJ was solemn at the beginning, basking in the attention, but then he started to use the information he learned about people to criticize and even make fun of them. His grandmother admonished him, saying, "Horse never know the ground is dry until he's hungry." Although SJ didn't understand quite what she meant, he knew it was a warning. It was only after he entered high school at ten years old that Sheldon Jerome realized that not only was the word *Friend* lost to him, but its very essence, and that although admired, he was completely and utterly friendless.

Now as Dr. Sheldon Jerome Bowen stood face-to-face with the jury of words that formed a tight circle in his living room, he wondered whether all of this was a result of what his grandmother and others had said, "You getting too boasty, too full of yourself. Seems like you think you and words are equals." He had gotten to think that he owned words, and that no one was beyond his reach; all he had to do was hurl words at them, and they couldn't hide from him. But now he, Sheldon Jerome Bowen was the one hiding out, afraid to speak or think, afraid and silenced by the very power of words. Dr. Bowen smiled just as *Dictate*, Grandfather Verb, pounced on him.

"You are smiling as if the charges we have brought before you are not serious, as if we are mere words to be ignored or discarded. Need I remind you we have no tongues to clip. You will be tried here tonight."

Instantly Dr. Bowen's head throbbed and he felt as if someone was inside it, pounding with a jackhammer. He was at a loss for words, and that scared him; he heard himself spluttering, but no coherent words would form in his head and find freedom on his tongue. Had the words succeeded in clipping his tongue? He knew, although he didn't know how he knew this, that this had been the fate of a maternal ancestor who had tried, three times, succeeding the fourth time, to run away and seek haven with Nannie of the Maroons. This was only after they had clipped her tongue and amputated her right big toe, yet still she made it to Nannie's camp in the mountains. His grandmother had told him this story, saying she was a direct descendant of the clipped-tongue woman, and had tried to impress upon SJ, that his gift of speech had surely come from this ancestor, her endowment to ensure that her line continued and her story was not forgotten. Sheldon Jerome had never told anyone about her life. In fact, that was one tale his grandmother told that he did not believe. He always asked her why they clipped his great, great, great maternal grandmother's tongue since it was her feet that allowed her to escape her enslavement, not her tongue, but always his grand-mother would reply with a deep guttural clicking in her throat:

"Is not only feet know path. Tongue does climb tree too."

What she said never made any sense to Sheldon Jerome, but now it did. He cleared his throat.

"Noname, my maternal great, great, great grandmother, re-fused to be a slave. She berated the slave master and the overseer. Weary of her nagging, they clipped her tongue, but still her story reached us here." Dr. Bowen did not recognize the sound of his own voice, but he had succeeded in silencing the words. He could hear his own breath, and sweat like blood from a new wound oozed from his body and cooled him down. *Dictate* nodded at him, then asked, "Why are you telling us this story now? Why have you kept concealed every essential thing about who you are? Why should we listen now? How do we know this is not a ploy or academic manoeuvring to throw us off or an attempt to win our sympathy?"

"Noname was seven months pregnant when she finally ran safely to the Maroon camp." Dr. Bowen spoke as if he didn't hear what *Dictate* said. "She had seven children, six boys and one girl. My grandmother was her only granddaughter." He paused, amazed at his own penchant for lying. His grandmother had never told him this about Noname. He didn't know how his grandmother was related to her, yet he felt that what he had just said was not a lie, but the truth come to him now. He couldn't know what this ex-slave looked like, but an image of a woman the colour of sandalwood, with three plaits, small round eyes, a braided scar by her upper left check and wearing a crocus-sack dress, with a piece of colourful African fabric in the shape of a diamond sown over her right breast, came into view. Dr. Bowen swayed as if he was on a boat navigating rough waves. He saw the woman step out of his head, touch him on his shoulder, and just as she walked away from him, he heard her say very clearly, "Now you talking!" but it wasn't her mouth that spoke, rather her heart. Sheldon Jerome heard her, heard every syllable loud and clear and he knew and understood what she meant. Now his talking had to have a purpose other than its own indulgence in hearing itself.

Dr. Bowen held on to the wall, ready now to listen to the words' accusation, ready to accept his just punishment. He was indeed a murderer. He would not ask for mercy, or plead innocent. He had consciously used words like weapons to hurt others and had in fact been delighted when he witnessed the pain he was able to inflict. Still leaning against the wall, he raised his head, looked into *Dictate's* eyes and said, "Read the charges."

At that very instant, there was a banging on the door.

"Open up! Open up!" a female's voice demanded.

The words shuffled, and Dr. Bowen wondered who it could be. Perhaps it was the new faculty member, Dr. Roseth Smalling, who was now the darling of the department, the very one who was being groomed to take his place. The same woman, with her unapologetic common speech and dreadlock hairstyle, who flaunted her island ways, as if where she came from was somehow on par with the US or even Europe; the same woman whose first book had won a prestigious award that he had coveted and had thought his third book should have received – in fact everyone had said as much – but there she was with a first book that focused, no less, on the culture of the island. It was even being touted as seminal and ground-breaking scholarship. This was the same woman who, at the reception they held for all shortlisted faculty, had come over to him the first day they met, after she interviewed for the associate position (he had voted against her outright) to say she had read his work, but was perplexed why he, a man of such sound scholarship, (*What audacity to feel she had the right, the qualifications to assess his research projects!*) should continue to write about Europeans rather than his own people (*Which people were these?*), and besides, she felt his last book was redundant (*The impertinence!*), and wondered if, after the party, which she said was boring and full of white people's pretence (*Who was she to assume that just by the virtue of colour or misfortune of birth that they had anything in common?*), if he would like to join her for a drink and give her the scoop on the department. All this she said to him forthrightly, and Dr. Bowen had wondered if she was also about to proposition him, he a respectable man of letters, who had never stooped to such things. He was well aware, or rather had heard through the grapevine, that several of his male colleagues and even one female faculty had engaged in sexual politics to get ahead, as well as dabbling in student liaisons in the bullying manner of the weak. He was above such indulgent acts, and had an unblemished record – at least until they hired that woman, Dr. Smalling, despite his threats to leave the department rather than be associated with the likes of her. So imagine his chagrin, when about five months ago, he turned up his pathway after a long day at his office, to find Dr. Smalling camping on his steps as if she belonged there. She'd smiled up at him as if they were friends, and spoken to him in that laconic, familiar tone. He was so aghast at such presumptuous familiarity that he stopped in his tracks.

"They said you didn't teach today. I knocked on your office door when I was on campus, but you weren't there. I called too, but they told me in the department that you seldom answered your phone, so I decided to drop by. I was just about to leave, but let me get up so you can get in." At which point, Roseth stood up, brushing off the shirtdress she wore that showed, to his disgust, her unshaven legs.

Dr. Bowen had disdained to speak to her. The unmitigated nerve! One didn't just drop in at another's house unless specifically invited. That was why he did not associate with island people, with their lack of social protocol, their insistence on assuming a commonality where none existed, their disregard for personal space, their predilection for speaking their minds, regardless of the audience's disposition to hear their story; their effrontery in inserting themselves in places where they were not welcome. Dr. Bowen stepped around the woman, without so much as a word, and slammed the door in her face. Even so, whenever she saw him on campus, she greeted him. He was sure it was merely to rile him, to make him lose his composure and descend to her level by engaging her in some heated quarrel. He had a reputation to preserve. It was well known on campus that he openly snubbed anyone, students and even administrators, whom he felt beneath him. As the years went by, more fell into that category.

"Is stalkin me, de damn woman, stalkin me." The words sprang from his mouth, awakening a memory of another tongue Dr. Bowen was sure he had long buried.

"Open the damn door, Professor, I know you're in there," the female's voice interrupted his reflection. He peered through the peephole and recognized the woman with thick-lenses from the bus. Her eyes were puffy and drooping as if she were tired. It was not Dr. Smalling, but who was this woman, and what did she want? Too weary to make sense of the muddle that his life had become, one water bottle slipped from Dr. Bowen's hand, wetting his feet and spreading on the floor. He opened the door and the woman pushed past him. He slammed the door shut quickly, hoping no neighbour had seen the woman enter. Should he ascertain who this woman was and what she wanted? Or should he just let the words deal with her. As if answering his thoughts, *Dictate* said, "Now that she has come, let's hear what you have to say to her."

"I know what you are trying to do and I only wish that you had intervened years ago before…" the woman shouted in a hoarse voice.

"Meddler!" *Dictate* shouted. "The esteemed doctor has wronged us, abused and misused us. Used us against the very people we wanted as allies. He is loathsome. He is a traitor, even to himself," *Dictate* ended, clasping his fingers and using the index fingers to tap his chin.

"But Professor Bowen did not murder those verbs. I saw them jump. They committed suicide," the woman insisted.

Dr. Bowen wondered why she was so determined to defend him. He didn't know her; at least, he didn't think he knew her. "Would you care to introduce yourself, Miss," Dr. Bowen said turning to the woman.

"How can you not recognize me? I am Sheri Washington Pringly, your first graduate student. I wanted to be just like you." Spittle flew from her mouth and sprayed Dr. Bowen's face. Her breath was hot and he saw her chest heaving. "I became you, until the day I looked into the mirror and could not see my own face, and didn't like or recognize the person whose face I was wearing. You told me *that* was the ticket to my success," she said, pointing her index finger at his chest.

Dr. Bowen gazed into the woman's face and still did not recognize her, although he well remembered Sheri, his first graduate student. He had groomed her for a professorship, had allowed her to practice on him, taken her through the process step-by-step, had helped her to peel away all of who and what she was that he thought was common and ordinary, criticizing her whenever she reverted to her former self. He had secretly desired her. And he had been successful. She had earned a prestigious position at one of the top ten universities in the country, her scholarship had been cited, she had made the circuit tour, and had even married – alas, her first error – one of them – and was doing well. This he knew from the occasional, concise notes she sent him yearly, or from reading the journals. Then he hadn't heard from her for a while, and was told

– she never informed him of this – that she had a child – her most tragic and egregious act. The news was like a stab in his chest (so many times he had wanted to caress her, to feel their bodies pressed together; she had stirred in him a desire he had not known he had) and he had banged on his desk and shook his head thinking *Black folks always go and mess up a good thing by wanting to reproduce themselves; they just can't leave well enough alone*. He knew that nothing good could come of this and lamented the wasted time: all his encouragement, reading and editing her articles, suggesting journals for publication, writing to the editors – all of his effort for naught. He prayed she would stop at one child, and hoped that perhaps it wouldn't be so bad since, after all, her husband was white. But alas, three years later her heard about another child. She had not sent him one article to critique and he heard nothing of her on the circuit, so he had washed his hands of her, erased her from his mind, as he did with everyone and everything that displeased him. Now she stood before him, unrecognizable.

"I heard you had a mental breakdown," Dr. Bowen said flatly.

The woman shook her head as if to deny the facts.

"You strayed from the well thought-out plan I had put in place for you. Noname took the freedom route." Dr. Bowen realized that Noname was inside his head again, and she was in control. "You must take the freedom route too. Be a runaway."

The words applauded and Sheri Washington Pringly gulped for breath.

"Dr. Bowen, you said that for us – you and I and a few selected others – freedom came through the manipulation of words, that the newest and most malleable plantation was the academy and we could garner coveted places in the Big House by gaining tenure and through publishing." Her voice was calmer now.

"Nonsense," interjected *Opulence*, Grandmother Noun, who had sat quietly throughout the entire proceeding, knitting a Rasta-colours cap for her grandson. "Freedom can never be gained through words, but rather with words. You need us as much as we need you to give us life, not drown us because you are too afraid of who you are. There can never be any freedom in someone else's house."

"You sure right," interrupted *Dictate*, Grandfather Verb. "If

156

you want to live on a plantation – though for the likes of me I can't understand why anyone would want to – but if you do, you'd best go and build it yourself rather than work to get a place on someone else's. That's just squatting. Seems to me, all that education should teach you the importance of owning your own house."

"You don't understand," Dr. Bowen finally boomed.

"What don't we understand?" the words chorused.

Dr. Bowen felt as if someone was hammering a nail into his forehead. He closed his eyes, massaged his temples and Noname stepped forward.

"Me always did know words had power. When me was enslave, it was the only thing dat was free. It was words that led me to de path of freedom. It was words that kept me running, even when me did tired and blister cover me feet. And every time de overseer say how we no good, how we lazy, how we is savage, me pepper him wid me mouth; me use words fi give de others faith; me use words fi remind meself me free, always free. Dat's why him have dem tie me to a pole, then him pry open me mouth wid sticks, pull out me tongue and chop off de tip wid him knife. Me blood spray him face and stain him permanently. Him go to him grave wid me blood still pan him face. And it still pan him people's face, as long as dem continue in him ways. But what de overseer don't know is dat clipped tongue have memory, and words and me is blood sister. We done made dat pack long time now, and some of us only have life in words."

The words listened to Noname in silent awe. Dr. Bowen kept massaging his temple and Sheri Washington Pringly fanned herself. Noname turned to her great, great, great grandson, and spoke a soft, but penetrating warning to him.

"You must do betta than that. Handle youself betta. Maybe me didn't prepare you well enough. But handle youself betta. Words are not de enemy, words are our friends." Sheldon Jerome cringed. He had not heard or used that word *Friend* since he was a boy wearing short pants. After he found words, and the children stopped teasing him, and the adults started to admire him, and come to sit and listen to him talk, he had wanted nothing else but to be friends with Delvine, the boy who lived in the house directly behind his and who was the same age. He remembered clearly now that Saturday afternoon, so unusually hot that even with his shirt off, sweat covered his body. He was sitting in the backyard, twirling a small ball on the ground, and he could see Delvine in his own backyard, directly behind his, doodling with a stick on the ground, while two puppies rested on his feet. SJ wanted to go over to Delvine's yard and play with him and his puppies, but he was afraid that if he asked he would be rebuffed, so instead he began to make up and recite out loud a poem about Delvine. Dr. Bowen laughs now recalling the nonsense of it:

"He who doodles doodles alone
He who idles, idles alone
Separated by a margin of space
An indolent boy sits, puppies at his feet
With nothing to do but doodle."

At which point, Delvine had looked over to Sheldon Jerome and asked, "Heah boy! Is who you a talk bout now? Mek you always talk like you have hot yam in you mouth a burn you tongue?"

At which point, Delvine stood up, sucked his teeth in a dismissive stretched-out sound, brushed off the bottom of his pants, picked up his puppies, one in each hand, and went inside, slamming the door so loud his mother shouted at him. It was that Saturday afternoon, fifty-two years ago that the word *Friend*, with all its attendant identification, intimacy and sense of belonging, evaporated from SJ. The tears trickled down Dr. Bowen's cheeks, before he wiped at them. He wanted to bawl for the missed friendships, for all that he lost, all that was stolen from him. He realized now that Delvine probably thought he was making fun of him rather than trying to befriend him. Sobs wracked his body.

Sheri touched his arm lightly. "I wanted to be your friend, Sheldon. For a long time, that was all I wanted. I would fantasize about us being together, but it seems that whenever you felt we were getting too relaxed with each other, you erected a higher wall to immure any threat of closeness."

"I never felt you saw me as a man, a man other than a mentor, or someone who knew how to navigate the system – someone to help you get over." Dr. Bowen slumped to the floor, his entire body flaccid. He did not notice that some of the words had begun creeping out and, more boldly, that the adverbs and conjunctions were skipping out the door and climbing through the windows. Sheri sat on the floor beside him.

"I spent twenty years of my life trying to be like someone who didn't exist. I don't know or even like the man who is my husband. My children are angry with me and I don't want to live this way any more. What do I do?" Sheri turned to Dr. Bowen who was gazing into space. "What do I do now that I've discovered that the path you sketched out for me was a maze whose exit is very carefully hidden." Again, anger crept into her voice.

"You must stop asking me and others, and find the way for yourself," Dr. Bowen said, taking her hand into his. "You have to find the way for yourself. I have been lost to myself too."

"We are done here," *Dictate*, Grandfather Verb declared.

"What says you the jury?" inquired *Opulence*, Grandmother Noun.

"Case dismissed," pronounced *Outdated*, Adjective Juror.

The words looked around at the mess. This had been the longest and hardest case to date. They were tired and anxious to return to their rightful places. Those that were still there quietly dusted themselves off and made a hasty exit.

Dr. Bowen and Sheri Washington Pringly sat on the floor until their legs cramped and the half-moon was slanted in the sky. She stood and helped him to his feet. She realized he was an old man now, and she was middle-aged. Although the words had led her back to the story of her ancestors, just as they had led Dr. Bowen to Noname, no new path was yet clear to her. She felt trepidation, but hope too, to start again, to invent who she would become. She looked around, found a piece of paper and a pen, wrote her address and phone number, and put it by the phone. As she walked to the door, she turned to see that Dr. Bowen had shuffled over to the easy chair and sat slumped in it. She knew he had a lot to think about and make right – if it was still possible at this late stage, but she was hopeful. However, she was not willing to stay and help him; she had two children and an estranged husband to try and make amends to, not to mention her family who had made great sacrifices to send her to college, whose love she had dismissed and ignored. Sheri Washington Pringly rubbed memory into her eyes, opened her mouth wide and stretched out her tongue.

"I wrote my number and address and left it by the phone," she said, looking at Dr. Bowen. "You may call me if you are prepared to talk. I must admit I am still somewhat angry at you, and at myself for allowing you to convince me, and for believing that the machinery of the academy was more important than me, than us. I am going now because there are things I must say to my children and my parents. There is an ancestor story I still must tell." She turned and grasped the door handle, then looked back at the man, her mentor. How flabbily he sat in the chair, yet she glimpsed the man whom she once desired. "Sheldon," she said with compassion, "Call me. Maybe now we can work at being friends."

Dr. Bowen looked up at Sheri and managed a faint smile before she stepped over the threshold and closed the door softly behind her.

The gracious light of dawn stole through the closed blinds. Dr. Bowen stood up, shuffled to the window, lifted the blinds softly and peeped out. He recollected that his grandmother would rise at dawn to begin baking. Often he awoke when she did, but almost always would fall back asleep to wake up later to find the house perfumed with the sweet aroma of pastries. Dr. Bowen jerked the blinds open and Noname entered his head again.

"You ever wonder what happen to you granny's house now dat you mammy and pappy dead? You ever wonder what is happening to dat place dat give you life? Maybe is time you go and see," and just as suddenly and noiselessly Noname vanished. Dr. Bowen panicked. He felt certain he would not see the school of words again, at least not for a long time he hoped, and for that he was relieved. But he needed Noname; she was the life-thread back to himself.

TEACHMENT VI:

"Withhold judgement, especially of those things that appear strange."

Life has a way of teaching us lessons – well, for those who are willing to learn, and Papa always said I was a quick learner. I know you not suppose to praise yourself, but I was smart in school. If Papa was alive he would say the same thing. I always came in first or in the top third in my class. I wanted to go further than 5th form, but we didn't have the money. Still I pass three subjects: English, Geography and History. Papa always say I was smart enough to work in a nice store or a get a job in the civil service, but I just couldn't see myself sitting behind a desk all day, locked up inside, longing to be outside. I like my freedom; that's more important to me than a nice office job.

I believe Ebenezer feel the same way. He moved into the community about seven years after I did. In fact his house was the first house at the opposite end of my street. I see him the day he moved in. I could just tell from the slow careful way he moved that he was a nice man that keep to himself. He was like me, live alone and keep a nice garden too.

Now, I know you not suppose to talk about people, but from the beginning I felt there was something strange about Ebenezer, not strange in a bad way, but strange like someone who has power, except he act like he didn't know it. Papa used to say certain people born with special power, a gift or a curse, he didn't know which one. I believe Ebenezer was born with power, and if he wanted to he could have been a good obeahman. Not the kind of obeahman that make people stupid, or lose what them have, but the kind that help people who are sick that doctor can't help, the kind that help you develop a business and keep bad-minded people from bringing you down. That's the kind of power he had, and I believe other people saw it too and that's why they keep away from him, even though he was a nice man. He was never in people's business, never go to anyone's yard and create contention. Just polite and clean for a single man. His clothes always clean and pressed. Many times I pass his yard and spot him in the back washing his own clothes.

You know lots of people believe it not normal for grown people to live alone, even people who come buy eggs and callaloo from me say that about me behind me back, and about Ebenezer, so I felt close to him.

But Papa always did say people only act on what they know, and I know from experience that most people don't spend the time to expand their minds. You see me; I read the *Gleaner* every day, from front to back, even the advertisements, and try to write some of my own. I even go to the library and borrow books and read about all kind of subjects. You see I know that an idle mind is a wasteland for the devil. So I read plenty books and I know that not everything folks think is strange is really so strange. People who stop in the morning to buy *Gleaner* and tea are always talking about how this not right and that not right, just because it's not their experience. I just shake my head, but keep my mouth closed. So after a while I just write in big, big letters and tack it up on the top of my stall: "Withhold Judgment, Especially of Those Things That Appear Strange!"

Some folks ask me what it mean, like them can't read. Others just act like they don't see it and continue to condemn everything and everyone, like Ebenezer, that they don't like or understand. Life strange for sure.

EBENEZER'S WATERMELON KNEE

By the time Ebenezer was put to bed with his knee swollen to the size of a large watermelon, he realized it had been six months since it had grown from a small wart, gradually getting larger, to the size a firm orange, the skin getting darker, then a smooth grapefruit, until now it was so heavy he was unable to walk. As he lay in bed his left knee propped up, and Miss Eleta's hot-water bag strapped to it, he resigned himself to fate: the doctors were at a loss, had not been able to find any scientific reason to explain the condition of his knee. The last specialist he went to consult at the University Hospital told him that since it didn't hurt and was clearly not infected, he should merely wear shorts or cut-off pants until, or if, he decided to have the swelling, which was "clearly a hard gigantic mole," removed. Ebenezer thanked the learned doctor, and caught the bus home.

It had begun when he felt a twitch in his knee and noticed it was slightly swollen, but since it didn't hurt he paid it no mind. Each evening when he came home from work, after eating his dinner on the veranda, he would hoist his leg on the bannister and massage the knee, feeling peaceful as he did so. It continued to swell, and he continued to massage it, sometimes experiencing the sensation that something was inside the knee, turning, but he dismissed this as his imagination. Perhaps his long-time friend Barrington was right; forty years without being married or even living with a woman was working on his mind, or as Barrington said, "Man, you nu fraid you nuts fly up in you brain and mad you? God neva mean for man to live alone. What wrong wid you? You not a bad-looking man. Plenty woman would love to share you bed. I can set you up wid Sheree's cousin." Ebenezer had met Barrington's wife's cousin before and was not interested in her. Frankly, he was not interested in any woman. He was content to live alone, coming home from the cigarette factory where he worked as a foreman, cooking his meals and sitting on the veranda of his one-bedroom house eating his dinner and watching the sunset. Sometimes he listened to the radio while he ate, but mostly he was quiet, filtering out the chatter of the men at the factory that often swam around in his head even after he left work, or the sounds of the children playing in the neighbourhood, or the women shouting demands, calling to one child or another, or speaking to neighbours over the fence. He couldn't imagine a woman sharing his house, but sometimes he watched the children at play and thought that he would be a good father; well at least he wouldn't shout at his child or flog him – a girl, he thought, might be too much, what with hair needing combing and all the frills that he associated with girls.

Regularly the same set of people paraded past his gate. Many offered salutations, some just nodded in his direction and others walked straight by. Ebenezer's response was always the same; he replied to each in the manner of their greeting, never encouraging anyone to linger and engage in further discussion as folk often did at Miss Eleta's gate, just two houses to the right, opposite his. On weekends, her yard was a stream of activities with her five children and their friends, her ex-husband and Butch, the father of her last three children – the youngest not yet a year old. Whenever Ebenezer was in his yard gardening or sweeping, there she was at her gate with a broom or a dust cloth in her hand, or a baby or laundry in her arms, running back and forth, exclaiming, "Praises, praises, hold on, let me run inside and turn down the pot so ah don't burn up all the food and leave my children hungry." Or he could hear her loud, laughing voice from the back of her yard, ping-ponging with a neighbour across the fence. He observed how she knew everyone in the community and their business. She would stop the young girls who passed by her house – those she thought were anxious to be women too quickly – and give them advice, and scold all the children she saw misbehaving, including the bang-belly, square-headed child of the woman who lived one street down, who several times he had seen come round and curse out Eleta for reprimanding her child. Despite getting involved with people in a way that was quite alien to him, Ebenezer conceded that Eleta did what she knew was right. She knew who was sick and visited them, often with her three stepping-stone children hanging onto the edge of her skirt and the baby hitched to her side. She was always neat and her children looked well cared for, and *they* were polite, because when they were playing on the street close to his gate and their ball rolled into his yard, *they* never just charged in like some of the other children, but always greeted him, and asked his permission to come and retrieve their ball, even though his was probably the only yard that did not have any dogs.

Apart from Barrington, who worked at the cigarette factory with him, and with whom he always ate his lunch, and who sometimes came to sit with him on the veranda and play checkers, or talk to him about Sheree while he worked in his garden, Eleta was the only other person in the neighbourhood who had entered Ebenezer's home in the fifteen years he had been living in Treesome Gardens. He hadn't invited her, but one Saturday about three months after he had moved there, as he stood in the back by the basin, hand-washing his clothes, he sensed a presence and when he turned there she was, smiling at him, with a covered dish in her hand; she had made him a sweet-potato pudding, the best he'd ever eaten. She had invited herself in and sat in his small kitchen, that only had one chair and no table at the time, so he stood and listened as she welcomed him to the community and told him about his neighbours to the right, left, behind and in front of him. Then she had walked through his house, that still only had a mattress on the floor and a few boxes in the bedroom for his clothes, and he followed her as if she was giving him a tour of his own house. Yet there was something about her manner that made him feel at ease and not in the least offended. Since then, she had decided that they were friends and would visit him, bringing him curtains that she had made, or just coming to sit and talk while he cooked or washed his clothes or gardened. Sometimes she brought him food, which led her first husband to get jealous and loudly accuse him of sleeping with her, even going so far as to toss stones and break Ebenezer's windows, and take a hammer and mash-up his bicycle. Ebenezer didn't think it was up to him to tell Eleta to stop visiting him. He sensed that she really needed to hear herself talk, and talk she did, about how Sam, her husband, did not know how to manage money, did not know how to love with gentleness, or how to play with the children – they had two. He realized she was talking to herself with him as witness so she could grow brave – which she eventually became. She told Sam to leave, which he did, but not before he broke every window in the house and pulled out their bed and set it on fire in front of the gate, and threatened to ruin her life and Ebenezer's. Throughout this show of rage, Eleta sat crocheting with her two children in Ebenezer's bedroom, while he kept vigil quietly on his veranda, his eyes seemingly mesmerized by the distant azure mountains. After Sam had spent his energy, well most of it, he barged up to Ebenezer's gate and put his hand on it as if to enter. For a brief moment Ebenezer diverted his eyes from the mountain range, leaned forward in his chair, and locked eyes with Sam. Although Ebenezer hadn't said a word, Sam must have read something in that gaze, because he took his hand off the gate, twisted his neck from side to side, placed his hands on his head as if to hold it in place and fumed: "Ah know you have me wife locked in you house. Ah know. Ah know you been carrying on with her behind me back. Ah know. But you can have her. Ah done with her. You can have me discarded goods." Sam had turned on his heels, got in his car, slammed the door so hard it flew open again and screeched off. Ebenezer hadn't moved, his eyes still scanning the horizon – even when an hour later Eleta emerged saying she thought it was safe to go home, to see what was left of it, leaving the children, who had fallen asleep on Ebenezer's bed, to complete their naps.

The incident sent rumours flowing like Dunn's River Falls, but since neither Eleta nor Ebenezer confessed to anyone that there *was* a relationship, the talk soon dried up like the soil under the July heat. Throughout the years they remained friends, and Ebenezer was the first person Eleta confided in before she took up with Butch, the father of her three youngest children and the man with whom she had been living with for the last five years. Butch was as easy-going as Eleta and was always polite to Ebenezer and friendly too, hailing him as he sped away in his taxicab, bringing him coconut from the tree in their yard, or crab after he had been out with other men in the community catching them. So later, Ebenezer had no fear that Butch might one day erupt in a senseless jealous rage about Eleta's daily visits, bringing food and boiling water for the hot-water bag that she placed on his knee, sitting on the side of the bed talking to him, her infant suckling her breast, or busying herself in his home, while the infant slept soundly beside him.

While Ebenezer lay propped up in bed, listening to Eleta move about in his kitchen, he thought to himself how much he liked her as his friend. She was a what-you-see-is-what-you-get kind of person, her actions and words as ebullient as stars on a dark night. Now she entered the room, sat on the edge of the bed, and placed her comforting palms on his knee.

"Ebenezer, don't worry. Doctors don't know everything. Let your knee do what it have to do. We go take care of you. I know you have savings because you work every day, and you don't have woman or child to mind. Don't lie in bed, languish away and get fat. Move around as much as you can. Butch and I will take care of you. Give me money for food and Butch will pay the water and electricity bills."

He directed her to his dresser drawer where he kept his credit union account passbook and told her to keep it and use what she needed.

He slept a lot, hobbled around, and sat on his veranda where he ate all his meals, rain or shine. Eleta sewed him cotton pants, one leg with elasticated stretch cotton at the knee, with buttons at the side. He had knitted his brow when she handed him the first pair, but they were practical and it didn't make sense, as she pointed out, to ruin all his pants by cutting off one leg at the knee.

"Ebenezer, I confident this knee thing not goin last forever," she said as she went through the door.

Barrington visited Ebenezer weekly, updating him on events at work, although mostly he gossiped about what was going on in their workmates' lives.

At night when the community was asleep, except for some of

167

the young men who congregated on the street directly behind Ebenezer's house, who talked loudly and played their dancehall music even louder, Ebenezer would sit massaging the knee and caressing the movements he felt inside. He only felt these at night and somehow it gave him a comforting feeling. Morning and evening, as people walked to and fro to catch buses for work, they asked about his knee, and offered numerous remedies and bits of advice, some even bringing him their own home remedies in old soda bottles, while others mentioned specialists he could consult – the priest, obeah men and the like.

One Sunday, after taking Eleta and the children to the beach, Butch told Ebenezer he was taking him to see an Indian man who was reportedly the best obeah practitioner on the island, who combined both African and Indian wisdom. As Ebenezer hobbled to Butch's taxi, Butch made him swear not to mention a word of this to Eleta because he didn't want her to throw him out the house, which she might if she thought him involved in these old-time things. They drove to Bernard Lodge, down a dirt road, to a one-room hut where Ebenezer could see a candle burning from the doorway. Otherwise the hut was dark and stuffy as there were no windows or electricity. A slim, bony Indian man sat on a crocus mat, red turban on his head, legs crossed flat. He beckoned with his middle and index fingers for Ebenezer to come closer. He shuffled in, Butch pushing him forward, telling him he would wait for him outside. Ebenezer sat with his watermelon-size knee stretched out in front of him. The Indian man touched it, then nodded knowingly.

"I seen dis kinda ting before," he said seriously, both his palms cradling Ebenezer's knee. "Yes, I seen dis ting before." As the Indian man talked, Ebenezer noticed that his knee contracted and it felt as if a lizard was under his skin, running inside his knee. The Indian man smiled beatifically, then rubbed some oil on his knee, with a smell Ebenezer could not place, except that it was sweet and made his head feel light. All he remembered was his eyes closing. The next thing he knew, Butch was pulling at him, tugging him to wake up. They sped away dangerously fast, Butch talking as rapidly as he drove, reminding Ebenezer not to whisper a word of this to Eleta, as he raced to get her and the children from the beach. Apparently Ebenezer had been with the Indian man for over two hours; he thought he'd been there for less than ten minutes.

"Well is a $1000 I tek from your credit union to pay him," Butch said, "so ah hope de man know what him a talk about. Plenty people tell me them go to him and him can do more miracle than Jesus himself, including bringing de dead back to life, so I figure him could well cure your knee. Anyway him seh is two more months, de most, and you knee back to normal-normal, just like before. Me only hope him right cause me no have $1000 fi give you back. But let we wait and see." Butch careered around a corner, overtook four cars in a row, shouting at other cars and people on the road.

"Get out de way, get out de way, oonuh don't see ah have to pick up me woman and children!"

Ebenezer closed his eyes and massaged his knee, which tingled curiously. He was not fond of vehicles, preferring to ride his bicycle or walk, only taking the bus when it was absolutely necessary. They arrived at the beach, scattering sand everywhere.

Butch jumped out almost before the car came to a full stop, with a mouth full of explanations for Eleta, who didn't seem the least disturbed as she chewed on fish and festival. Then Butch was back, helping Ebenezer out the car, his knee looking larger than ever, and leading him to sit on the blanket with Eleta and the children, sand, fish-bones and crumbs of festival everywhere.

"So Butch take you for a drive, Ebenezer. That's good. Have a piece of fish, then let the seawater bathe your knee. It will do it good."

Ebenezer was reluctant, but Butch, Eleta and the children kept encouraging him, so he eventually waddled to the water's edge and allowed the waves to wash over him. It was a day like no other that he could remember, and when they took him home, and he closed the door behind him, there was a smile on his face that made his face glow and he could almost imagine his knee was smiling too.

He continued to work in his garden as best as he could, using a cane to steady himself while he attended to his eggplants, chocho and cabbage. He had four chickens from which he gathered eggs and several fruit trees as well as tomatoes, carrots, mint and thyme, which grew wild in the front of his yard, the surplus of which Eleta distributed to the other local women.

It had been almost three months since he had last been to work. Barrington told him that no one liked the new foreman.

"De promotion gwane to him head. Him want boss-boss everyone. Ebenezer, let me put a cutlass to this bump pan you knee and let the blood drain. You knee sure to get better then."

Ebenezer frowned at Barrington as his knee contracted into a hard knot.

His swollen knee was no longer a topic of discussion; nine months was too long for any one subject to dominate the talk in a community that thrived on novelty and made up stories when there was nothing true to report. People greeted him as usual as he sat on the veranda eating his meal, his left leg resting on a small stool. But one Wednesday evening, just as he went to get the plate of food Eleta's oldest child had brought over and left covered on the table, his left leg cramped so badly he had to hold on to the counter to keep his balance. He could not place his foot flat on the floor. Perspiration drenched his body and he felt weak. He hobbled, holding onto the wall to get to the bedroom, where he slumped on his bed. He had only ever felt such intense pain before when he was a small boy and fell out of a guinep tree, crashing into the fowl-coop, fracturing his collar bone and breaking his arm. He faded in and out of consciousness, until he awoke groggy, the sun streaming through the window, and heard the insistent sound of a baby crying. He couldn't tell if he was awake or dreaming because the baby sounded as if it was on the bed beside him, but his eyes felt as if sealed with the crust of sleep and his throat was parched. The next thing Ebenezer remembered was Eleta calling his name and saying, "Lawd, Puppa-God is what this eh? Look how Ebenezer knee all bloody and where this baby come from? Lawd Puppa-God, is how this happen? I have seen strange things in my life but this is surely the strangest. Ebenezer knee all busted open, and this baby is all bloody on the bed beside him. Lawd Puppa-God, help me to understand."

Ebenezer shook his head and managed to brace himself on his elbows.

"Look Ebenezer, is baby you get, is baby," Eleta said, holding out the baby to him.

His left knee was split open, smashed in like a watermelon, bloody and stinging. Eleta was at the foot of the bed, cradling what looked like a wet rat in her arms that cried like a baby. His abhorrence for blood was even worse than his anxiety about vehicles so he promptly blacked out and fell back on his bed. He slept on and off for the next three days, Eleta told him, when he finally emerged on the veranda, his eyes blinking in the sun.

Butch saw Ebenezer as he drove past. He stopped, reversed and, leaving the car running and the door wide open, walked up to the first step of the veranda, scratched his head and asked, "So, Ebenezer man, is whe you get de baby from? I go to police station and hospital and no baby missing or born. I want to know whe de baby come from? I don't care what Eleta seh, man can't have baby." And he ran down the steps as if afraid, got back in his taxi and sped off.

Ebenezer pinched his arm to confirm that he was awake. He walked to the edge of the veranda, and then he realized that he was walking normally. He looked down and discovered that he had on regular pajama pants. He pulled up the left leg of his pajamas and saw his knee was bandaged. He tried to remember if it was the same knee scarred from the cut he suffered when he'd been dared to jump over a jagged tin drum when he was nine years old. Ebenezer sat on the step, his middle finger scratching the top of his head, his tongue heavy in his mouth. He sat like that for thirty minutes enjoying the feel of the sun on his body and noticing that his yard had been swept and the garden watered.

"Mama! Mama! Mister Nezer sit down pon him steps."

Ebenezer looked across the street, and saw one of Eleta's daughters pointing at him and hollering for her mother, as if the house was on fire. He looked down at his knee, wiggled his toes as the girl's voice caterwauled, and sensed and heard women's movements and voices around and about, and felt eyes peering at him out of windows. A few women stood boldly at their gates staring at him. Then Eleta was running towards him, cradling something in her arms, calling out even before she was inside his gate.

"Ebenezer, Ah never did think you was ever going to wake up. Ah had my hands full with this baby and all the questions. Is time you take over," and she put her bundle in his arms. "Is a good baby boy you have, Ebenezer. Him real good and quiet like you. You and him going to get along. Is what you go name him?"

Ebenezer looked at the baby and saw his own face, well the face he'd had when he was a little boy, looking back at him. The baby smiled and Ebenezer cradled him to his chest.

"Him name Kneezer," he said looking down at the baby. He was about to smile when he heard the accusing voice of Mother Taylor who lived directly across from him and looked after seven grandchildren belonging to her three children, who were in Toronto, the Bronx and Brooklyn.

"Whose baby you steal, Ebenezer, whose?"

Ebenezer raised his eyes to meet Mother Taylor's and saw five other women from the community bunched around her. He lowered his eyes and once again looked at the baby in his arms. Eleta spoke for him.

"Mother Taylor, come and take this baby and care for him with your seven grandchildren until his mother come for him? Come take him." Eleta took Kneezer from his father and held him up over the gate. "Who want to come and take care of this baby until his mother come?" She offered the baby to each of the women in turn but none moved forward. They had seen the baby. Had all gone over to Eleta's house and inspected the baby. Although he seemed normal in every way, there was also something not quite normal about him too. His head was too large. His skin seemed to be spattered and streaked green. His gums were too red, and his eyes looked like tiny little black seeds. They were superstitious people, afraid, unsure. It was best to leave the unknown to God or the Devil, both being accustomed to the extraordinary. They were, after all, only women with their own children to care and provide for. They hung their heads under Eleta's scrutiny.

"So none of you want to take and protect this baby. Let's see if this evening *Star* or tomorrow *Gleaner* announce a missing baby boy, and if so let's call Policeman Trigger who lives by the square to come and arrest Ebenezer, but until then, let's leave him with his son." She turned and put the baby back in Ebenezer's arms.

"Eleta, you is an educated woman and I respect you, but you and I well know, man can't have baby." Mother Taylor had to have the last word, and she brushed her hands together indicating that she was done for now, walking slowly back to her gate with a few of the other women lingering with her, the group talking and still gesticulating towards Ebenezer.

That evening while Barrington and Butch drilled Ebenezer, the boys from the next street, and about twenty other people from the community, took up vigil in front of Ebenezer's gate and a loud and heated discussion ensued. The group carried on well after Ebenezer turned off his lights, and did what Eleta advised: "Put pillows between you and the baby so you don't crush him in you sleep. You have to buy crib soon." Ebenezer and the baby both slept soundly while arguments about them still raged outside.

A few days later, Butch quietly visited Ebenezer, returning his credit union account passbook, with most of the money intact, and whispered to him, although they were alone.

"Ebenezer, you still can't tell Eleta nothing bout the Indian man, you know. Finally, she promise to marry me come Christmas – after all these years. I put back the $1000 in your account. I went to the Indian man and demand back the money. Ah tell him, him is fake, but all him do is smile. Then him say, 'Everybody get what them want.' Ebenezer, I didn't tell that Indian man to give you baby. Ah just wanted him to fix you knee, and him could a well do that without the baby. But don't worry. Is the money I save up and work extra hours I give you. Eleta say me have to be godfather, so we cool. Remember now, don't breathe a word." Butch even peered out of the window to make sure no one had heard their conversation. Ebenezer, who rarely spoke, though few noticed this, broke his silence.

"De Indian man did good. You did well to take me to see him. I get what *I* want, so no need give me back money that spend on me. You keep what's yours. Kneezer lucky to have you and Eleta as godparents."

Butch grinned widely and thanked Ebenezer again for keeping his confidence.

For the next two weeks, several groups of sisters from different churches, a pastor, a priest and the chief inspector of police, visited Ebenezer. Respectively, they prayed for his soul, invited him to confess and attempted to intimidate him into revealing the true origins of the baby, but eventually they all had to leave him with his son. And like every other bit of news that gets old, Ebenezer and Kneezer were summarily forgotten when a high-school student, returning home at eight o'clock from an evening class, was pulled into some bushes and almost raped. The community was up in arms both figuratively and literally – machetes and butcher knives were sharpened, sturdy limbs from trees were pruned and even young children were armed with stones in their pockets. Everyone was on the lookout for the would-be rapist, and in the midst of the community's fear for the safety of their girl-children and women, Ebenezer returned to work, leaving his son in Eleta's care.

Barrington sat with Ebenezer at lunchtime, as usual, and chuckled frequently as he ate his food, glancing at Ebenezer. A few minutes before it was time to return to work, he nudged his friend.

"So Ebenezer man, what's the story? Sheree seh you bring in woman and hide her, then when she have the child fah you, you send her way. People ah talk bout you, me friend. Now is not the time to keep you mouth shut. Man, ah don't know about you and this baby. How man alone can care fah baby? That's why God made woman. Sheree cousin still don't have a man, you know, and she love children; she have a little girl, and she is a good mother and ambitious too, going to night school. Ah can set you up with her, just say the word."

Lunch was over so Ebenezer walked back to his post, saying nothing. Barrington shook his head and cursed under his breath, "What a blood-claat! Massa-God must soon come tek his world!"

Kneezer grew like all normal babies, walking at eleven months, saying his first sentence, *Go Mama Eta's house*, at eighteen months, bursting his knee when he fell from the top of the steps from the veranda at twenty-three months and beginning kinder-garten when he was three and a half, tagging along with Eleta's youngest child. But he was not all together normal, at least in the view of many in the community. His head was as large as a watermelon, and he always appeared to have a faint pattern of streaks on his legs and arms. His eyes remained small and the pupils much too black. But Ebenezer, if he heard any gossip, gave it no heed. Everyone remarked that he certainly seemed happier and smiled more. Kneezer was good company for him.

Just when Kneezer began kindergarten, Ebenezer decided to expand his house by building on another room for his son. At school Kneezer learned that he was not normal, that he had no mother, and had been born out of a watermelon which grew on his father's knee. He cried like any normal child who was being teased and would not be consoled, not even when Uncle Butch came to pick him and his son up in his taxi. He would not even eat what Mama Eta fed him – guava jelly on crackers, his favourite. Tear marks spread like faint white lines all over his face. That evening when Ebenezer came to get him, he at first hugged him around his legs, then dug his teeth deep and hard into Ebenezer's left knee, screaming, "No knee, no knee."

Ebenezer stooped and held his son firmly by the wrists. Eleta and her children crowded around them.

"You here," Ebenezer spoke softly to the boy. "You here now. From air, from woman, from knee – don't matter. You here now and we family." Kneezer grew calm, looked into his father's eyes, smiled and then leaned into him. Ebenezer picked up his son and headed for home, thinking that it was late and he had to give the boy a bath, wash clothes, make him lunch for school the next day, and water the melons growing in the backyard.

TEACHMENT VII:

"For each of us judgement day finds us unaware." Papa used to say that to me at bedtime, after he had me recite my prayers. I was never quite sure what he meant, but when Jeremiah moved into the community I understood.

That was the time I had started to sell where the roads make a cross, just below the cotton tree where all the buses going to town stop. No matter how hot the day was, that spot was always cool. I was not a higgler, I was quick to point that out to everyone. I don't have anything against higglers. I was just not one of them. I was a seller – the first one out here selling – *Gleaner* in the morning with sweet-sweet oranges that I peel; the skin come off in one-even circle that I wash and hang to dry. When the skin dry I use it make tea and other stuff. I also sell fritter in the morning and a hot cup of peppermint tea from mint that I grow myself or cerasee tea for those who need to clean their system out. Only that I sell.

Same way I was attending to my regular customers one morning when I see this man step off the bus and he remind me of a boy I knew in Potosi. But I couldn't see him well, especially since him face looking at him shoes like he fraid he will lose his feet, and him shoulders round bad-bad, telling me that he wasn't feeling too good about life. Even though I attending to my customers, my eyes see everything, and I watch him cross the road and walk down the street heading to the settlement. I know he don't live there, so I watching his back to see if he's walking like criminal.

Two days later, I see him just when night begin to creep in like a little girl dragging her blanket. I was watering my garden, and he

176

walked pass my gate, his head hung so low, I wonder if his neck
go break. I say howdy, because that is what I say to everyone who
pass my yard, but he don't say a thing. So I decide to watch out for
him, and I stand by the corner of my yard, where the street light
is. I see him coming back from the store with a bag hook in the
crook of his arm. I step out so he can't pretend as if he don't see
or hear me, and I say, "Good night," just as bright and friendly as
you please. Him nod him head, but don't look at me and he keep
walking. I think what a bad-minded and rude man this is. So I call
after him. "Is live, you live around here? Welcome." He don't say
one word, just walk fast with his head hanging like it go fall off.
I trail behind him and stand and watch until he turn into the
house at the end of the road, the one that the yard never take care
of, because the man who own it don't live there; he rent it out. I
say to myself that with this man, who reminds me of a boy I knew
in Potosi, that makes three different set of people living in that
renters-house. I say to myself that can't good.

I go to the house several times, but I don't see him. Mabel ,who
live in the front apartment with her two children and common-
law-husband, say she hardly see him. Him always inside. Queenie,
who live in the back apartment with her rough-wrangling man
say she never hear him, him is like duppy for true. Nobody know
anything about him or where him from.

I knock at his door, calling out that I bring him a dozen eggs as
welcome, but no answer, even though Mabel says she sure as the
day she born that he's in there. So I wait for about a half hour then
I leave. It take two weeks before I waylay him, and the moment
he open the door I recognize him: Jeremiah from Potosi, whose
mother use to beat him like preacher chastise sin. He go like he
don't recognize me. I just smile. True, I have about eleven years
on him, but he knows me. I could see it in his eyes that he
recognized me, but I respect people who don't want to know, so
I say, "Sorry, I must make mistake." You see I remember what
Papa says: "Judgement finds us unaware," so who is to say is me
that know.

UNTIL JUDGEMENT COMES

When a coconut stays too long on the tree, the sweet juice and soft jelly that quench and cool the heat burning one's throat grows tough with age. Its smooth, green, protective skin turns brown and rough, bitter at its wasted life. The juice evaporates, rancid from the wind and heat that batter it daily. Finally it falls to the ground with a thud that is the sound of a dozen men turning over the vanishing soil on the side of a hill. Someone comes along, picks up the neglected fruit, uses a machete to free the husky skin that's good for polishing floors to a sheen. Then its hard flesh is dug out with a knife, grated and juiced, sweetening rice and peas or boiled to a thick oil. The trash of the coconut meat is thrown to feed fowls.

He is a dry coconut not yet husked or grated.

It has seemed an eternity of long, endless days, and restless nights that merge into each other, none distinguishable from another, but now, finally, it is coming to an end. He isn't sure when he realized this, but he feels it as he awakens and just before he falls asleep. Release from having dragged around a heavy burden is how he puts it to himself. This knowledge kindles in him a desire to be with someone other than himself, to hear something other than his own voice, but he has dwelt so long inside, silent but for an occasional pursing of his lips, or gleam in his eyes. He knows he is awkward at communicating, so his attempts are often mistaken as madness, vulgarity or foolishness. Nonetheless, he keeps practising.

That is what he is doing, trying to make contact, because he has to have someone who knows him, and wants to be with him. Regardless.

Through the cracked louvre window, which, when open, looks out on a wrought-iron fence painted green and yellow, he peers at sturdy brown legs passing by on the street, on trips to the market, to work, to visit, to gossip. As he stares at them he wills the swell in his groin to deflate. He is as afraid of his sexual arousal as he is disturbed by the aggression displayed by many of the youths who congregate in front of the gate leading to his apartment, whose only profession appears to be to whistle and undress women with their eyes and words, to pull at their arms, or even run their hands over their behinds, or try to pinch their breasts. He notes the resistance and loud protests from some of the young women and teenage girls they try to seduce. Yet, the daring of these young men also inspires awe in him. He, though, confines himself to his secret spying, which often leaves him in agony, curled on his bed, a pillow thrust between his legs, perspiration covering his entire body.

Large brown stains circle his merino vest, all the way down to his waist. The room is dark and the air is heavy with the stench of a spoilt meal – steamed king fish, rice, boiled sweet-potato, cabbage and carrots – that is partially covered on the small table pushed up against the window. Ants trek across the table to the plate. A fly buzzes, circling the room drunkenly, trying to deny the death which is pitched on its wing. His hands, fat and solid, with fingers like banana pegs, are folded tightly together, resting on the black book on his lap. Sweat runs down his cheeks, drips, blots the pages. He appears to be asleep, sitting up on his bed, his breathing audible, vulgar in the quiet of the room that entombs him.

"How much longer, Lord, must thine servant repent?"

He muffles the cough that tickles at his throat, swallows phlegm and swiftly, with a ruthlessness that surprises him, cracks his fingers, the sound like exploding gunshots to his ears.

He hears the women outside in the communal backyard that he shares with the other tenants. Opposite his apartment is the largest unit, occupied by two sisters with four children between them, and sometimes one of their common-law husbands. Behind his unit, there's a one-bedroom apartment occupied by a bulldozer-looking man and his beautiful woman, deep ebony-toned, with lips that curl like lace and a laugh as quenching as a snow-cone. Often when the sun is at its zenith, all three women, if they are home, sit on the veranda in front, taking refuge from the midday sun, talking softly and giggling, occasionally cursing out and shooing away the boys who hang by the gate. He cannot see them now from his sitting position on the bed, especially not the one he has been seeking – he strains to hear if he can pick out her voice – and though the women cannot see him, they know he is there listening and watching them, although he does not know this.

The sky is a clear blue, and the red and yellow hibiscus flowers glow and sway in the slight breeze. He hopes the women – Mabel, Stephanie and Queenie – will all move at Mabel's suggestion to sit on the veranda where he can see them clearly, just by glancing out his bedroom window. He cannot resist the temptation, so slides off the bed, tiptoes to the window, and though afraid to open the louvre any wider and be discovered, peers out. He only wants to gaze at Queenie, who makes his heart push against his chest, and goosebumps cover his body, but she is not with the women today. He recognizes the third woman as Shirley who lives a few houses to the left and is good friends with the sisters, whom she visits often. Nonetheless, he does not retreat, but listens to the women chatter.

"Dat man a mine sweet more than condensed milk. Him put a piece ah loving on me last night, is wonder ah ain't melt like butter in heat."

The speaker sighs deeply, then emits a quiet laugh. He can't tell whether it is Stephanie or Mabel, because the sisters both sound alike – flat, uneven voices like brown paper bags. Shirley's voice was like quicksand; it was hers that now captured his attention. As she walks closer to the sisters, he creaks the window open a little wider, ducks down when the women turn in unison to look in his direction, then chuckle before resuming their conversation. Shirley pulls the shoulder of her dress down, and invites the others to witness the love marks that decorate her breasts. After they have feasted their eyes, Stephanie declares melodramatically, "Lawd God, Shirley, is vampire you livin wid. Just now one mornin we gwane wake up, and is dead you dead from dat gravalicous lovin. No chile, me like me stuff soft an easy."

Mabel cuts in impatiently, "Well, Stephanie, ah can understand yu likin it soft and easy, cause no matter how much Irish-moss you give Desmond, you still only comin up with me big finger."

Stephanie sucks air between her teeth, turns in her chair, presenting her back to the other women, although she does not move away. Shirley continues with her story, and after a while Stephanie's voice can be heard probing for more details.

Jeremiah's legs are cramped from holding himself still, but just as he is about to get up and return to the bed, he hears the front gate open, and he knows it is her; he can smell her, smell his desire. The conversation ends abruptly and he follows the gazes of the other women. Queenie stands about two feet away from the gate with a large red snapper in her hand. He licks his lips tasting her deep sweetness, pungent molasses stirred in tangerine juice, her skin, shiny and glossy like starapple – though without the purplish tint. Just as he is about to enfold her in his arms, her voice, high-pitched yet easy, stops him.

"De fish-lady comin. She have nice-nice snapper, king fish and parrot, but ah get de best snapper."

She turns on the balls of her feet, heading for her apartment, the fish held like a prize. He stubs his toe, tries to suppress the hurt, but his hand flails, knocking a glass to the floor. He scrambles but hears the raucous laughter of the women and knows he is exposed.

★   ★   ★

All week he has fasted, staying indoors, his eyes sealed against daylight and the temptation of sin. He did not even look at his mother when she crept into his room and poured him more water, his irritation rising each time she entered the darkened room, disregarding his wish and need for isolation. Nor did he speak to her; no word would issue from his mouth to cast transgression against anyone or call attention to himself. He was making himself safe from evil eyes, preparing himself for the important path that he would be taking. On the third day the hallucinations began.

He drove the devil from her body until it became pure. Her breasts were like twin varnished dry coconuts, glossy and brown, but he did not caress them, his nobility and restraint unquestionable. All he wanted was to look upon her, imagine gliding his fingers over her pointed firmness, sally over the rest of her body until his fingers grasped the tight rump that was an Athenaeum where men were schooled in the art of ecstasy. Before him she was a goddess, flawless sculptured gold, and he stood hesitant for so long that when he opened his eyes all that assailed him, like an ancient curse, was the old, faded brown curtain, fluttering slightly in the breeze which forced its way through the cracks in the wall, apologetic for arousing him. Once again his rancour had saved him from ravage.

"None but the righteous shall see..."

Wobbling like an old man, he mounted the steps, his right hand gliding over the cold blue marble wall, as if for assurance. Once at the dais he tried to avoid his mother's furrowed forehead, but she was the only person he saw, sitting there, a vivid reminder of her sacrifice, her every breath a testament of martyrdom, surviving abandonment by the one who had begotten him. Her eyes cornered him; he felt the saliva bubble in his mouth and the muscles at the backs of his legs tensed. His fingers grasped the podium; he swayed; the women moaned, "Thank yu Lawd," freeing him from his mother's domination.

★ ★ ★

He stretches, retrieving yesterday's newspaper from the brown-tiled floor, cracked in a few places, but which still reflects the sheen and care it once received. Methodically he folds the paper into a slender rectangular shape, rests it in his lap, his eyes following the fly orbiting the room. Suddenly, like a phantom that appears in the night, the wind picks up the loose dirt outside and swirls it into the air with such force that he imagines women's wide skirts billowing, exposing their thighs and the private flesh that men's eyes feast on; while the women, eyes blinded by the dirt, gag with the same agonizing bleat that comes from deep within the throat of a goat who looks at the knife and knows that it will spill its guts into the basin set just for that purpose. The wind blows against the house and Jeremiah, attracted by the swashing sound, glances through the partially open louvre in time to witness the dance and rhythm in the skirt of the young woman, Queenie, who has come back out of her apartment. She moved in just a little over two months ago, exactly two weeks after him, with her man, obviously jealous as he had already challenged two of the young boys idling about, warning them in a voice that reeked of menace and blood pudding that he would "chop-up any man who look pan his woman." Seeing her almost naked, as she is now, standing direct in his view, her skirt almost above her head, her thighs visible like succulent banana stalks, not wearing a panty, her pubic hair black and shiny, he holds his breath, his heart racing, racing, while semen leaks through his pants, already starched from last night's dream. Then, just as suddenly, the wind dies and her skirt falls, protecting her beauty from him. Without being aware of it, a deep wounded groan echoes from his body, so loud that Queenie, out of view from all, she assumed, looks around trying to find the source of the anguish. For a moment she stares at the window, but shakes her head, dismissing the possibility that he has peeped her exposure. But she has been watching him and suspects that they have been playing cat and mouse.

She moves from his view; he slumps over, head to his chest, hands pressed tightly between his thighs, his entire body trembling.

"Lord, I'm but a lowly man, and a sinner."

Almost an hour passes then he stirs again, roused by the fly that is now happily buzzing by his ear, then lands on his shoulder. The voice of a woman street vendor jolts him, the similarity to his mother's voice so strong that he shrinks into himself, trying to be invisible, until he remembers where he is, far, although not free, from the tyranny of his mother. The voice of the street vendor trails off, announcing the going of yellow yam, plantain, and nice red tomato fresh from the country. He returns to himself, and plots to rid the fly, still perched on his shoulder, of its misery. His right hand calmly reaches out, and fingers accustomed to grasping things clutch the folded newspaper and, with precision and force, he smashes the fly on his left shoulder. The black skin and blood of its body makes a weird design on his khaki shirt starched and pressed to a silver crispness, although he does not go anywhere, has scarcely left his room since he moved in. The blade of his shoulder hurts and his fingers are numbed, the blood purpling his fingertips.

★　★　★

He had never seen his father, and this was uncommon because even though he was not the only child whose father did not live with his mother, all the other children knew their fathers, had seen them at least once, knew where they were, periodically heard from them, or had surprise visits from some man claiming to be their father whom their mothers, to their utter surprise and total resentment, fed the best that was put on the table, and made much of, as if they were long lost saviours. Sometimes, their mothers even closed the bedroom door behind them, from which only muffled moans and giggles escaped, the paradoxical sounds bewildering. Afterwards there were boys who for days would be sore at the world, converging in some field, or at the riverbank to cut away at grass or toss stones to vent their anger and share with each other their feelings of exclusion, swearing under their breaths that they would never be like those men who claimed to be their fathers. Yet many would grow to be just like the men their fathers were. They too would never be able to question their actions, articulate their failure; they too would wear smiles to disguise their impotency – their walk confident, detached, a camouflage for their displacement; they too would go around as predators devouring every woman, fooling themselves into believing that all females were available to them. They would touch each and all possessively, but never savour any, not even for the moment. Underneath these boys' loud denials of affiliation, their actions indicated that they envied the men who fathered them, their ease, their nomadic existence, which ensured them a bed in every town. And, after all, women obviously expected nothing more, or why else would they allow their fathers to come whenever they felt like it, eat their food, then leave them with another child growing in their bellies.

But he, Jeremiah, was spared such reflections. No man ever once came to call him son, even though many nights he had lain on his bed, eyes wide open, watching the ceiling and the mosquitoes that buzzed there, praying that his father would come at least once, hoping against hope that his mother would tell him something more than, "You just like that piece a man who father you." Perhaps that was why he had invented a visit, so that he could belong to the group of boys with whom he hung. Lindsey, one of the boys, was overheard by his mother telling another about Jeremiah's father's visit. Lindsey's mother felt as if her heart would jump from her mouth. She left her machete in the field she was digging and hurried to her friend, Miss Hortense, Jeremiah's mother. How had she greeted this man who had ruined her life? How come this man who had driven her from the garden of Eden (for which expulsion she was in complete repentance, denying herself any other man) was, according to Jeremiah, being lavished with kisses and food?

He had not witnessed his mother's response when she was informed of this returned lover. Perhaps if he had seen her consternation, he would have understood the reason for the merciless flogging he received. Had he been there, he would have wanted to embrace her and draw out the tears hemmed behind her proud eyelids; he would have massaged the calcium hardened to stone in her lumped shoulders; fanned the heat rising under her dress; cradled his head in the folds of her bosom and allowed her to open wide the dam so the pain could flow – but he had not been there. He who had caused her grief, who had made her heart fly to her mouth, who had caused perspiration to drench her body so that patches of water seeped through her dress – as if she had hurriedly bathed and dressed without time to dry – had not been there. He hadn't been there to see her lips harden and pout – more like the snout of a pig – hadn't seen how suddenly she had been transformed so that death seemed to dance in her eyes, hadn't felt the cold stillness of her palms when she realized that she had misunderstood what her dear friend was saying. Wilfred was not coming, she had told her friend, her hunger for him still so evident after ten years. He must have already come and gone, and she hadn't got to see him, to shower him with kisses, to touch him, to cook him the coco yam and cabbage he used so to love; she hadn't felt his breath – the hot sweetness of the parched earth after a sudden rain; she hadn't got to see him; Jeremiah had sent him away before she got to see him.

"Oh dear God, wha sin me commit so, wha sin, to be so denied?"

Her voice was the dry wail of something dying; her knees buckled as her arms embraced her longing in a tragic dance. Then embarrassment took over; she had been tricked, exposed; her bravado was bared like the terror of one whose lids are turned over exposing the raw vulnerability of the eye; she was cornered, forced to open her mouth and have her teeth counted, forced to spread her legs for the stranger to feel her, forced to offer her hand and have the tender flesh between her fingers slit. But he, Jeremiah, the son she had kept out of love for the man who had abandoned her, had not been there, disobeying her as he often did, to go with the other boys far up the river to catch crayfish. It was lucky for him, for if he had been there and had heard and responded to the tremble of her voice that ringed the mountainside searching for him, that long gravel howl that stopped the wind and made the chickens flutter their wings, that long howl that burned with the heat that rose from the melted tar road at noon time, he would have surely died, a clean sharp death; but he hadn't been there, his disobedience saved him. For when he did not appear, and only the silence of the day responded to her vexation, she grabbed the sharpened axe that was resting by the kitchen door and axed down the sweetsop tree which fell like a betrayed person, charged for simply being there in place of the real culprit. Jeremiah had not meant to stay out until dark, but he and his friends had gotten lost. He and the others had built a fire, made a large bush-pot of crayfish soup, rested, then discovered they had not marked their tracks. His waywardness had been his salvation for the sweetsop tree was not the only victim: a pot, three chickens, the bench he often sat on in the evenings to do his homework, and the beautifully carved mahogany table that sat in a corner in the living room (always free from dust or any objects) were also axed. (The latter, he would later learn, was the only tangible evidence that his father had existed and loved her, carved as it was by his own hand, the depth of skill and care so boldly evident.) These objects were all piled in the middle of the yard to be set ablaze almost a year later under her guidance, after the hacked-up pieces of mahogany table were removed, roped and put in a box which was shoved under her bed.

When she had started to flog him with the leather strap, he had succumbed, feeling contrite for going off all day, but when the lashes intensified and he felt the wetness, that was too sticky to be sweat, and saw the leather stained red circling him, he knew he was not being flogged for going off all day, but for some great crime, which would remain nameless, but always quietly audible between them. So he had fallen on his knees and had prayed for deliverance. None came but the safe darkness which exploded in his head, the lashes circling, making his penis stiffen, bumps and ridges designing his back, bile frothing his mouth, the lashes circling, circling, blood spraying into the cool evening air, their breaths pushing out, ringing up, falling, the leather strap circling, her breath hard and suppressed, his tears gone inward, too choked, trapped in the moment, the pain becoming her own, mocking her, stroking her nipples hard against her dress dyed red and wet, the trickle of urine that had glided down his legs, circling, circling.

For ten days he had lain curled in a corner, naked, ointment greasing his back, the shadow of a man, buff skin and grey, every so often looming over him with hot liquids that he must have drunk, his breath stifled, fearing calling attention to himself, unable to move, shuddering every time he heard a sound, a creak in the floor, terrified that his mother might appear, the tension in his head and his alert body exacerbating his wounds. But she had never appeared, and two weeks later, when he had faced the outside world again, he had discovered that he had been removed from her by his godfather, Mas Tomlin. He had always showed him love and compassion, was the only adult he felt safe and comfortable to talk with about anything, especially his feelings, but who, after weeks of care, had deposited him like an inanimate object quietly at her steps, leaving him standing there too unsure to do anything else but sway there until his feet collapsed from under him and she had caught him and bore him to his room. Since then, whenever overcome by the world and the malicious feelings that people guard, he would shut himself away in his darkened room and peer at others outside without being seen. The darkness of his room was a cool gown which draped his back, and tenderly caressed him as he yearned for love but never found it, especially since that night when the leather strap had circled him, spraying the air with red sweat and the deep even breathing of their anguish.

Neither Jeremiah nor his mother ever said anything about that incident, nor did anyone, including his friends, remark at his raked back, scarred cheek, or his three weeks' absence. It had never happened and soon life returned to a benighted normalcy.

Who's going to save him from his fate, who will save him?

★　★　★

"I want to be saved, to be saved, to be saved."

Jeremiah awakes into the present, and still feels on his body the blood and sweat from that boyhood memory almost twenty-three years ago. He tenderly touches the welts, and is surprised at the absolute anger he feels. He stretches on the bed, and the stench of the stale food reminds him of his inertia, his cursed attraction to women: to sturdy legs, arms' lissome grace, dark-hued bodies that glisten and glow, ripple and ruffle, tease and confuse. He cannot hide away forever, stealing glances through slit windows, dreaming, longing. Only of her, not all of them.

It is evening.

"Mackey, lend me two shillings til Friday," Desmond pleads, but Stephanie, Mackey's woman, answers for him.

"Mackey look like Mista Nova Scotia Bank to you? Two shillings can buy me drawers fi cover meself and food fah de picknie dem."

Neville, Mabel's man comes to Desmond's defence. "Stephanie, Mackey need more than two shillin fi cova wha you carry behind you."

All the men, including Mackey, laugh. Stephanie fans out her hand at Neville, chupses, turns around, shakes her behind, then stalks off. The men laugh and joke with each other as they head through the gate.

Jeremiah rises on his elbow and surveys his small room – a bed, a dresser, a table with two chairs – and ponders when his exile will end. Will he ever return to the pulpit where his mother always claimed he belonged? He rises, walks to the small bathroom, pisses, spits and returns to bed. The playful bickering of children returning from school provokes him. When will he father one? Whose bed awaits him, ready with food, moans and giggles? None! His right fist beats his left palm. None! His balled hands beat the bed. None! Balled hands pound, head shakes from side to side. Denial! Denial! There would have been one.

★   ★   ★

He had thought it was all a dream; that she was a dream, no more than one of his secret desires. But she was flesh and blood and he had met her flesh with his flesh and their desire had made a child that he had killed, and killed her too. She had drowned when he had held her down for too long. All he had wanted to do was wash her clean, and let her enter into the bosom of the Lord. It was not as they claimed.

"Drownin him sin, yes sah, dat's wha him did do," the old women mumbled.

"Is a damn shame, a fearful shame," the younger church sisters lamented.

The men were more philosophical, less condemning.

"De good Lord can judge fah himself; Him will embrace de righteous, and dash out de sinner."

The nail that sealed the coffin of that foolish, innocent girl was driven by her own mother who, rather than weep for the sixteen-year-old daughter she had lost, sought to protect her own position when she said dry-eyed and haughty, "She spread she leg like whore, and die like one; me neva did raise she fi shame me."

So it had ended with his excommunication, but not immediately, and he was never directly accused of any wrongdoing.

He was not even sure of her name, and would be hard pressed to describe what she looked like, but the feel of her supple body next to his, and her hot breath on his neck stayed with him. He had known that he had drowned her when they pulled her bloated body from the river. His knees had buckled when they laid her on the bank, her dress busted open and the big swelling of her stomach bared for all to see. He had looked transfixed at her stomach, trying to figure out how she had held it secret for so long, banding it down with cloth. He had laughed out loud at the perversity of her will and had kept laughing until he fell at her side and rested his head on her stomach and smelled her. Then he remembered he had known her, and understood the silent accusatory stares, the disapproving glares, the cloaked hostility. But there were no words to be spoken. He had stood there, his arms extended in plea, but they all turned from him, and turned from her – with the finality of brushing off their hands as if to free them of dirt. After they walked away, he had looked down at her body and asked forgiveness, but she did not respond, and it was then that he observed her skin was so much like dried bamboo. After they had left him alone with her, the John-crows had perched in anticipation of a feast. He had not known what to do, looked around bewildered, until he saw the young girls, four of them, also dressed in white, approaching. When they reached her, their friend, they formed a circle around her body and fell to their knees and wept, excluding him. He stood around awkwardly for a time then, feeling futile, spat at the carrion birds and walked dejectedly to his mother's house where he stayed cooped up for two days without eating. He would probably have stayed there until he wasted away, but a few of her young friends came and begged him to bury her.

It was a burial, if it can be called that, that would have made the devil weep. Having disowned her, the girl's mother refused to bury her, so it was left to her young friends to dig a hole way out in the bushes, dress her in the same dress she wore when he had baptized and drowned her, and laid her body, now disfigured and ashen gray, in a clumsily built wooden box. There were no songs, and no sermon to speak of, because he couldn't find any words to say. Every time he tried to say something kind, he kept smelling her, and her bloated stomach rose like rotten food shoved in his mouth. He did not even know her name, so whom could he ask the Lord to take unto his bosom? Her friends made a beautiful crown from pink and white oleander flowers, which was the only beauty to suggest that someone had lived and had been loved.

The weeks that followed the girl's baptism, drowning and burial were, strangely enough, the most peaceful he had since becoming an adult. All was quiet. Though no family was grieving her, nature seemed to mourn her passing. No wind blew for days on end. At night, the crickets and other insects did not sing their songs to liven up the darkness. During the day, the sun parched the soil, and in the year that followed many went to bed hungry, and the lush valley witnessed its first drought in the memory of the oldest living person. As devastating as the drought was the death of four healthy female infants, all of whom were found dead the morning after many claimed they saw and heard a rolling calf – that terrible ghost that appeared in the form of a cow with a long chain dragging behind it – near the edge of the river.

Jeremiah had been oblivious to most of these events. He had gone on a prolonged fast and stayed indoors. Then he had gotten dengue fever from mosquitoes' bites, and perhaps would have died if his godfather, Mas Tomlin, had not come again to rescue him and nurse him well. Between fits of sleep, and being spoon-fed a nasty-tasting liquid while recovering from the fever, Jeremiah heard snatches of Mas Tomlin's life, and his great undying love for his mother and for him, Jeremiah, the son Mas Tomlin never had.

Mas Tomlin and Miss Hortense had grown up in the same valley and had attended the same primary school to Standard Six, which was the age most country children left school to devote their time to some trade, or to help cultivate the land their parents owned. Mas Tomlin did not like farming, and was not interested in any trade, so wondered around aimlessly until he had the chance to go to Cuba where he ended up working on a tobacco estate. He hated this work but made good money and planned to return home, seek out Hortense and make her his wife. But after leaving Cuba, he went to Costa Rica where he gambled and lost most of his money, spent five years there, working in all sorts of jobs until he saved his passage and had a little money in his pocket.

Never having much skill in writing, he had not written or kept in touch with Hortense, or anyone else in the valley, so his return was a sad homecoming. His father had died, a younger brother had migrated to England, and his Hortense had married and was five months with child. Wilfred, a skilled carpenter, had built her a cottage (where Jeremiah still lived), and everyone said they were happy.

Close to recovery, Jeremiah had listened to the soft, sad voice of Mas Tomlin and saw the sun cast a shaft of light, like a spotlight on his regretful face.

"Yuh moda was de finest woman inside dis valley. Skin as smooth as banana leaf, an lawd, de woman could talk sweet, just like bombay mango juice. Ah did want her from long, long time, but she was a lady, and deserve more dan de likes of de nothin me had to offer she. Dat's why me went to Cuba, but de money tun me head, and by de time me find back me senses, yu fada Wilfred marry her off, and see you dey now fi prove it."

Jeremiah drifted off into sleep and when he awoke, hoping to learn more about his absent father, Mas Tomlin had gone, and Jeremiah did not see him again until the next day. Much to his disappointment, Mas Tomlin did not resume the story about his mother or father, but rather spoke of others in the valley. Jeremiah, still feeling like the ten-year-old boy who had been rescued by this kind man, refrained from asking what he desperately needed to know.

★ ★ ★

The bed creaks and he hauls himself up on shaky feet. He hears the women bantering back and forth, and as he peers through the window he sees them sitting on the veranda while the children play under their mothers' watchful eyes; they appear oblivious of all the children's bustle, but nonetheless are always vigilant, cautioning a child with an abrupt pause in their conversation, a slight gesture of the hand, head or a look, a knowing, voiceless, but understood glare.

They are sitting there, he knows, hoping he will emerge – his nightly trek to the store, or just to stretch his legs – to add fuel to their gossip about him, to taunt him, their every gesture an invitation – though if he were to respond to their flirtation, they would withdraw just for the pleasure of rebuking him.

"Look on de unquenchable bags of desire," Jeremiah spits in the women's direction, but they don't hear him as it is murmured. How he would like to sally up to them, and playfully slap them on the arm or on the behind, as he has seen more than one man doing; how he would like to feel their strong working hands on him; how he would like to say "Beg pardon" as he purposely opens the door when they are drying from a shower, pretending it was an innocent accident; how he would like to have one of them, Queenie, cook him a meal and bring it to him, to have her in his bed, to kiss her full lips open wide in laughter, to nibble at her long neck – Lord, he would be satisfied just to touch her hands, to kiss her fingers, to look at her unashamedly, openly.

He is done with repentance. He has sinned, he has gone without, he has exiled himself, and now he will live.

This is decided in a flash as he continues to peer at the women.

They are very different from the women in his valley who are circumspect and keep their desires a hidden secret. Maybe these women are free to be themselves, to revel in their desires, because they are away from the scrutiny of rural villages where many of them grew; or maybe they have discovered their beauty, as natural and bountiful as the fruits, flowers and animals, so make each day a celebration of the joy which is their life. Still, these are not women to trifle with or practice on. They are all physically able, but even if they cannot match a man muscle for muscle, their tongues are as caustic as they are sweet, and woe to the person who mistakes their friendly ease as an invitation to be familiar. Jeremiah will not risk their outright condemnation. Their lives are unfulfilled in many ways, and their appetites insatiable. He has overheard their men frequently both applauding and lamenting these women's endless needs and the weak backs which resulted. No, he will not make himself their prey. Jeremiah breathes deeply, takes in the stifling stench of the room.

He goes to the partially open window, and quietly, but determinedly closes it. He holds his breath as he shuts out the outside world to his view. Closed in his darkened room, Jeremiah lets out a whimper, feeble at first, like that of a day-old puppy. Then it grows louder, and all the women stare in the direction of his room and two of the dogs in the yard begin to yap and suddenly the entire street is besieged with yapping dogs. Mabel stomps her feet and uses the hem of her dress to fan the mosquitoes buzzing around her legs. She is made uncomfortable and very angry by this exposure of pain; she speaks to no one in particular, but to everyone who will hear her.

"Wha kind a madness dis man bring pan we, eh?"

Stephanie snaps at her two daughters who have drifted outside the gate, and as she heads for her room she cautions Mabel, "Yuh no know what cross dat man a carry round wid him. Him need some lovin fi ease up him load." She slams the door behind her.

Everyone scurries away to avoid meeting Jeremiah's pain. They know such pain is lethal; they have all separately and communally witnessed how such a pain can drag stout men out in the street and whip them until they are mere bones; they have heard the screams and weeping that pain demands from young girls; they have seen the anguish it inflicts on women and the old; they have heard it all too often whispering at their windows, seducing them to submit to it.

Queenie, though, creeps up to and presses her ear to Jeremiah's door. The cry dissipates; the dogs cease their yapping, and for a few minutes all is quiet. Queenie looks along the street, then confident that no one is watching, she tries the knob of Jeremiah's door. At that very moment Jeremiah has collected his pain and folded it like a handkerchief for his pocket. He turns on the 25-watt bulb, too faint to render details, sits at the table, and pulls the black book close, almost to his chest, opens it, reads.

"But as God is true, our word toward you was not yea and nay." Pausing, he ponders and reads again, "But as God is true, our word toward you was not yea and nay."

Was he true? Is he true? Does such a thing exist any more? Quietly he pushes back the chair and as he begins to pace the tiny room – six long paces, then beginning the pattern again – the phrase *Yea and nay* leaps, jumps, turns over and somersaults in his head. *Yea and nay*. He is true. Life is true. It matters, if he matters.

Queenie listens, then goes to make Jeremiah a tall glass of Ovaltine, and bring him some of her dinner of rice, boiled plantain, and corned-beef simmered in tomatoes and onion. Again she surveys the street to make sure no one is watching her; confident of being unobserved, she taps on Jeremiah's door. He hears her before she taps; he is behind his door, his cheek pressed against the wood, drinking in her smell, wet sugar being rubbed into butter to make a cake, wet sugar rolled into tamarind balls, wet sugar melted and baked into peanut-drops, wet sugar, scooped from a can and tossed in the mouth, wet sugar, dark, textured, sweet.

"Yes?" Her voice awakens him from his reverie. He waits.

"Open de door so ah can come in." Her words are full and her breathing is rapid. No word will leave Jeremiah's lips; they won't even come up out of his throat. He caresses the door where he imagines her face is, and affirms to himself that it matters after all, and he is worthy of love.

Queenie places the food by the door, and before leaving she whispers, "Ah leavin sometin fah you to eat. Take it up soon so ants don't get to it."

He knows she is gone, but still cannot bring himself to open the door and take the food. So he stands until the silence calls to him. He creaks open the door and picks up the plate and covered mug quickly, glancing around to see if anyone is in sight.

★   ★   ★

Sweat covered his body, and the thick black robe, which came to his ankles and swished around his feet when he moved, mocked him. The heavy linen fabric rubbed against the scars on his back, reminding him of his first sin. He must not look at his mother; to do so was to be reminded of transgression, to wallow in damnation. A lone, withered voice began the song, then other voices, gravelled and desperate, joined in the chant:

"Release him, release him, release him let him live
Release him, release him, release him until morning
Release him, release him, release him to glory's hand..."

On and on the voices lifted him up, and pulled him down, rocked him, and pushed him, held him and soothed him, then released him, sending him reeling. He swayed, trapped by their voices, the twin starapples, the sturdy legs, and death flaunting in his mother's eyes.

Then all eyes were on him. Sweat like a river bathed him, his fingers gripped the dais while his tongue lay heavy in his mouth, ungraceful, a rotted breadfruit, frothing on the ground where it fell. It was then he was certain he wasn't worthy to be up there before them, that he had sinned too many times. But how was he to turn around, retrace his steps, apologize for his audacity, rebuke his mother further. Where would he go? If he denied his mother salvation, he could not return to his room in her house, the house for which she 'd had to eat hunger and grief for dinner, or smiled lovingly at loneliness and call it friend just to maintain it. No, he would not be allowed back there, and where else could he sepulchre himself from temptation?

Nowhere.

But despite his doubts, he found he was able to give the people down below him something to feed on, and no longer felt their eyes stripping him. He ventured to look at his mother, whose head hung heavy like a ripe fruit. Of course, his confidence was premature; he mistook their compliance for gratitude, and fancied himself saved, immune from temptation. That was the first time his mother had walked with the other women rather than alone, doing what she had always admonished him for, needing to be with others.

All through his childhood Jeremiah had heard bits and pieces of a story that he knew were references to his and his mother's life. Now that he was cloaked in the clothes of the Lord, more of the stories surfaced. Fond of taking walks, he often wandered in the bush, cutting through other people's fields, sniffing at the air and drinking in the different aromas that issued from the earth. A few days after his first sermon, he went on an early morning stroll and found himself at the far end of the river where a few women washed clothes. Two women, somewhat older than his mother, were busy scrubbing clothes against a rock, their voices keeping up with the vigour of their hands.

"So Miss Hortense son tun preacher man."

"Ma'am! Ain't dat sometin. Mark yu, ah wasn't in de church but ah hear from good-good source."

"Is wha yuh hear?" the other woman interrupted the first.

"Well, Miss Coolie daughta seh him tongue heavy like a bag a cement."

"Same ting me hear."

With that the speaker put aside her washing, wiped her hands on the wet apron around her waist, and took a few steps towards her listener, whose hands did not pause for a moment.

"Shame," she said with such finality that Jeremiah felt as if he had been slapped. He was about to move away and retrace his steps, when the speaker continued in a louder tone, as if sensing him, and wanting to make sure he heard what she said.

"De poor boy didn't tek not even a ounce of him daddy charm. Now, dat was a man wid a butter tongue. Wha was him name again?"

At this, the listener paused, her arms in suds to her elbows, cocked her head, squinted one eye, made a clicking sound, and then resumed washing. When she spoke it was as if declaring great news.

"Wilfred Moore. Ah remember him. Him colour did like nutmeg. De boy is tall like him, but not as strapping, not as dashing. Him was a proud man. Him was a man dat walk by yu, an yu couldn't help but pull up yuself. Wilfred Moore. Ah remember him well."

At last Jeremiah had a picture to go with his invention of this man, his father, around whom he had created a story, but to hear that he was less him, lacking the very qualities that esteemed his father to others' memory, would gnaw at him for the remainder of his life. As he retraced his steps towards his mother's cottage, he understood why, whenever he looked at her, he saw nothing but dissatisfaction written on her face; he was not even a pleasant reminder of the man she loved.

★　★　★

He moves quickly in the semidarkness, splashes water on his face, gargles, spits, wipes his armpits, then goes and sits at the table and slowly savours the food she left for him, pretending she is seated on the other chair, so close to him, their knees brush against each other.

"Wha de blood-claat do yu?" a crass male voice just outside the gate breaks the spell.

197

Jeremiah bows his head. "I'm weak Lord, but thou art strong..."

He isn't going to read the black book any more tonight. His head throbs with memories that live too close to the surface of his pain. He opens the windows and the cool night air blows through the room lessening the stuffy smell. He uncovers the mug, discovers the warm Ovaltine, and sips it slowly. Soon footsteps and voices tell him that others are returning home; he switches off his light. Two men, seemingly on the street a house away, begin a heated debate. Their shouting stirs Jeremiah's sadness, so much so that he wants to shout at the men to stop arguing. Instead, long accustomed to burying his emotions, he turns within, strips off all of his clothes, lies spread-eagled on the bed and ponders his life.

Next week will be two years since his exile and expulsion from the church. Jeremiah turns on his stomach, closes his eyes and travels backward to the period before he was derobed.

★ ★ ★

After Jeremiah's three years of apprenticeship with Brother Jonah, who also doubled as a very successful plumber, Jeremiah was ready for his robe. It was his mother who informed him of this; Brother Jonah discussed everything with her before speaking to Jeremiah. He was excited and felt humble yet privileged. If he were to succeed at saving sinners' souls perhaps he would also be able to restore his mother to a place of salvation. Throughout his childhood, she had accused him of causing her to fall from grace, to fall from love. Whenever she accused him he felt like a sinner. However, now that he could free her guilt, he would also make himself free from sin, pure, unblemished. The same day his mother gave him his robe, Jeremiah learned from her the reason for the flogging he had withstood at ten, the memory of which still haunted him, the leather strap, red and wet, circling, circling him.

Exactly ten years had passed, and as a young man of twenty he was no more assured than he was at ten. His mother still directed his life and he followed without questioning. After parting from Brother Jonah, Jeremiah took the bus, which stopped at the junction of his valley, about two miles from his mother's house. Disembarking from the bus his mind suddenly went back to that day his mother flogged him so mercilessly. It was a day similar to the present one, in July, in the season of drought that bled the colour from the land, and even took the sheen from people's skin.

The children in the valley so often teased him that he was a mama's boy, he was always trying to prove to them that he was not. That was why he had agreed to go off with Monroe, Karl and Chapman, Monroe's older brother, whom he admired. Besides which, he liked crayfish, and enjoyed exploring the river to find its different outlets into the sea. They had walked for what seemed like an eternity, with a big pan of crayfish, and finally, well after the sun was behind their shoulders, they made their way inland. There they met a man working in his field who gave them green bananas and cocoa yam to cook. The food was the sweetest Jeremiah had ever had, and this discovery that his mother was not the best cook displeased him, worried him in fact. Perhaps what the children chanted was true; he was a mama's boy, even though he couldn't remember his mother ever holding him gently, kissing him, or cooking any food especially for him. He could not recall, not even once, when she asked him what he wanted either for breakfast, lunch or dinner. But she always made his meals, and maybe that was enough. Still, after eating his fill of Chapman's crayfish pot, Jeremiah felt as if his mother had been tricking him, lying to him. When they were done with the meal and had cleaned up, Chapman asked them if they knew any rude-boy stories, and Jeremiah felt more isolated still because Karl and Monroe both told stories, but he could not remember any to share. As hard as he tried, all he could remember were snatches of stories about Big-Boy, a notorious folk character who was said to be dunce and dense, and apt to get into trouble at school. However, at Chapman's prodding, Jeremiah ventured to tell the story, snatches of memory, but mostly invention. Not sure of his ability, he looked at his feet as he began.

"Well one day, when Big-Boy was in Sixth Standard, Teacha gave him ten words to look up and tell him to write about one of de words fah homework. Well Big-Boy fool-fool around as usual an nuh do nuh work. Next morning come, Big-Boy late fi school, but reach in time fah vocabulary words. Big-Boy neva did no homework so him crouch down in de back, hoping Teacha wouldn't call pan him. Teacha start by callin on dose in de front, and dose who volunteer, till all de words but one left. Big-Boy, feelin happier now, sit up, forget himself and start to whistle. You could a hear straw drop. Everybody stare pan Big-Boy, and de lines in Teacha forehead stand out big so and ripple, as Teacha breathe harder and harder. Teacha walk over to Big-Boy and use de cane to tap him pan him shoulder. Big-Boy jump like hot water fall pan him back. Den Teacha clear him throat, an in him most proper voice Teacha say to Big-Boy, 'Now Mister Bertram Bendexter Bigger,' an everyone bust out laughin cause dem didn't know or did forget is so Big-Boy name. But de look pan Teacha face soon put dem straight, and everyone fix dem face as if dem listenin to de most important ting in de world. Den Teacha tun to Big-Boy again an in de same tone, Teacha say, 'Suppose you tell de class de meaning of drawstring.' Big-Boy scratch him head, scratch him arm, scratch him whole body before him stand up, makin much noise wid de bench and desk. By now everybody ah sputter behind dem hand, but Teacha face mek up. Big-Boy a stand up now, but him nah say nutten. Teacha bang down de cane pan Big-Boy desk, who jump in de air, an knock him knee on de bench. Teacha well mad now. Him say to Big-Boy, 'Boy, are you a dunce or a fool? Which one?'

"Big-Boy hang him head, then smile up at teacher and say, 'I's a fool, Teacha.'

"Laughter fah days. Teacha say him gwane give de whole class detention.

"'Well, fool,' Teacha say in the same proper tone, 'Tell the class what a drawstring is.'

"Big-Boy chuckle, hang him head, look pan Teacha and ask, 'Yuh really wan me fi tell de class, sarh.'

"'Don't waste my time, boy,' snap Teacha, 'just tell me what a drawstring is.'

"Big-Boy start big cryin, and snot run down him nose, and so him wipe it, so more run down. Den Big-Boy quiet down and, playing wid him finger like likkle pickney, he begin.

"'You see how tings go. Me neva go look fi trouble, but trouble always fine me. Well, Mister Teacha sarh, is passin me was passin you house when Mistress Teacha call to me to come help her.'

"By now all was wondering what Teacha wife have to do with the definition, but Big-Boy continue wid him story.

" 'Me go inside you bedroom, an Mistress Teacher say how her drawers string pop an if me can help her fix it. Mistress Teacha have a nice big bottom, you see. Well to tell you de truth, Teacha, me neva did know till Mistress Teacha show me dat women need string fi hold up dem drawers, sarh, Mista Teacha.'

"De whole class fall out dem seat from laughin, and Teacha storm out de classroom widout givin Big-Boy a caning, an de class never get no detention either."

Chapman laughed until his eyes were wet, and even Monroe and Karl said that was a good Big-Boy story. Jeremiah felt proud of himself, and just before joining the others in taking a nap before heading home, he smiled at his victory.

Little did Jeremiah know what was in store for him. Chapman got them lost returning home when he claimed he knew a short-cut, which actually turned out to be a long, roundabout way which cost them two additional hours. Jeremiah knew his mother was going to be mad, but he didn't guess at her wrath. The happiest memory of his childhood, telling a story that made him an equal in the eyes of his friends, was connected to the saddest incident in his life, the flogging that almost cost him his life.

Jeremiah wiped the perspiration from his face. His hands trembled. He told himself that he was not a ten-year-old boy but a twenty-year-old man; his mother couldn't flog him any more. However, he wasn't sure of this fact. He had completed his training. His mother was proud. Brother Jonah said so, so what was it that Jeremiah feared? Happiness? He had felt completely happy when he told that Big-Boy story. It was his story; he hadn't heard it from anyone, he had made it up as he went along, and it was a good story. Being away from his mother was happiness, even though he did nothing but what Brother Jonah told him to do, but his mother was not there watching his every move, comparing him to that invisible but ever present person – his father. Brother Jonah did not like him or dislike him for not being someone else rather than being himself. Living with his mother was to live with that constant burden, and though he would not allow himself to think the words, or accept the idea, he hated his mother for never liking or wanting him; indeed, he wished that she had given him away the day he was born. Such were Jeremiah's thoughts as he walked home. Trepidation marked his progress, especially since he hadn't been home in several months.

In addition to teaching Jeremiah how to drive the devil out of the sinner's soul, and cure the evil ways of others, Brother Jonah had taught him his plumbing trade. Jeremiah had been going on jobs with Brother Jonah for almost three years and, although quite proficient, he was never given any money for his services. Since he did not know what arrangements his mother had made with Brother Jonah about his accommodations and training, he had not thought to request compensation. Didn't his mother say Brother Jonah was doing her a special favour out of the goodness of his heart? Jeremiah was treated and fed well at Brother Jonah's home. In fact he was treated better than Brother Jonah's own children and wife. He was allowed to sit at the table with Brother Jonah for meals, being urged to eat as much as he wanted, while Brother Jonah's many children peeped through the door, silent, with open mouths, and his wife was busy in the kitchen, yet always right at his elbow if he needed water or something he fancied that she had failed to anticipate. Jeremiah never asked Brother Jonah why he did not allow his family to sit with him, although he felt great pity for his wife, and especially the children, so he never ate more than the first helping that was put on his plate. However, after one year in Brother Jonah's company, one Friday evening as they sat at the table long after it had been cleared away, sipping a little orange wine that Brother Jonah's wife had made, the preacher imparted some of the details of his life to Jeremiah.

He rubbed his hands together as he always did before launching into a sermon. Jeremiah knew a long story was coming so settled himself in the straightback chair.

"Now, my boy," Brother Jonah began; he almost always addressed Jeremiah as *my boy*, not in a disrespectful way, but affectionately, and it was at the beginning of this story that Jeremiah realized that he and Brother Jonah were the only males in the house. Brother Jonah had six daughters. No wonder he took such an interest in Jeremiah, the son he wanted but never had. Brother Jonah interrupted Jeremiah's train of thought.

"You listening, my boy? I want you to listen closely. You see me here, a poor humble black man. I'm well schooled. Attended Oxford College in England for two years, but life for a black man is hard, my boy. You will soon learn just how hard. But I'm not dwelling on the hardness of my life because I have much to be thankful for. Now I see you watching my wife and children, and you wondering why I don't allow them to sit with me. Well, I used to let me wife sit with me, but she disappoint me bad. How many children you see she give me, how many?"

Startled by this question, and not being sure an answer was wanted, Jeremiah remained silent.

"You right to not answer. Six! Six gal picknie fah me one to mind."

Jeremiah observed that Brother Jonah had broken into the dialect that he often decried. Then he continued in a calmer tone.

"Now you tell me, my boy, what is one man to do with all those females? Them vex me bad, well vex me. I wouldn't even touch that woman again because I do believe my father was right. Him say when I was a baby one of me sisters walk over me, and turn me back. That is my crosses, my boy, and a heavy one it is too. My loving father, may his soul forever rest in eternal bliss, died after me fourth girl was born. He took one look at her and fall dead. Shocked. He knew, and told me I shouldn't have any more and I should have known too and stopped then, but, my son, those species of human beings," and Brother Jonah paused, pointed in his wife's direction, "are the vilest corruption you can imagine. Keep away from them, my boy. They will pull you down every time. Just look how that woman walk." Brother Jonah got up from his chair and went to stand at the doorway from where he could observe his wife. He beckoned to Jeremiah to join him. Together they stood in the doorway, Jeremiah feeling uncomfortable staring at Mrs. Roberts. "Now you tell me, my boy, who can resist that wanton flesh of desire. Surely not me, my boy. Remember how we came about? No doubt another wanton flesh tempted poor humble Adam who was trying to obey the words of his God. Mark my words," and Brother Jonah strode to the table and smashed his hand hard on the smooth wooden surface, "mark my words, my boy, women will tempt you ever time, so you must resist them, or treat them with indifference."

Brother Jonah strode onto his veranda and looked out, waved at his neighbour, responded to greetings from a few people passing by. Jeremiah didn't know whether he was excused so he sat, feeling foolish. Mrs. Roberts came, smiled at him and poured him more wine; she refilled her husband's glass and took it to him. Passing back to the kitchen and seeing Jeremiah sitting alone in the living room, she spoke to him in a gentle, yet conspiratorial voice. "Go and sit wid him. Him need to hear himself talk. You allow him to practice. Just don't take half of what him say to heart."

Jeremiah went obediently to the veranda to join Brother Jonah.

Jonah Roberts was the last of seven children, and the only boy. His father was overjoyed but his mother was disgusted at another baby, and a boy who wet the bed for the first eleven years of his life. Jonah feared his mother who whipped him at the slightest infraction, but his father showered him with love, and indulged him, which only added fuel to his mother's wrath. Nonetheless, his mother was as fair as she was mean, and she whipped his sisters as well for the slightest misdemeanour. All his life Jonah was puzzled why she didn't want a boy, when everyone else seemed to want boys. It was only after he returned from England that he was brave enough to ask her. She had looked at him, shook her head, and rephrased his own question. "Why I should want a boy, what special bout you?" Jonah hadn't been able to answer right away, and his inability to make a rejoinder scared him because he had always assumed boys were better, but why they were, he couldn't say. His mother told him not to worry his head to find an answer because there wasn't one. She said it wasn't that she didn't want a boy, it was that she didn't want another child, and if he had been a girl she would have felt the same way. Jonah had been hurt beyond reason. He had wanted to hear her tell him why she hated him, instead he learned that he was not even part of her hate, just a reminder of what she didn't want.

Jeremiah felt the tears running down his cheeks, and quickly wiped them with his hands. He understood why he instinctively liked Brother Jonah. They shared the same pain. To their respective mothers they were never themselves, just a reminder of something or someone else. Together both men sat on the veranda, well after all were in their beds. They didn't speak; they were very still, but they were not asleep; they had shared their scars, and were trying to continue to live with themselves in a world which was not of their making, and seldom to their liking.

But Jeremiah was still stunned when, about seven months before his apprenticeship was over, Brother Jonah handed him an envelope containing more money than he had ever had, when they completed a job they had worked at all week. Ever since that Friday, each week Brother Jonah gave him money, most of which Jeremiah kept hidden under the mattress. Moreover, the week before he left his mentor's charge, he was told to visit his mother who had special news for him. Brother Jonah had taken him to his own tailor and had three pants made for him from the woollen cloth from England that was sold by young lads in front of many of the stores in town, and then bought him sturdy black shoes from Bata shoe store, and although they rubbed against his heels, and pinched his broad feet, Jeremiah felt as Moses must have done when he crossed the Red Sea and turned it into blood in which the wicked Egyptians drowned and were washed away. So he was beside himself with pride that Friday afternoon as he took the road that led to his house, with three new pants – black, navy blue and grey; five new white cotton long-sleeve shirts, merinos, and the prized shoes.

That entire day was special; the sun played in and out of the clouds so that its rays did not sting the skin as it often did; the breeze was cool and soothing, and as Jeremiah walked in the valley, protected by trees whose names he did not know, out of the slender amber grass a host of butterflies, their wings a golden yellow with delicate black designs, flitted before him for most of the four miles to his home. So happy was Jeremiah that he temporarily forgot one of Brother Jonah's cardinal rules and started to whistle. He soon caught himself, and immediately prayed for forgiveness and understanding. After all, Brother Jonah often said every man was allowed a few mistakes as long as they caught themselves in the wrong and eagerly prayed for guidance and forgiveness. Still, whistling was worse, he had said, than even sleeping with three men's wives, so Jeremiah was quite remorseful, and cursed his tongue for tempting him. As Brother Jonah repeatedly said, "There are enough things in life to tempt a good man, so all one can hope for is the will to not wallow in sin, but rather catch oneself, ask for forgiveness and move on."

The butterflies were not the only creatures that opened the way for Jeremiah; he heard the high-pitched chirpings of birds and low coos that fluttered in cool peacefulness. The colour of the sky, azure, not just blue, seemed to be welcoming him; it closely mirrored the sea in all its subtle nuance of blues, greens and opals, and the clouds, too, were spectacular, puffy-white, yet thin, translucent, so that the yellow of the sun and the milky azure of the sky made the clouds appear as rainbow mats that glided and twirled. Half a mile from his mother's house, Jeremiah stopped, sat on the banking, one leg pulled to his chest the other extended on the gravel road with its white marl and cracked limestone. There he sat while time stopped and he transported himself to the verdant mountains, splendid against the yellow-brownish valleys, struggling for life where there was no water. Never before had he experienced such a sense of peace and power; he felt as if his heart was the mountain from which sprang trees, tall and strong, and where the best coffee trees blossomed. So enraptured was he that he did not see her until she was right by his side, her jar cocked to pour him some water which he thirstily drank from his cupped hands, a little spilling to mark his pants. She had a quiet beauty that one might take for granted, like dew on leaves in the morning. As always, in the presence of what he desired, Jeremiah was speechless. But he smiled at her, and his hand brushed her chin lightly. Then just as quickly as she had appeared, she disappeared down a track and he wondered if she were a duppy or a vision from one of his hallucinations.

Finally he was home, his mother's house, looking as it had always done from as far back as his memory was stored; the small brown bungalow with its three small rooms and the recent addition, the veranda, nestled behind red and mauve bougainvillea vines that ran all the way to the roof. The wood was painted deep brown and even the inside walls were stained that colour, with only two tiny windows in the parlour and one tiny window in each bedroom so that the house always seemed dark and stuffy; and since his mother thought any colour other than deep blue, brown, black, white or grey was an indication of one's willingness to take life too easily and frolic, the furniture was all darkly stained, the chairs covered with plain brown cloth, the same material as the curtains. This was not a home to live in; it was a place to sleep, to hide oneself away from the obdurate ways of others.

That was why, as a child, having to be home during the rain season was so painful for Jeremiah. He was not allowed to lie on the bed, except at nights when it was time to sleep, nor even sit on the edge of it because his mother criticized this as slovenly behaviour, as was stretching out on the floor on the mat spread in front of the bed. The only chair that graced his room was hard, without a cushion, and it faced a blank wall on which the only thing to see was a poor drawing of Christ on a calendar that was then ten years old, but his mother insisted should remain intact. In her eyes, to tear off the yellowed bottom portion on which the faded months were printed would be an act of defilement against the Lord. The only window in the room was above his bed, and he had to kneel or stand on his bed to see out of it, and of course his mother strictly forbade standing or kneeling on the bed. He couldn't remember ever once sitting in the parlour, did not dare even when his mother was not around; in fact, he was quite sure his mother had never ever sat in there either, although she had stood in the parlour when Brother Jonah came to visit. So, when it rained, he felt imprisoned in his room, and dreamed of committing unspeakable acts so he could spend the remainder of the day repenting.

As he stood by the front gate, he recalled the first time he met Brother Jonah. He and his mother were in the backyard; she was preparing the evening meal and he was building something, he could not remember what. When Brother Jonah arrived, his mother greeted him formally. Jeremiah nodded to their visitor, but his mother did not introduce them before they went indoors, though she ordered him to bring them the pitcher of fruit punch she had just made and the ice that she had chipped and covered up in the glass jar, and which he was to carry very carefully into the parlour without spilling or letting his fingers smear the glass.

Jeremiah smiles now at the memory.

He had performed the task under his mother's burning eyes, feeling the pee burning at the tip of his penis where it was waiting to spill out and shame him, but he managed not to pee himself. He noted, just as he stepped out from the parlour, how self-assured Brother Jonah was, sitting waiting to be served, as if he owned the house and the very chair on which he, who had lived there sixteen years, and even his mother, had not dared to sit. He noted, too, the pleasure his mother felt at his ability to serve the drinks without a spill. Although the stern features of her face didn't alter – not even a muscle twitched – her skin, purple-black as it was, changed colour and the tiny hairs on her arms ruffled. That was perhaps the first compliment his mother paid him. Usually anything he did, positive or negative, was met with indifference.

It did not take Jeremiah long to know there was something different about his reception when he finally entered the house on his return from Brother Jonah's, and from thenceforth his relationship with his mother would be transformed from one of terror, blind obedience and secret defiance to one of dependency and expectation. He couldn't explain how he knew this, but as he walked around the house, he shivered, as if ice water had been thrown on his back. The yard had been swept clean, not a leaf or blade of grass was out of place and the pattern that the broom made in the dirt had a design more complex than he could decipher. As always, he had walked around to the backyard; no one ever entered the house from the front, and even when she began to permit him and herself to sit on the veranda, they still – even if they had been inside – walked to the back of the house, went around the side, then entered the veranda from the front. He had long known the front door was permanently locked, and no key for it was ever found. (Later, he learned that his mysterious father had pocketed the key after locking the door on the night, forever indelible in his mother's memory, when he left, promising to return, but never did – so the door remained barred.) When he got to the side of the house he noticed that she had dug another garden bed and planted eggplants and cabbage, and around the stump of the sweetsop tree she had chopped down that memorable evening, Joseph-coat flowers sprouted and a circular bench seat had been fitted.

Then he saw her sitting on the stool she always sat on, looking queenly, her back against the kitchen wall. She was wearing a new white church dress, the high neckline dwarfing her neck, and the long sleeves concealing the muscular strength of her arms. That was the first and last time he wondered about how he felt about her and knew that he both loved and hated her, and that both feelings were born in the same place, therefore were the same. He would always be her burden, she his terror. He wished it did not have to be so. He wanted to know her, and have her know him. They had lived all his life together. She was the closest person he knew and he probably knew her better than anyone, yet he did not know what was her favourite fruit and she did not know the pleasure he got from looking at the mountains or listening to birdsong. Seeing her as she was, looking so vulnerable, Jeremiah had wanted to run up to his mother, fling his arms around her, and protect her – from what he wasn't sure. He sensed that there was something unnameable that she feared. However, his fear of her, of her rejection, her quickness to anger, quickly dispelled his desire to run and embrace her.

Hortense Moore was not a pretty woman, but that only made her more handsome in an uneasy way. A hard muscle line zigzagged from her forehead to the tip of her nose; her eyes were death cold and glazed, yet her face had deep determination, a resolute chin and cheekbones that were high, haughty, befitting a queen in some distant time. She was in deep thought, and did not see him; he knew she was aware of his presence but had to complete the journey she was taking. She was the only child of old parents. Her mother had been forty when she was born; having suffered four miscarriages in her early twenties, she and her husband had resigned themselves to not having any child of their own, so had helped to raise a number of nieces and nephews, and even cousins' children. Then she came along, unexpectedly. She was not expected to live, being sickly the first two years of her life. When she started to grow, they planted an avocado pear tree for her life support and celebrated their second life. All through her childhood, Hortense was called Second-Life. Hortense's mother had education and trained her to be a lady, to demand respect, especially from boys, and later men. After she completed Standard Six, her mother wanted her to train to be a teacher, but she refused, preferring instead to work the land. She had often accompanied her father to the field, and believed it was simply magic to be able to put something in the ground, and reap food in return. Her mother had protested at first, claiming field work was not for a lady, but relented, accustomed to indulging this only child of hers, only demanding that she wore a hat to shield her face from the sun.

For a long time Hortense wasn't interested in boys, though she enjoyed going to the open-air dances where she had as much fun dancing with the men her father's age as the boys of her own age group. Her life was uneventful and happy. She was never flogged, seldom scolded, and her every wish was granted. Everyone said she was spoilt, and she readily agreed. Then close to her seventeenth birthday her mother died, quite unexpectedly, not having been ill, and three months later, before she had recovered from her grief, her father also passed away. For Hortense it was the most painful and desolate experience. For all her life, before she saw the sun she saw her parents, before she heard the crickets at night, she heard her parents; they were her best friends; she had not imagined life without them. When the gravediggers started to throw the dirt on her father's coffin, she jumped in and had to be pulled out. For several months after her parents' death she slept on their graves and prayed for her own death. She had not believed that there could be a life without them. Sleeping out in the damp air, she caught a cold, which soon turned into pneumonia; then, to her complete surprise, when she felt pain cruising through her bones, she began to fight for her life, and returned to sleeping in her bed, but not before swearing never to love anyone as much as she loved her parents.

But promises are often broken, and memory sometimes has amnesia.

Hortense picked up her life and turned all her energy to cultivating her land. Everything thrived under her touch, and soon others came to her for advice about planting one kind of yam over another, cabbage, turnip, carrots, tomatoes, all kinds of vegetables and fruits. After a while men came, under the guise of seeking advice, but it was soon clear to Hortense that they cared little for the advice, and really only came to waste her time with small talk. She was very impatient with such men. They, after repeatedly being rejected, stopped visiting her, claiming she was arrogant. Having always enjoyed the dances, about a year and a half after her parents' death, Hortense got dressed up, and walked the three-quarter mile to the open-air meeting hall where a dance was in progress. Not being choosy about her partner, in less than five minutes she was on the floor, and remained there for the next two hours, having changed several partners. That was where she first saw Wilfred. He stood out, but he did not make her heart beat fast, nor did she flutter and tremble under his gaze. It would be a year before that happened. She went home alone that night, and several other nights after the dances she attended.

Yet her path and Wilfred's kept crossing: going to the store, to church, or for a walk. One day, when she returned tired from the field, she saw him sitting on the stool by her kitchen, carving a woman whose arms were tree branches and whose stomach was the trunk. She was about to demand to know what he was doing, sitting as if he belonged on her stool, when he looked up at her, smiled, and said in the most matter-of-fact voice, which was a request and a command in one, "Long time ah waiting on some food." Her heart skipped a beat, and as much as she wanted to say something sharp back to him, she could think of nothing appropriate, so went in the kitchen and cooked them dinner. At the end of the meal he gave her the statue he had carved and left.

The next day, when she finished work in her field, she went looking for him, and after inquiring from four different persons, tracked him down ten miles away, building a house. She didn't greet him, but stood watching him work, and although he saw her, and paused for a moment, he continued at his task. Then he took a break, and cut them both coconut water to drink.

She drank it, then looked him straight in the eyes and said, "After you finish dis house, come build me one."

That marked the beginning of their courtship, which continued for a year. After he completed the new cottage for her, they got married – without even drinking a toast or eating any cake.

Hortense knew she was doomed the first time they went to a

211

dance and he danced with someone else. She was surprised that she only wanted to dance with him, was surprised that when he winked at her from across the room, her feet wobbled, and she felt foolish. Now she was surprised that she no longer missed her parents, in fact she seldom thought of them. There was not a moment of her waking day that she didn't long to be near Wilfred, to feel his hand on her thigh, to smell his breath as he kissed her face, to delight in the sight of his walk, his very existence. Actions suggested that he shared her intensity, was faithful beyond reproach, got excited every time he looked at her, and could not resist touching her affectionately, even in the presence of others. For two years, five months and three days they shared such bliss until that night he tried to walk away from her, claiming he had to leave, but would send for her.

"Oh Lord! Oh Lord!" she wailed when she saw Jeremiah, her arms coming together on her chest, then extending to the sides, her finger spread. Her eyes, however, were dry, as if she was living someone else's emotions.

Jeremiah bowed to his mother, for at the least she deserved his respect, his humility. To Jeremiah's surprise she repaid his greeting with a similar bow of her head, and her eyes directed him to his room where he stood speechless and his grip dropped from his hand. A long black robe, shiny from the pressing and starching, hung on a hanger over the nape of the door. Was this a vision?

"Humble thyself, my servant, and I shall put the world at your feet."

He dared not touch it, even as his hands were magnetized to it, stopping a breath away from the actual feel of the fabric, so close to it that he could feel the heat it generated against his skin. Whenever overcome with desire, he was foolstruck, and so he stood there until the croaking of a frog sent him running from the room, into another memory that gave him deep satisfaction.

Jeremiah was not a bright student, but he was far from being a dunce. He was thoughtful, and took his time to ponder every problem and question before responding. This habit caused some teachers to label him as slow. Jeremiah's fifth form teacher,

Mr. Stradmore, was very impatient with his students, and quick to show his displeasure by rapping them on their heads, shaming, verbally abusing and even caning them. This was what led Jeremiah to drop out of school when he was sixteen. *He* would never again have Mr. Stradmore's knuckles rap him on the forehead, or be made to stand in the corner, wearing the dunce cap because he was too slow in responding to a question. He remembered one Wednesday afternoon vividly. Just after lunch break, Mr. Stradmore called him to the blackboard to solve some algebra problems. Jeremiah had sat at his desk, not in disobedience, but merely to recall the formulas. Mr. Stradmore sprang on him, pulled him up by the front of his shirt, sending buttons rolling on the tiled floor, and rebuked him for his defiance. Then the teacher had begun a barrage of insults, calling him an imbecile, an ignoramus, a moron.

Jeremiah had lost all restraint and blared, "Ah might be stupid, but least ah know me left shoe from right."

The private joke among the students was that Mr. Stradmore always wore two left shoes, didn't know left from right. Snickers resounded in the classroom for an eternal minute, then died as suddenly as a deflated balloon. Mr. Stradmore looked down at his feet, so obviously mis-shoed, that like a child attempting to cover up his error, he quickly crossed his feet at the ankle, but in the process lost his balance and fell on his bottom. The students' amusement was uncontrollable. Some of the larger boys fell off their already too small chairs onto the floor in stitches. Jeremiah didn't stay around to learn of the outcome, but neither he nor his mother was ever summoned to school, and soon this became another incident that was never talked about. Mr. Stradmore retired at the end of that term after repeatedly being hailed as "Left Shoe".

Jeremiah remembered the incident with mixed emotion. While he was proud of his assertiveness, he felt bad that it was at the expense of Mr. Stradmore, who was, after all, a good teacher, concerned about his students' learning, even though his methods often achieved the opposite result. He realized that Mr. Stradmore had triggered in him the same feeling of terror as his mother. That was why the confrontation had frightened him so. He had fled from the classroom, running all the way to the river that was more than a mile from the school. There he had stripped off his clothes before diving in, and trying to hold himself down, until he realized that he did not want to drown himself, that nothing Mr. Stradmore had done was so terrible as to prompt his death.

When Jeremiah ran from his room, trembling at the sight of the robe, he almost knocked over his mother. He was ashamed to face her, sweat pouring under his arms and around his waist. What would she think of him, bursting out like that, after she had made his robe with such care and fine detail. He shortly returned, glanced at her, and then hung his head. She said nothing so he sat, as she often sat in the evenings, by the back door. But where her eyes never saw beyond her yesteryears, Jeremiah surveyed the valley, the mountain range; scrutinized the varying shades of green and brown of the trees; observed, as if for the first time, their frailty and verdure, their variety of shape, the bend of a branch, the pointed or round shape of a leaf, its lines and veins, the sheen or flatness of surfaces and the prickly or soft spikes that broke that surface. Whilst his mother marvelled at the earth's ability to yield food, Jeremiah was in awe of the texture of the brown-red earth, the hollow and uneven surface of its belly; or of the many different ants – tiny black ones that crawled with their bellies close to the ground or the large red ones that stung worse than wasps and seemed always to be in a jog; or the many coloured lizards – the ground lizards, silver-turquoise, that people said couldn't climb trees and whose eyes were a sad grey – probably from that realization; or the duppy lizards that could change from the deepest green of a leaf to the light brown of a tree trunk or whitish like fever grass; or those other monstrous-looking ones, called saw lizard – because they appeared to be carrying saws on their backs, their skin like old crocus bags washed and sunned too much; or the tiny lizards that were cold and clammy, the polly lizards that were always hidden in dark crevices, on window slabs, in the openings of doors. All these things Jeremiah saw and marvelled at that Friday evening when he returned to his mother's house and received his robe.

She made him boiled green bananas and mackerel rundown,

the coconut milk sweetening the salty mackerel and making the bananas buttery. He thought that perhaps this was his favourite meal, and she knew this. Could it be that she wanted to please him? Maybe she was just celebrating her own success in having him complete what she had instructed him to do. She stood to his right while he ate, her body rigid. Her voice, which was often cutlass-swift and blade-sharp, now assailed him like soggy bread. At first, when she began talking he didn't hear it, because the voice did not seem to be coming from her, but from someone he wished he had met back when love danced around her.

"Ah love him as much as ah love life. Ah love him more dan ah did love me mother and father, more dan it safe to love anyone. Is sin ah commit lovin him so. Ah did swear after my father dead dat ah wouldn't love anyone else like dat. But Wilfred come sit on me stool, and ah love him more dan... more dan anyting else. For him ah would leave no stone unturn. Is him ah been keepin myself for all dese years. How ah love him! And same way him did love me, love me until me weak. We did make for each other, and night time before we go bed we would lie down in de dark room seeing each odder eyes and talk and talk all kind a foolishness, tings we want and so forth. Is love bring you here, and is only love why you live and is almost man now; de love for him, de love of him."

She paused and he stole a glance at her face, so different from the flavour of her voice; the red undertone of her skin like burning amber. Such a love could cause one to forget oneself, forget one was mortal, responsible for the feelings that others harboured for them.

The food was tasteless in Jeremiah's mouth. He was a love child, but not loved, merely the memory that stored such passion. His stomach grumbled, and his hands grew weary and rested on the edge of the table. He no longer wanted to hear about the man who had fathered him, this man so loved that it sent him fleeing, too burdened by the sense of obligation that such a love de-manded. Through the corner of his eyes he could see the even contraction and exhalation of her stomach; he thought he saw tears at the rim of her eyes, but was too jealous to bother; what he wanted to do was to place his hand on her heart and massage it, stuff a cloth in her mouth to stop her from spilling her load. He didn't want to hear it any more.

"Him still alive somewhere, me know it. Ah don't know why him can't come home; him must know ah waiting for him; ah will wait for him all me life. We neva quarrel, neva fight; every night ah would rub him palm dem with liniment to smooth and soothe dem. Me was wid belly when him left. We did happy. Is my fault. Dat night me did have a craving for something; can't even remember what it was now, but him say him would go out street and get it for me. Dat's how much him did love me. Me fall asleep and when me wake up, day breaking and de bed empty. Me call out; me get up and look outside; me walk up and down de street days and weeks; me put word in the paper; me pray; me ask everybody; me belly with you in it get bigger; me cry; me fling meself pan de ground and beg for death; me wait; me wait; me wait; me waiting; me waiting; me waiting..."

How many times or for how long she repeated "me waiting" he could not say, but after a while he could no longer stand the repeated drone of her voice, so he got up from the table, went to sit at the doorway, his eyes fixed on the mountain range that seemed so far, but was so near. It was long after the night orchestra of insects had begun their concert and the peeni walis were flitting about that he was jolted back into the moment, and realized that her voice no longer droned on, and he was free again to not feel anything but the night which blanketed his anxieties and concealed her suffering. Since then darkness became his solace.

★   ★   ★

Springing up from his bed, bathed in perspiration, Jeremiah looks around, thinking he has slept through another day, pursued by the same pregnant, nameless drowned woman. What does she want from him? Will she never leave him alone? He doesn't know her, can't even describe what she looks like, so why does she persist in torturing him. He hadn't meant to drown her, had not drowned her. It was discovered, before she was buried, that she had swallowed rat poison. Jeremiah pulls at the sheet, a mound at his feet, and uses it to wipe his tense body. In the adjacent

216

apartment, he hears the light prance of Queenie's feet, which send shivers through him. She is there before him, unclothed, unashamed, but more than an arm's distance from him so that to touch her he would have to move. But he knows that the slightest shift on his part will send her outside the range of his vision, so he lies watching her, desiring her, yet unable to touch her. Tormented by his futility, she laughs, a hollow, tight sound that escapes from between clenched teeth, offers him the glory of her behind and vapours into the air. This time was to have been different; his fingers were as close to her as they could be without touching, but not even that satisfied him, when he could feel the heat of her body seeding through his fingers.

Still sitting up in bed, Jeremiah watches the morning steal upon the world, urging sleepers to begin their day. He will begin to work, soon; his time off has been passed shut in darkness, but now he longs to give flesh to his yearnings.

"And the word was made flesh, and blood baked and made skin real."

He springs from the bed, stretches, and resolves to boldly enter the yard and face the women. He stands by the door, his fingers on the knob and pauses. What if the words refuse to leave his mouth as they so often do? Fear beats down his resolve. Then he hears Brother Jonah's voice, like a loud burst of thunder.

"The weak fail from not trying, so always try, my boy, even if failure is certain."

Jeremiah pulls open his door and greets Mabel, who stands with her mouth agape.

"Mornin, sister Mabel." He steps out onto the veranda, yawns and looks up and down the street at those heading to the bus stop. He wishes he was brave enough to walk around to the side and knock on Queenie's door and thank her for the dinner, and the Ovaltine, but he knows her man has returned. Heard him come in loudly a few hours ago from the bauxite job that keeps him away a few days at a time. Jeremiah sighs, then returns to his apartment. He does not need to hurry. His cousin, the same one who secured him this apartment after it was clear that he had to leave the village of his birth, had convinced her husband, who was in construction, to hire Jeremiah as his plumber, and today, at ten

217

o'clock, Jeremiah is meeting with his cousin's husband and his partner to discuss the job. He isn't sure what there is to discuss really. He has no idea what salary he should demand, and Brother Jonah is too far away to ask. What Jeremiah feels certain of is that there is no plumbing issue that he will not be able to fix or figure out in time. Brother Jonah is the best there is, has trained him well.

Jeremiah pulls the sheets from his bed, then scrapes all the leftover food in a plastic bag, and takes it outside and tosses it in the garbage. He returns to his room, takes Queenie's plates into the bathroom and washes them, as he doesn't have a kitchen, just a bedroom and bathroom. Since it is only seven o'clock, he decides to clean his room, gather all his dirty clothes and drop them off on his way to the interview; he has a woman who does his clothes – another arrangement his cousin had made. He hears the women in the larger apartment opposite his loudly preparing breakfast, getting their children ready for school, and themselves ready for work. He moves to the hallway that leads to his bathroom, and past the barred door that separates his room from Queenie's apartment. Behind the door, he knows, is her living room. During the day she keeps the front door open, and whenever he walks to the backyard, to sit or wash something in the communal washtub, he can't help but see her spotless living room, with its stereo case, and buffet filled with plates and glasses, centre table on which sits a vase with artificial red roses, and her sofa and two armchairs. He has seen inside her kitchen too, as that door opens into the backyard, and that is similarly neat, with a small icebox, a round wooden table with four chairs and other kitchen stuff. He has never seen inside her bedroom, but he images that it too is neat, with its pink and white curtains that sometimes flutter. He knows it is a sin to covet another man's wife, although Queenie is not Mackey's wife – they just live together. Jeremiah remembers overhearing her tell one of the sisters that she and Mackey were not married, and that she wasn't sure she wanted to marry him because he had changed a lot since they met over three years ago, and he was too jealous and didn't want her to work, and she was tired of staying home all day, with little to do. Now Jeremiah presses his ears to the wall, hoping to hear Queenie, but the only sound he hears is the radio. He sighs and resumes sweeping his room. He then takes a long shower and dresses slowly.

He is ready to leave, but has not yet seen her. He looks at her plates and the empty mug. He hesitates, but not wanting to be late, heads for the gate. And there she is. She stops in her tracks, her face open to the wind, the fleshy part of her breasts full through the sleeveless blouse she wears, holding the freshly baked bread she has just bought close to her chest and nose, so she can drink in the aroma. She stands in his path; he fears others, especially her man, might be observing them, but she does not move. He stares at her, but feeling his desires awaking, looks away to the mountain range on the horizon. He hears children chatter as they walk merrily to school. He feels the sweat spreading under his arms. *Wha she want from me, out here in de open? Is playing she fooling wid me?* He hopes he isn't dreaming, praying it isn't his imagination playing tricks on him again.

He forces himself to look at her; she stares at him; they stand looking at each other, the bread cradled to her chest like a lover's head, her nostrils flaring, drinking in the aroma; he hopeful, his desire sticky like jackfruit; her breasts juicy starapples, her belly smooth-roundness, her thighs supple banana trunks, standing there, daring him to take her, teasing him, offering herself so openly, with her man threatening in their room, waiting on the bread for his breakfast.

Jeremiah clears his throat. "Mornin, Miss Queenie," is all he can manage, although he wants to say much more. To thank her for the dinner, to tell her how every time he sees her his heart rushes to his mouth, how he dreams of her all the time, despite Brother Jonah's warning, and that he wants to get to know her, to spend some time with her.

"Mornin back to you, Mister Jeremiah. Me hope you enjoyed the little dinner I left for you last evening."

He nods his head, unable to speak on hearing her voice, a song to his ears. The sun salutes them, and a lone doctor bird begins to chirp. Her lips part, revealing teeth as white as the fleshy meat of a coconut. She breaks off a piece of the still warm bread, wets it to her lips, then offers it to him; he swallows it in one gulp, then hurries through the gate as if his feet are on fire.

The Sunday morning after he had returned to his mother's house from residing with Brother Jonah, Jeremiah was officially robed and gave his first sermon under the vigilant eyes of the women of the church, his mother the major guard. His disappointment at the ordinariness of the day only equalled the tremendous release his mother felt. That moment signalled the beginning of her death that would be slow, although not painful, ending one Thursday night, exactly twenty-four years after Wilfred, his father, her lover, went away.

Jeremiah hadn't thought about what he would do after he got his robe; neither Brother Jonah nor his mother offered any suggestions, so he continued with his life, returning to his mother's house, the both of them respectful of each other, distant and disconnected. After many months of watching the mountain range, wandering through the valley and reliving a time he felt, but which he knew he had never experienced, Jeremiah found odd plumbing jobs, mostly outside his village, which was only slowly acquiring running water. The work was sporadic and during the slow periods Jeremiah took up gardening. He experimented with grafting fruits and growing those vegetable not commonly grown in his village: beetroot, chocho, Indian-cane, and Irish potato, many of which thrived under the care of his banana fingers, perhaps because he placed no investment in the success of what he did. It was also at this point in his life that he discovered, quite by accident, that he had an aptitude for weaving animals from coconut leaves. His first piece was a dog, which he left on the kitchen shelf for his mother. She never acknowledged that she received it, but a week later he saw it on the table in the living room. He made more pieces and left them for her; she displayed them all over the house. Once when he went to visit Mas Tomlin, he gave him one of his weavings, and that was when he learned of his father's talent. This resulted in the suppression of his own.

"Tank yuh kindly, Jeremy," Mas Tomlin intoned, handling the statue of a bird, perched on a tree, that Jeremiah had just given him. "Dis is fine work indeed. Haven't seen anything as good, for a long, long time." Jeremiah helped Mas Tomlin husk dry coconut. When he was about to leave, Mas Tomlin stopped him.

"Hold on, hold on. Ah have someting fi gi you. It will help full you out." He went inside his house and was a long time returning. As Jeremiah stood waiting, he wondered if Mas Tomlin had forgotten about him. But being patient and not having anything that he needed to do urgently, he waited until at last Mas Tomlin returned, triumph written on his face. He extended his hand to Jeremiah, who took the package offered to him. Slowly and carefully he unwrapped the musty smelling cloth to reveal an expertly carved statue of a woman whose arms were the branches of a tree and a pregnant belly the trunk. He ran his fingers gently over the smooth surface, then closed his palm around the object. Mas Tomlin smiled at him.

"Is long time ah been waitin fi give yu dat. Is yu inheritance. Same day yu did born, yu moda give it to me, say she no want it nuh more. Me was de only one dere wid you moda; is me help her bring yu into dis world. Yu undastan now why me couldn't mek her kill yu cause yu not yu fada. Is him did carve dat, give her."

Jeremiah wanted to fling down the statue, but instead his fingers grasped it more tightly. Each time he tried to release it, to give it back to Mas Tomlin, he felt his hand frozen, and Mas Tomlin seemed to have understood his dilemma.

"Don't feel nuh way bout it. Just keep it. Yu don't have fi do noting wid it."

Jeremiah just managed to say, "Thank yu Mas Tomlin," as he headed home. That night, he lay restless in his bed, unable to sleep. Finally he got up, took the statue from off his bureau where he had placed it, and carefully fingered the details. That was how he fell asleep.

★ ★ ★

As Jeremiah climbs into the bus, he remembers his father's statue that he still has wrapped in a handkerchief and he smiles, thinking that he will give it to Queenie one day soon.

His cousin's husband, Mr. Davis, seems fair and, after speaking with Jeremiah for less than ten minutes, tells him he is hired

– unless it is discovered that he cannot do what he claims he can do. He is also Jeremiah's landlord and asks him how he likes his living arrangements, and would he, Jeremiah, be interested in managing the home and another that he owns in the community. "It too little money fi me one deal wid de headache, but ah ave to be able to trust you," Mr. Davis says.

"What involve?" Jeremiah inquires.

"Make sure de yards dem tek care of; fix anything dat break down and collect rent."

Jeremiah nods his head to indicate his willingness.

"Well, let we shake on it, man to man," Mr. Davis says, extending his hand. "De Misses speak well of you, so ah goin out on the limb fah you."

"Thank yu, sar," Jeremiah says, bowing his head slightly in gratitude.

"Yu thank me by doing what yu seh, and mekin sure me can rely pan you," Davis remarks, giving Jeremiah a once over with his eyes. "Well, yu can start managing me property today. De construction delay til sometime next week. Me will get word to yu, but let me gi yu de address of de odder house so yu can go by today and see wha need to be done. Me will come by afta work and let everyone know is you in charge," Mr. Davis ends, dismissing Jeremiah.

Outside the office, which is next to a car repair garage on Slipen Road, the sun is hot. It is just eleven o'clock. He'd waited almost forty-five minutes after his appointment time to see Mr. Davis, and emerged somewhat stunned by all that transpired in such a short time. His own land and property left to him by his mother was going to ruin, except for the little care that Mas Tomlin was able to provide, and here he was put in charge of two properties, without knowing exactly what was expected of him. He stands leaning against the building for a long time, before he crosses the street and walks to the bus stop. Managing the house in which he lives would require, at least monthly, speaking to Queenie to collect the rent. Maybe she has some repairs that need to be done. His heart races. The bus stops and he gets on, feeling as if he has been washed clean.

"Surrender thy burden, and I will give thee rest."

He is so lost in his daydream that he misses his bus stop and has to walk back. At the crossroads, under the usual tree, he sees the egg woman. He stops by her stand, buys two fritters and a glass of fresh papaya juice – just like he likes it, not too sweet, with a hint of lime added. He nods at her and she responds with a nod. She has one *Gleaner* left, so he buys it, suddenly wanting to know what is happening in the world. He thanks her, and as he is walking a way she says, "Live long enough and the sun must shine on you." She smiles at him, and he returns her smile. He wants to live, to really live, to throw off the duppies of his mother and father.

He opens the door to his room, and reaches for his grip on the top of the cupboard. He fumbles around in it, then brings out a discoloured white handkerchief in which is wrapped the beautifully carved tree woman. He rubs it clean of dust, heads for the door where he pauses. "Ah can't just go and knock on her door," he says to the air. He wraps the statue back in the handkerchief, places it on the table and goes and sits on the veranda.

Mabel, the only other woman beside Queenie who doesn't work, watches him out the corners of her eyes as she sweeps off the veranda. She hums, moving closer to where he is sitting.

"If yu stay dere, dirt gwane blow in yu eye," she states flatly. Jeremiah remains silent, but does not move. Mabel continues to sweep. She begins to hum again, moving away from Jeremiah who stands up and begins pacing, walking up and down the steps.

"Is waitin yu waitin to see someone?" Mabel pauses by the steps.

Jeremiah looks at her as if deciding, then looks toward Queenie's and her man's apartment. He shakes his head to indicate no, then opens the gate and steps through, heading toward the second house he is to manage.

★   ★   ★

It had been a long while before Jeremiah got his own church. Every three months, when Brother Jonah went to a village more remote than his own, he would have Jeremiah accompany him and lead the people gathered under the shade of a tree in someone's backyard, in someone's living room, or on a veranda in some type of sermon. It was on such a visit that Jeremiah had first assisted with the washing away of sins, when, following Brother Jonah's urging, he held the left hands of the women, blindfolded and dressed in white, who were led, one at a time, into the river, and held underneath until they began to struggle, so that all of their sins and fornicating ways were washed away. But barring these quarterly religious rites, Jeremiah's life had continued with the same monotony it had before he went to apprentice with Brother Jonah. And since he had given up his short-lived love – weaving – his days again dragged, and he prayed for something, even death, to enter his life. It was about that time, too, that the women of the village with marriageable daughters started dropping by his mother's house, pulling their giggling daughters with them – who often brought some pastry which they had allegedly cooked, just for him. At first, his mother was polite and tolerant, but after the fifth mother came with her daughter bearing gifts, his mother traced her out, sending her and her daughter and their bread pudding packing.

"A beg yu, please don't bring no temptation in me house. Ah is a decent woman, and ah trying to live a decent life. Tek yu daughter and clear out ah me house with yu presumptuous self. Me son is a man of God."

After that incident, the gossip about Jeremiah and his mother surfaced. Unidentified voices speculated and insinuated.

"She mus fraid if him marry someone, she gwane have fi live by sheself."

"She must no know say is sin fi a mother want her son always under her frock."

"Seems to me like she feel her one so-so son is prize possession."

"Ah wouldn't want tell oonuh all wha me ting a burn she. Is jealous, she jealous a people pretty daughter."

Each day the gossip increased, until Jeremiah became deaf whenever he was in the presence of others. But he was bored, hungering for some big change, something to indicate that he mattered. One day, while inspecting a very tiny beet, he acknowledged that three more years of his life had passed, and he could not distinguish one day different from the next. He had to do something.

He repainted his mother's bungalow as he heard death shuffling through the cracks. His mother heard it too, and she conceded to the call after reasoning that she and Jeremiah had long outlived each other's need for the other, and that since she was the older, and he was after all the child, then it was right for her to depart because she could no longer save him or herself from abomination. Jeremiah was indifferent to the whole affair and only wanted some change in the pattern of his life. That death was not the only option never occurred to either of them, so narrowly did they live, always accepting crumbs, eating them from a plate as if it was a meal, and even offering up prayers of thanks. So that when she stopped preparing his dinner he never questioned her actions, rather went about the task with surprising creativity and enjoyment.

On a Thursday night, exactly twenty-four years after Wilfred's departure, she accepted sleep, knowing that he, her husband, lover and Jeremiah's father, would join her. At last she had found him, her waiting had been rewarded, found him waiting as she had been waiting, guarding her love for him, waiting by the side of the road, waiting her coming. So with a sweet breath that did not smear any mirrors, with hands folded over her stomach where he was always embraced, her waiting ended, his hand feeling for the key in his pocket, turning the key in the door that had not been entered since his going, bringing her the plantain tart she thought she had to have, he leaving with the promise to return, leaving with her waiting, her belly round with his life, waiting for him to come, she not going beyond the village boundary, so fearful that he would return and she would miss him, waiting because she loved, loves, loves him, waiting until he came, turning the key in the door, bring her the plantain tart that she no longer wanted and which she had never liked or eaten since that night.

Before life left her body, Hortense thought of her son, and all the things she had planned to give him. How could she have forgotten how much she'd wanted him, wanted him and prayed that he was healthy, as Wilfred rubbed her stomach and kissed her swollen feet? When did she forget? How had she forgotten? Tears streamed down her face as she reflected how she had wasted her life, given her all to Wilfred, so that after he left she could not find it, even after her son was born. He deserved more than what she had given him. He deserved her love, but she did not have it to give to him. When did she lose it, and would he ever find it? Hortense wept silently for Jeremiah whom she had almost flogged to death because he had trespassed on her memory and claimed a part of her lover for himself.

"Wilfred! Wilfred... " she screamed inside her head, her hands clutching at the sheet. "Wilfred! Why yu go away? Why yu go away til now?" Her body stiffened, and she struggled with death a little longer. She had to get it all out. Jeremiah deserved something. She eased herself from the bed, pulled out the little wooden box in which she kept money and a few treasures from her parents. From it she took the key which she placed in the front door, before collapsing in her bed. She had waited long enough.

It was almost over for her. She could not lie to herself any more. She had not meant to kill him, but the thought of him leaving her was more than she could bear. He had said he would send for her after the baby was born, but she did not believe him, did not want to be left again like her mother and father had left her. She had sworn not to love again, but he had come and sat on her bench by the kitchen, and she had made him food, and he had loved her, and married her, but there he had been with ticket and passport in hand, telling her he was leaving in a month. One month! – and she was two months away from having their child. She couldn't lose him. So after he left to get her the plantain tart that she begged him for, she followed him, knowing he would cut through the bamboo track on his return, and there she brought the hammer down on his head. Why had she waited so long? The corner of her mouth puckered and furrowed lines washed her face. How could he have been so conceited to think that she would allow him to leave her? All her life was wrapped up inside the love she felt for him. He would not leave her; she had waited long enough.

Jeremiah was not surprised when he woke and did not smell the smoke that she always sent curling into the air every morning, or the aroma of the chocolate tea that she boiled, the top oily with a thin layer of skin that signalled to the duppies that their time for wandering had ended. He knew she was gone, had known it the moment she left. He was in bed, not asleep, his eyes wide open, looking at the ceiling, pretending that he was up there, looking down and judging others. He had heard the shuffling of her feet on the wooden floor, had heard her try the front door before coming to his room. She hadn't come beyond the threshold, but stood by the door looking in the direction of where he lay on the bed. Several times he had wanted to call to her, once he even whispered, "Mama, Mama, come to me." He didn't know why he said that because he had always called her Miss Hortense. Then she went, without him seeing her leave or hearing her shuffle across the floor. Strangely, he had not been startled, just quietly prepared, knowing that the moment would come. When at last he heard her fall on her bed and sigh loudly, he had loved her then and felt that she loved him, not seeing him as his father, the man she loved who deserted them, but loving him for himself, Jeremiah. After that he had closed his eyes and slept.

A circle of flies hovered at Miss Hortense's door too afraid to enter, the final signal of her demise. Jeremiah wondered if he had dreamt her last night, or had she in flesh or spirit descended upon him to say goodbye? He dressed slowly and as he reached the side of the house, Mas Tomlin, the only real father and companion he'd ever had, greeted him, even though the mist was still blowing over the hills. Mas Tomlin, leaving Jeremiah standing by the side of the house, entered the cottage, went straight into Hortense's room and closed the door behind him.

Her mouth was open as if she had been choking, but apart from that, she seemed as if she welcomed death. Mas Tomlin wiped his eyes. He felt deep relief, and regret too. He knew he wouldn't have a chance later, so he pulled up the chair, and sat with his deceased love.

Twenty-four years and a night ago, Mas Tomlin had been in bed, planning to leave the valley again, this time for good, since he had missed his opportunity and Hortense was happily married and pregnant with child. He heard the pounding on his door and when he got there he saw her, blood splattered all over her nightdress. He thought she had fallen, and hurt herself, but she kept babbling, "Him gwane leave me, and a swear ah wouldn't love again." He couldn't calm her so he went to make her some tea. He heard her stumble out and he ran after her. She led him to where Wilfred's battered body lay. He never knew exactly what had happened, but he carried the body back to his place on his donkey, more than a half mile, and buried it down by the banana field, wrapped only in old crocus sacks. They never spoke about it after that night, and she seemed to have forgotten what she did, because the next morning while he was still nodding in and out of sleep on the chair in her living room, she had gotten up and gone asking if anyone saw Wilfred... For months, years after, Tomlin was convinced the body would be discovered; that they would be found out, but it never happened. Apparently, Wilfred had confided in someone in the village that he had gotten a job as a chauffeur in America and would be leaving in a few days to go there and work. When he was reported missing, it was assumed he had left without telling Hortense or anyone. He wouldn't have been the first.

Mas Tomlin wiped his face, kissed Hortense on the cheek, and went out to join Jeremiah.

By mid-morning, the others came, and Jeremiah, along with three men of the village, dug her a deep grave by the jackfruit tree where she had lately taken to sitting, bracing her back on the trunk, resting on her love, for it was his father, her man, who had planted the tree on the slight gradient from where the road and the three traversing tracks in the village could be seen.

Jeremiah presided over his mother's farewell, and many of the villagers later remarked at his kind words for her, although they lamented that he, a Reverend-Brother and a grown man, should so openly weep at her grave. He was like a child crying for the breasts he once enjoyed that were now the exclusive right of the new baby who sucked greedily and whose tiny hand clutched at the fleshy conical mound, a further indication of his privilege and right. But Jeremiah gave no indication that he heard any of this gossip nor did he seem to care. A month after she was laid to rest he built a tomb, sculpting the chopped-up wooden table (*that* all the time had been roped in a box under her bed) into a headstone, and people remarked how it looked like a pregnant woman holding her stomach as an offering to someone. The only words he engraved – no name or birth or death date – were *She waits, waited, have been waiting, but waits no more for He who has returned*.

The very night of her farewell, during the wake, Mas Tomlin took Jeremiah aside, held him by the shoulder, looked hard into his eyes and said, "Him dead yu know. Yu father dead long time, and him did love yu, and love yu moda." Jeremiah had walked away from the people who had gathered to help him mourn. He was happy at the news. Finally, he was free to embrace the father and mother he never had. When Jeremiah had rejoined the gathering, Mas Tomlin shook his hand, and said, "Is well pity yu didn't get de opportunity fi meet yu daddy. Yu would ah like him."

After his mother's death, the people of the valley had, through some private miracle that they kept a secret, gotten together and built a part-concrete bungalow in which Jeremiah was privileged to preach. It was the only concrete building in the entire village, and it looked an absurdity in the middle of the clearing near the river where they erected it, with a thatched roof, rough, unpainted outside surface and cool blue interior, clay-packed floor, stained maroon with Bismarck, and buffed to a shine with dried coconut husks. This was to be his first and last church, with a wooden platform with two steps up to advance onto it, and upon which he paced back and forth as he tried to lead them from the path of temptation and deliver them from evil.

It had been less than a year since he was installed in his church when one hurricane after another threatened to blow them all away. Several people lost their homes, so he offered to share his cottage with a mother and her three daughters. Ever since his mother's death, mothers had been more bold, almost demanding that he marry their daughters. This was the case with this mother and her daughters so he moved out from his cottage into his church. There followed a week of great storms. Many invited him to share their homes, but he knew their dwellings well enough. He knew how many bodies shared a bed, how stuffy was the air in the rooms, so declined their generous offers while still seeming gracious, a dutiful shepherd of God who would suffer inconvenience for his flock. This way he deprived no one or their children of a place to lay their heads, staying instead within the sanctuary of the Rock, their name for the church they had built him, and where, if not comfort, he would be assured privacy. After securing him two long benches to sleep on, his followers all rushed home during a pause in the torrent. During the course of the evening and early night, food was brought to him, and in the pouring rain a child, obviously used to such a task, brought him a very hot and strong cup of coffee, still full to the rim, with the banana leaf that covered it turning brown from the heat. So Jeremiah settled for the night, thinking, just before he fell asleep, how Christ must have felt being out in the open with only a stone for his pillar.

Before long, as the rain poured down like rocks tossed in a barrel, the worn thatched roof of the Rock streamed with water and soon the floor ran red with blood. In the darkness there was only the beating of his heart and the thump, thumping sound of the rain falling on the trees and ground. He shivered and curled himself more foetally, remembering the warm quilt his mother had made for him many years ago. He didn't know what he was longing for, because he had never had it, but it was heat, the spread of heat that two bodies in communion produce, so that when she materialized from the darkness, no more than the sound of his heart, pulling his curled body close in to hers, pressing her body to his back, heating his bottom, covering him in her heat, he responded in gratitude. Even though the floor beneath him bled, and the rain sprayed its vengeance on him, he was warm, nestled in the protection of her body. How was he to know that the word would be made flesh and the flesh would make demands?

For five days the rain raged, and he stayed cooped up in the Rock. Food and a change of clothing were relayed to him, and in the darkness of night, and even day, the heat of her passion kept him warm and his heart pounding. He was dreaming was he not? Surely he was dreaming. This heat that seemed another skin, this heat that made his body tremble, not from cold, but passion, this heat was not flesh like his flesh.

When, on the third night, out of gratitude he sought her face, she held his head firm, away from her eyes and whispered, "The fear of man bringeth a snare: but whosoever putteth his trust in the Lord shall be safe."

He was safe; the Rock was the Lord's home where he had been fed and sheltered. Still, he, a Reverend-Brother, lacked trust, even though in darkness his every want and comfort were taken care of. He settled on the hard bench and shuddered each time the heat of her body sent warmth to cover him. It must have been a dream, surely it must have been a dream.

But he was also troubled. His black book had fallen onto the floor, and when he plucked it up he discovered that it was stained with blood, as were the bench and bedding on which he had been sleeping, as were his clothes, stained with the blood on the floor.

Four months after the storm, Brother Jonah succumbed to death, so now Jeremiah was without a spiritual leader. This meant that he had to preside over the Rock as well as perform the next washing away of sins completely on his own. He felt uneasy about this latter task, not because he felt ill prepared but rather from an instinct about danger, like raising one's cake above one's head. But how was he to deny his calling, the people's need to air their sins, shower someone with the power they lacked? No. He would continue and wash away his own sins as he washed away theirs.

Months after the storm which had kept him in the Rock for those many nights, whenever Jeremiah went about the community, he sensed that he was being watched, that a pair of eyes was piercing into him. He felt uneasy and wondered who wanted him, and for what. Then he began hearing whispers wherever he went. Nothing made sense to him. He felt as if he was a small part of a large puzzle, with many pieces missing.

"Yu know him or someone like him breed de girl."

"What a shame."

"Wha gwane happen to her now?"

"De worst is how him acting like him nuh ave noting fi do wid her condition."

"Mark me word, neva trust a man, as long as him wear pants."

Jeremiah tried to figure out who they were referring to. Surely, if one of his members was in trouble, she would come to him for guidance, and no one tracked his steps or sought to speak to him in private. Still, every so often, he felt young girls staring at him, and once one tried to speak to him, but when he had extended his hand to greet her, she pulled back and ran from him. After that incident, Jeremiah began to feel that the whispers were directed at him, but of what was he guilty?

Six months after the great storm, as Jeremiah prepared to perform his first baptism at the river, he brushed against one of the sisters who was to be baptized. The contact of her skin made him shiver and he was puzzled that she smelled so familiar, like his own sweat. During the preparation service in the Rock, he knew he was being watched, that there were quiet, knowing smiles. Jeremiah sensed that the one he no longer saw, whose smell had wrapped itself around him when he brushed against her, knew him more intimately than anyone else had, even more intimately than his deceased mother. Yet he could not place the moment when such an exposure could have taken place, but each time the words to call on his followers to release their sins formed in his mouth, and he looked down at his congregation, he felt a pair of eyes, indistinguishable, yet ever present, seeking him, holding him down, demanding that he make redress, but for what he honestly did not know. He cowered, faltered, paused in mid air, his thoughts confused, lost, a memory stored somewhere, too frightened to fly on clipped wings. As the Sunday for the washing away of sins drew nearer, Jeremiah trembled at the slightest sound, and he wished, as he had never done before, that he could be relieved of his duties. His groin throbbed unceasingly, and he sought to drive out the source of his yearning. If at that time he had known how to say no, he would never have performed the ritual.

The morning that Jeremiah lead his first washing away of sins without the guidance and help of Brother Jonah, he took the key for the front door of his mother's house that she had kept hidden until the night before she died, put it on a chain and hung it around his neck. When he found it that morning of her death, he placed it with his other boyhood treasures: two emerald green marbles, a sling-shot that he had made himself with rubber and wood, a matchbox with the flimsy remains of a butterfly, a silly bow-tie that someone had given him, a neatly folded white handkerchief with the letter "J" embroidered in all four corners (the handiwork of his mother), and the statue his father made that Mas Tomlin had given him. Jeremiah wasn't sure why he sought the key, but he felt that it belonged to part of the missing puzzle. Something distant yet familiar about the key caused him to massage it as he walked to the Rock.

The people were gathered, all draped in white, dazzling in the sun. The path that led downhill from the Rock to the river was swept to a smooth cleanliness, and plaited palm fronds were spread like a mat along its entire length. Jeremiah gazed at the people standing, heads bowed, eyes glued to their feet, bodies placid in front of him, and tried to remember how Brother Jonah began the washing away of sins. As hard as Jeremiah tried, he could not remember and his head throbbed. He felt the key hard against his chest, reached for it, and discovered it had the shape of a cross without a figure imprisoned on it. He held it to the sun and it seemed to dazzle and burn.

Jeremiah closed his eyes, and asked his congregation to join him in prayer, but he could not pray because the nights of the storm sped through his head. He saw someone like himself, wrapped up with another, skin supple, the colour of dried bamboo; and he heard their moans, which were not of pain but of release, and he saw, rather smelled, her body mixed with the rain, skin satin-soft. He heard the rain dripping and the blood-washed floor danced before his eyes as he swayed and moaned, swayed and moaned, and the older women of the Rock joined him until soon everyone swayed and moaned, swayed and moaned until the reason for their collective grief became a distant pain, the very idea of which would later produce silence among them.

In front of the Rock the people spread their food, in covered baskets or tied and cradled in stained towels; they shared with abundant generosity all that each family had provided. By the time the sun was near the valley, all bones had been scraped clean. The men reclined, snores rising from some of them; children played by the banks of the river and women chatted, their voices soft and comforting; dogs yapped at the fleas that insisted on torturing them; and ants toddled away, their legs and backs braced with a feast of crumbs.

Jeremiah brushed the creases from the back of his robe and led the way to the mouth of the river. Sometimes incongruous to the mouths from which it issued, the singing, spirited, high pitched, resounded. At the water that was clear and cool, Jeremiah swayed, ready to wash away their sins, wash the sins from their bodies, wash his own sins away. He could not carry the unnameable guilt any longer. He opened his black book and started with the second verse of Titus 3: "To speak evil of no man, to be no brawlers, but gentle, shewing all meekness unto all men." Why did he feel as if he had spoken evil of someone? Who but himself had he sinned against? He dismissed the question and pressed on, opening the gate to their salvation. "For we ourselves also were sometimes foolish, disobedient, deceived, serving divers lusts and pleasure, living in malice and envy, hateful and hating one another..." He didn't hate anyone, not even his deceased mother any more, not even the one whose eyes bore into him, demanding so much of him, more than he could ever understand, much less give. Whoever she was, he wasn't sure, but he meant her no harm, didn't wish to banish her from his sight either. He felt her eyes, her presence as familiar as his sweat, the glint of her eyes so bright in the darkness and the rain sending water into the Rock, the floor washed red, the leather strap circling wet, sticky, circling, her supple body pressed against his back, the heat against his bottom. Lord, if only he could find her before he had to wash away their sins.

They had lined up, the wrinkled skin ones in front. His heart pounded against his chest; there were more of them than he had anticipated. He walked into the water, his feet testing jagged rocks, moving to the middle, the water at his knees, his black robe floating out at his knees, dragging him down. A rock cut his sole and he looked at the red quickly washed away in the stream, flowing to distant shores. So his blood had to be sacrificed for their salvation, so his blood must be spilled for their deliverance. He bent down, scooped water into his mouth, swished it around then spat it back into the flow. Finally, his mouth rinsed clean, he drank and drank and drank.

The first one came; he touched his key-cross to her forehead, held her shaking flabby arms, placed his left hand on the top of her head and pressed her face below the surface of the water. She emerged eyes closed, lips trembling, her feeble arms flailing, clutching for him. Another one came and her sins were also washed away with the flow that took the red that bubbled at his feet and quickly carried it away to shores unknown. One after another they came, until well after the sun had gone home to rest, until the dingy flies pitched about blindly, until the owl was perched on the bombay mango tree that was like a sentinel by the Rock; they came and were immersed, the water bubbling at their noses and mouths, pulling him down with them, reluctant to let go of their sins, afraid he would not allow them to rise above temptation, grasping his wrist, pleading to be lifted from their sins, delivered from evil. So much to promise when eyes stripped him to his flesh, so much to offer when one's own sins burned like a smouldering fire, so much when temptation was always at one's door, so much, the strap circling, the floor running blood, the darkness and rain crushing his spirit, circling, her body pressed against his back.

He thought he was through, and hoped they would leave him so he could wash away his own sins, but they stood, trembling, humming a strange tune. That was when he saw her coming towards him. He had wanted to run, to scream no, but did not. She stood in front of him, and raised her bowed head, and looked into his eyes, and a shiver surged through his body. He could not touch her, but they would not free him.

"Let we see yu wash her free."

"Help deliver her from her pain."

"Cleanse her wid yu healin hands."

"Set her spirit free."

Different voices shouted at him. He placed her in front of him, held her by the back of the arms, and lead her into the river. As he was about to dunk her, he smelled her, the familiarity so over-powering that he stumbled, found himself gasping, unable to rise up, unable to wash his sins free, until he felt hands raising him up, setting him free. He emerged from the river with their voices like waves splaying his body.

Set him free, Lord, set him free
Set him free, Lord, set him free
You have washed him free of sin
Now set him free…

235

They lifted him up out of the water and led the way to the Rock, water dripping from their clothes, their faces and hands held up to the sky, their feet and tambourines thumping, their voices unrestrained. Jeremiah didn't know how long they were in the Rock before he remembered the young girl who had come forward to be washed of sin just before he fell. He scanned the congregation, but did not see her amongst them. He looked around wildly, all the while fearing, instinctively knowing that she was still in the river. His feet felt glued to the ground, but not for long. He pushed past them, running to the river, and soon he heard them behind him.

He waded in the river, searching for her. Even though it was just the eve of night, it was dark, and all he could see when he looked out were his followers on the bank, their white dresses and shirts the only light. Then someone got a torch, and Jeremiah pulled off his robe and dove and dove, but still he did not find her.

Early the next morning, when a woman went to wash her baby's clothes, she saw the body, caught on a branch. The village gathered and stood around as if dazed, staring at the body, buoyant, arms floating by her side and the band around her belly burst away releasing the hill that she had sought to hide. Had he held her below the surface of the water too long? His eyes trailed the white band that had secured her secret, and the white, loosely fitting cotton dress clinging to her body that had once pressed hard against his back, the floor washed red, her arms encircling him, protecting him from the rain and his ignorance. They all knew it was an accident. Others had drowned before at the washing away of sins, though only sinners. Surely.

They laid her on the rocks like the clothes they scrubbed and spread to dry on the bank of the river and there she stayed for many hours while the dogs sniffed her. Water gurgled from her mouth, her mountain stomach looked like a bloated fish washed ashore, her once tan-coloured skin was dull and streaked white, and her eyes wide open in acceptance. The key, his cross, was wedged in the flesh of her palm.

> Take me to the river to wash away my sins
> Take me to the river where all deeds are done.

On and on their voices took the words and wrung them, squeezing the water caught in the fabric, rinsing the suds buried in the dirt, mouthing the words, wringing the melody, giving them voice and flesh and spirit, accusing the guilty, redeeming the repenter, offering to the hopeful, praising the humble, wringing the words, lifting the meaning from the words, licking the sounds into shape, squeezing all the water from the fabric, washing away all the dirt, washing his torn sole bubbling red in the stream, washing their fearful and guilty hearts beating against their chests, their hands holding fast to his, demanding salvation, washing away their sins, cleansing their souls – and there is her belly public, the wide band that held it in, trapped between a stone and a bramble, the water clear, floating, floating out to glory.

★   ★   ★

He weeps now that this memory awakes in him. Why hadn't they told him? Why had they allowed him? Jeremiah runs from the house he is to manage, back to the house where he lives, hastily locks himself inside his room, and closes all the windows. What else happened at the Rock that he has buried? He feels the tears mist his eyes and sniffs. He thinks about Queenie, she who seems always partially exposed, who blocked his way this morning, who wet the bread in her mouth then gave it to him to eat, who has awakened a desire in him that he thought permanently buried. Will she leave her man for him? Will she want him, if he tells her of the Rock and the drowning? Jeremiah falls to his knees and begins to pray. His tears run. Why couldn't his mother have loved him? Had she known all along that his father would never come back? Why had he spent most of his life stumbling, trapped inside someone else's dream? He wipes his eyes with the back of his hands, and thinks of Queenie, of his desire to tell her, to confide in someone; wondering how he is going to tell her. He has been sleeping all this time, and now that he is awaking, he has to fit the pieces of his life together. He is not his mother, and he will not be his father. He will be himself despite the memories crowding him. He hopes that his sins are forgivable, as long as he is able to live with and learn from them. He is not going to be a Reverend-

Brother again; that was his mother's dream, and that dream died when he buried her.

Jeremiah rises from his knees, goes and washes his face and pledges to welcome each day, to try and live in the present and honour his needs. He walks to the gate and stands leaning on it. He looks up at the sky, blue, shimmering. He is no one's boy any more. His mother sought to entomb him, to keep her broken heart alive, Brother Jonah moulded him to assure his continuity, Mas Tomlin healed him to be benevolent and the young woman seduced him to satisfy the selfish ambitions of her mother.

"I am a man, a man," he says over and over inside his head. "I am a man." He walks back to his room, picks up the black book from the dresser and traces its shape with his fingers. It was a gift from Mas Tomlin. After much hesitation he opens the stiff leather cover and reads the inscription, his index finger following each word like a child learning to read: "To a good lad, Jeremiah, who will be the man his mother always needed." His fingers trace and retrace the outline of the words. To be such a man! He bangs the black book closed, reaches for his grip, takes out a white embroidered cloth, wraps the Bible in it, then places it at the very bottom of the grip which he closes and returns on the top of the closet. He hears sounds coming from Queenie's apartment, and stands still, his ears alert. Although he hears her voice and that of her man, he cannot decipher what they are saying as the radio is playing. Jeremiah admonishes himself. Be a man and declare your intentions.

★ ★ ★

What greatly disturbed Jeremiah as a boy, and gnawed at him even more after he had buried the young woman, was the complete passivity of the village. They refused to directly accuse anyone; they never sought reparation, and they never made any decisions or took any steps to act on their own behalf. They accepted every act as a matter of faith, the will of the almighty, so surrendered their lives to whomever seized it and wrestled it from their hands. He had waited for them to come for him, to try and condemn him, but they never did. They often whispered when he passed, but no one declined to speak to him. If he said, "Good morning," they replied, "Mornin Reverend-Brother." Although some only mumbled this, and others avoided his eyes, they never outrightly stopped speaking to him. The women stopped sending their daughters to prepare him meals, but they never avoided him directly, nor demanded that he keep out of their way.

About seven months after the drowning, he woke one morning to the smell of smoke. He hurriedly dressed and went out to see how he could help. Someone shouted that the Rock was on fire. As he approached it he saw that it was indeed in flames, and the women, dressed in white, with blue head-ties and sashes slung from shoulder to waist, had formed a circle around the burning building and were singing loudly,

"Let it burn, let it burn
The Lord says let it burn."

At the mouth of the path leading to the entrance of the Rock, four machetes had been stuck in the ground in the shape of two Xs. No one needed to restrain Jeremiah. He heard the women singing and knew they sung for all; it was their most defiant act, a signal that he was no longer welcome among them.

Nonetheless, Jeremiah had remained there almost two years after the incident, isolated except for Mas Tomlin, who finally convinced him that it was time to leave. It was Mas Tomlin who had sought out Mrs. Davis, Hortense's cousin, and asked her if she had a place for Jeremiah to stay, and could she help him to find work as a plumber in St Catherine where she lived.

Mas Tomlin promised Jeremiah that he would look after his cottage and land, and would write him about happenings in the village, including the new yearly occurrence when the river spilled over its banks, washing the land with red frothy water for almost a week, staining everything.

★　★　★

He is remembering more.

★　★　★

They had lain there for hours, the four of them, just to steal a glance at the women. Jeremiah had been fourteen then, and his friend William had found out from his female teenage cousin where she and some of her friends went to bathe. What they had not known at the time was that some of the older women also bathed there. With friends Zack and Joseph, they had stolen to the river where it nestled in tall grass, and for many evenings, week after week, they lay flat on their stomachs, the weeds itching their skins, their shirts growing damp as they crawled in the grass to get as close as they could without being seen, to feast on the small firm breasts of the girls. Then he had gotten caught. Red ants had penetrated his clothes and he had jumped up squealing, agonized by the bites; that was how one of the women had taken a hold of him and pulled him to the river where they all were, many naked, some half clothed. They had stripped him, and thinking they were going to flog him, then send him to his mother for another, Jeremiah had begged for mercy, but soon he realized that flogging him was not their intention; he was to be their game, their plaything for believing himself man enough to spy on them while they bathed. They had pulled him into the river, all of them naked then, surrounded him and dared him to look at them. They splashed water in his face, pulled him to them, then tossed him into the water; they laughed so raucously that it scared him, and their flapping breasts, the roundness of their bellies rocking in the water had dazzled, blinded him. One woman even shoved her breasts between his parted lips, laughing at him. Made him their game. His friends had escaped, but Jeremiah had been trapped, tossed from one woman to the next, until they got tired of him, and sent him on his way shivering.

He had thought that would be an end of the incident, but the women had told their daughters. A few days later, when Jeremiah had gone to bathe, further down the river where the boys and men went, he heard giggling, and when he looked around, a crowd of girls was staring at him. The braver ones dove into the river and swam around him, splashing him with water. Then they took his clothes, and since it was already late, he had to walk through the bushes, the tall grass and vines scratching his naked body. Still they wouldn't let it end. Even the friends who had been with him when the women discovered him teased him, and when a girl he

240

liked in school declined his offer to walk her home – her friends would have teased her for walking home with "River-Mirror", his new nickname – Jeremiah withdrew into himself, and if he looked at women, spied on them from afar.

★ ★ ★

He does not intend to admire Queenie secretly from afar, neither is he prepared to stay locked in his room and listen to her talk with her man. Jeremiah decides to go into Spanish Town and purchase some tools. As he walks around the town, looking for the hardware stores, he wishes he had a friend. He wonders what happened to Lindsey, Monroe, Karl and Chapman, his boyhood friends. They left the village as soon as they were through with school. He has heard that Monroe is in Canada, but as far as he knows Lindsey and Chapman are still on the island; Chapman had gotten a scholarship to the university, and Jeremiah is sure that Lindsey, who was always bright in school and quick to respond, is probably in a nice civil service position, maybe he is even in politics, the chatterer that he was. Jeremiah smiles, flooded with the memory. Perhaps he will try to find them. He spends about an hour in the hardware store, purchases a few essential tools, then heads back home. However, on his way, he realizes that he is hungry so stops at a small eatery, with only three tables and twelve chairs and sits at the only table that's empty. Before his food arrives, two other men enter, and seeing no free table, ask if they can join him. Jeremiah welcomes them, glad for the company although he doesn't know them.

"My name is Ivan," says the shorter of the two men as he sits. He extends his hand to Jeremiah.

"Dem call me Bigger." The other man pats his spare-tyre stomach and chuckles. Before Jeremiah can introduce himself, Bigger says, "So wha yu go by?"

Jeremiah suddenly feels awkward, unsure. He reflects that he never really liked the name Jeremiah, but always smiled when Mas Tomlin called him Jeremy.

"De name is Jeremy," he says, extending his hand first to Bigger, then Ivan.

Almost immediately Bigger turns away and addresses the woman behind the counter.

Ivan asks Jeremy if he lives in the area, and between wolfing down their food, they exchange information, and Jeremiah is hopeful that Ivan will be his first new friend in years.

He hears her the second her hand lightly taps at his door, the sound meant only for his ears. It is late, he knows, because the indigo of the night has gone, leaving a cool blue. With two leaps, panther lithe, he reaches the door, his left hand turns the knob gently and his right pulls her in, pressing her back against the closed door.

"Me don't tink anyone see me."

"Me did wonder how long you go mek me wait."

"Me wasn't sure ah could come. Sometimes Mackey seh him workin, but him just go a street, den sneak back to spy on me."

"Me want you."

"Mackey seh if me leave him, him will always find me."

Her breath perfumes his face so he lifts her off her feet and carries her to the bed.

Jeremiah has had this same dream three nights in a row. Queenie's man has been home for four days straight, and hardly anyone has seen her or him. Even the sisters, Mabel and Stephanie, have remarked as much. Jeremiah doesn't think he can take much more of not seeing her. On several occasions in the last four days, he has heard what sounded like arguing, but maybe he only imagined it. He knows he didn't imagine the laughter, both Queenie's and Mackey's. Consequently he has been spending a lot of time at the other house he is now managing, fixing up the yard, including doing some planting, and repainting the fence. Although he has ideas for the house in which he lives, and has already cut the grass and trimmed the trees so that a few neighbours have re-marked how much better it is already looking, he has not been able to do much more than that as he is reluctant to run into either Queenie or her man. He still has her plates and mug, and has rehearsed over and over exactly what he will say to her the first opportunity that arises.

Last evening, while taking his nightly walk, he ran into Ivan who invited him for a beer. While not a drinker, Jeremiah was thankful for the excuse to postpone returning home. In fact he'd wished that he could forego returning because just before he left, Mackey had come to sit on the veranda, shirtless, and hollered for Queenie to join him and bring something cold to drink. He had two beers with Ivan, and one of Ivan's friends. Although he sat with them for almost two hours, nursing his two beers, Jeremiah did not like the bar scene. He was thankful when he returned to his apartment that the veranda was deserted and the house relatively quiet. He had fallen into bed and was asleep almost immediately.

Now the voices of children saying goodbye startle him awake, his mouth sour, head slightly groggy. As he enters the hallway leading to the bathroom and the barred door that separates his and Queenie's apartment, he hears her singing a calypso and suddenly feels happy. He pauses and listens for Mackey's voice, but only Queenie's serenades his ear. He showers hurriedly, determined, regardless, to call on her, but before he is fully dressed, he is startled by a knock on his door. He pulls on his merino and goes to answer it. It is only Mr. Davis informing him that there is work today. Jeremiah is thankful, but also disappointed. He hoped it was Queenie. Mr. Davis tells him to hurry and says that he will be waiting for him in his jeep. As Jeremiah locks the door, he glances to the left and sees Queenie framed in the threshold of her door, one leg just outside, her cotton pink nightie just above her knee.

She sticks her head out and asks: "Yu leavin already, Jeremiah?"

"Yes, ah start work today."

"Mackey lef for work before day break."

He steals a glance directly at her, but says nothing, dumb again at the most inopportune times.

"You don't need get anythin dis evenin; ah will save dinna fah yu," Queenie states like a question.

"Ah like yu, Miss Queenie," Jeremiah manages and hurries off, a small victorious smile on his face.

Jeremiah works harder and longer than he has ever done before. By the time he returns home, it is dark and the boys have begun to congregate. Jeremiah pushes the gate full of anticipation. Throughout the day he has replayed in his head his brief exchange with Queenie and hopes he has not misunderstood what she said. At first he doesn't see her because she is sitting on the dark veranda with one of the sisters, Stephanie, he thinks.

"Evening," he says addressing them both, and although Queenie's name is on the tip of his tongue, he refrains from speaking to her directly, but she does not harbour such restraint.

"How was your first day, Jeremiah?" she asks, sitting forward in her chair. He cannot avoid her. He can feel Stephanie's eyes searching his face.

"It was hard but good," he says.

"Mine was de same as usual," she replies smiling. "Den yu mus hungry, ready fah a good dinna."

"After ah shower, dat would be most satisfyin."

"Ah was just going in fi tek care of something," Queenie says, rising. "Stephanie, ah will see yu lata," and she skips onto the path in front of Jeremiah, and walks ahead of him. Jeremiah feels his heart pound against his chest. He follows behind her, then remembers Stephanie.

"Good night, Miss Stephanie."

"Night," she replies.

Neither Jeremiah nor Queenie sees Stephanie's curious look as she watches them walking down the path that leads to their respective apartments. She senses something is going on between them, but isn't sure what. It's the first time she has witnessed them speak directly to each other – almost like lovers, she thinks, but dismisses the idea since Queenie's man left just this morning, *and he jealous like hell*. Still, disposed to being nosey she decides, *Ah gwane watch dem close*.

By her door, Queenie turns, places her index finger over her lips, then mouths that she will soon come, and slips inside her apartment. Jeremiah goes into his room, showers quickly, not taking time to dry himself properly before he pulls on a clean shirt and pants. Then he goes to the barred door that separates their apartments and taps softly. Almost immediately, he hears Queenie begin to hum. He moves to his door and waits until he hears her there. He half opens it; she's there carrying a tray; he isn't sure if he should take it from her, or invite her in. She settles the matter, whispering: "Let me come in and put it down fah yu."

He steps aside and her shoulder brushes his chest as she passes him. He cannot speak. In his small room, she immediately spreads a cloth on the table and sets out his dinner, including something to drink. As he watches her, he is so moved by her grace and tenderness, so grateful she wants to be with him, he has to fight the tears that want to wet his eyes. He hears the taunts of his childhood, *Mama-Boy, Mama-Boy*, but quickly gains control of his emotions, certain that a woman such as Queenie deserves a man, and he does not want to do anything that might jeopardize her feelings for him.

Queenie sits and watches Jeremiah eat; neither says anything. When he is through, she waits, and still neither seems able to speak, so after a while she gathers the plates and rises. Jeremiah watches her walk to the door, and there she pauses. Missing her already, he rises awkwardly, knocking over the chair. She looks at him and laughs, covering her mouth. He laughs at his own clumsiness. At the door he finds his tongue.

"Tank yu, Miss Queenie. Dat was a most delicious meal."

"My pleasure, Jeremiah," she smiles at him.

"Ah would be very happy to taste yu hand again," he says, his eyes fixed on her lips, imagining his mouth on hers. She smiles, steps back so he can open the door for her, and he watches from his door as she enters her apartment, less than twenty feet away.

Thus the beginning of Jeremiah's and Queenie's relationship. By the end of the week, he has insisted on paying her to prepare his meals. Their conversation began tentatively, mostly Queenie telling Jeremiah about her life, and questioning him, trying to tease out his emotions and feelings.

Queenie's uncomplicated passion for him, for life itself, adds fuel to Jeremiah's resolve to live life more fully. He is inspired by her ability to reject pain, to deny it entrance into her life. Mostly he likes the fact that he has someone to talk to, someone who listens to him, as if every word he speaks is important. They laugh, they cry, and sometimes they are silent, especially after she probes into one of his memories.

"So you haven't love anyone before. But did yu ever feel sympathy?"

"Wha good is sympathy?" he demands.

"Is de same medicine like kindness."

245

"Me mother had no sympathy fah me."

"And yu had no kindness fah her," Queenie snaps at him.

"Ah did everyting she wanted."

"But yu never knew wha she want, so how could yu?"

There is a tap on Jeremiah's door. They both hold their breaths. He's trying to decide whether he should answer or not. They hear a male voice; it's Mr. Davis, and Jeremiah feels his body go limp. Queenie whispers to him to answer. She sits on the edge of the bed as Jeremiah goes to the door and cracks it.

"Howdy," says Mr. Davis. "Listen ah need yu help right-right now. A big leak. Get yu tools and come quick."

Before he leaves, Queenie says, "We lucky it wasn't Mackey. Go do wha yu affi do. Me will be here."

"Ah tired ah pretendin. Ah want to love yuh all de time."

He takes her face between his hands and kisses her on the cheek.

Every opportunity they have, Queenie and Jeremiah get together. Soon their conversations take on more depth. Queenie relates her relationship with her family and Mackey. She has grown up in a loving and cantankerous family, unlike Jeremiah. She and her siblings had many fights, but they were always the prelude for them to display their deep affection and commitment to each other. Queenie's mother and all her maternal aunts adored her; they said she reminded them of their own mother who died young, somewhat beaten down by her husband. But like Queenie, her grandmother had always been optimistic, able to see a way out of any situation, even when everyone else declared doom. Jeremiah also thinks that Queenie's beauty, so open, so complete in itself, so unpretentious, would win any heart. Her skin is the colour of wet raw sugar, smooth and flawless like varnished mahogany with a red lustrous undertone. Her hair is jet black, thick and fibrous, and her strong white teeth are perfectly even. But he adores her not just for her physical beauty, or the bounce of her walk, or her flirtatious smile but because, from all the evidence, she is a person without malice, who always seems to see the best in others.

Although a victim of childhood asthma and whooping-cough,

Jeremiah deduces that Queenie never bemoaned her condition or demanded special treats or attention from her mother or others. He gets a picture of her as a child jumping rope, playing hopscotch, or dashing about. She confesses that as a child her main badness was that she liked to wander, and often went off without telling anyone. Her mother was never able to beat that habit out of her. She completed school at sixteen, where she learned religious studies, domestic skills, and soared in literature. Then she joined her aunt and some cousins in Kingston. They secured her a job at a small bakery, and it was there five years later she met Mackey when he came to buy bread. He soon made it his daily stop. One evening, as she left work, Mackey was by the door waiting on her. He bought her some peanuts and walked her home.

Mackey had courted her for over a year, even travelling with her to the country to visit her parents and family. Shortly after, Mackey had asked her to marry him and was deflated when she said no, but he'd been persistent and finally she'd agreed to live with him.

Queenie liked Mackey, but she didn't think she was in love with him. He was her first man, and although she had nothing to compare him with, except what she had overheard her sisters and girlfriends boasting about their loves, she hoped love was more than what she felt for Mackey. He should make her heart beat faster, or throb with desire, but no such feeling visited her. She appreciated his kindness, but he did not excite her. She had lived with him for almost six years. More recently he'd been taking her for granted. What she could not stand was his jealousy and possessiveness. That's why she'd refused to marry him – and not wanting to tie herself to someone whom she could easily live without.

It had not all been bad. The first year of their life together was comfortable. Rather than sharing a room with her four cousins, she had a room of her own, since Mackey was only occasionally there, when he was not working. He was very ambitious, and worked every opportunity he got; he said he wanted to build her a house before they had a family. This news had not excited her. He'd expected her to throw her arms around his neck, kiss him and

247

declare her love, but she'd merely said, "Dat sound nice," and walked away. That was the first time he'd accused her of cheating on him. She'd laughed, then walked out, not returning for more than a week. She'd gone back because her sister told her she was tired of Mackey coming round to make his pleas.

He'd been less hasty to accuse her after that. Instead whenever he saw, or thought he saw, a man in the house where they'd rented a room looking at her, he'd quickly secure them another room, and give her some lame excuse about why they had to move. Mackey was stupid about her, she said. He seemed to love everything about her, including her indifference to him. He went to great lengths to please her, and to keep her to himself. After two years of living together, he'd suggested that she leave the bakery and keep house for him. She didn't particularly like working at the bakery so happily quit.

But stuck in the room, she'd tired of Mackey's possessiveness. Sometimes she could stand no more of it and went off for days, which drove him mad, sent him wandering the streets seeking her. She'd never gone off with any man, except once, and that was only to the beach to swim and eat fried fish. Mostly she went to visit one of her many relatives, helping them with their many children and chores, telling the children stories since she was a good storyteller. She'd been thinking about leaving Mackey when he moved them yet again, this time to their current apartment. She'd been so annoyed about moving, she'd refused to pack any of their belongings, leaving Mackey to do everything by himself. Mabel and Stephanie had told her she acted like a queen with her footman.

She wanted to have a child, but didn't want Mackey's, so she kept drinking bush tea to make sure no child came and bound her to him. Moreover, she feared that Mackey's threats were no longer just words. On two occasions she'd witnessed how badly he'd beaten men with whom he'd seen her smiling and talking. And even though he'd never hit her (though he had threatened to – and she'd told him that she would pour hot oil in his ears if he ever did), she had felt his firm grasp on her wrists, and seen the insane possessiveness in his eyes.

She confessed to Jeremiah that the first time she'd seen him, his handsome round face, his gentle, shy eyes, his large fingers, she'd shivered and felt ashamed to be seen with Mackey. She'd tried to ignore this feeling, but daily she'd found herself waiting around to see him, to make sure that he saw her, and each time she'd felt more drawn to him.

Queenie keeps to herself a conversation she'd had with one of her cousins in whom she'd confided. The cousin had responded in her usual dismissive tone: "Is bout time someone slip you, mek you fall." Queenie wonders if that is what love is, falling. She certainly feels as if she's about to fall each time she sees Jeremiah.

Months go by. Everyone in the house knows there's something going on between Jeremiah and Queenie, everyone except Mackey. On several occasions when he'd returned from being away at work for four day stretches, she refused to sleep with him, and told him that that she was leaving. He'd stormed out, then returned, alternating between threatening and begging.

She ignores Mackey, and continues sharing her dreams with Jeremiah; he is the first and only one to whom she reveals her desire to be a journalist and write for the newspaper. She tells Jeremiah that daily she reads the *Gleaner* from front to back.

He asks, "So yu ever write anyting?"

She shakes her head and smiles.

"Well yu ave to write someting, den tek it show dem."

"Yu tink ah could do dat?" she inquires, her eyes bright. He nods. "Me big sista always say me ave talent. Me use to write poems in school. And me know me can't write fah paper like how me talk. If ah write someting and give yu to read, yu will read it and tell me what yu think, since yu used to be preacha man?"

At that moment Mackey returns from work and passes by Jeremiah's partially opened door, but does not see Queenie sitting at the table. In unison, they draw in their breaths and freeze. Somehow in the two months they have been developing their friendship, Mackey has never returned and found Queenie in Jeremiah's place. A couple of times, when they were in the backyard talking, he arrived unexpectedly and heard them in conversation. On another occasion, Stephanie had spotted Mackey as he came through the gate and hollered a loud greeting to him, and detained him with questions about his work. This had allowed Queenie time to slip into her apartment, and Jeremiah to go around the other side of the house, and back to his room. Stephanie is their ally, even though Queenie insists that she and Jeremiah are just friends, and in deed they are not yet intimate, even though they spend lots of time together.

They hear Mackey holler for her. Jeremiah closes his door and window quietly. They listen as Mackey walks to the backyard, still hollering her name. He goes and knocks on the sisters' door but no one is home, not even their children. It is Saturday evening and everyone is out. Queenie and Jeremiah stare at each other and when he reaches across the table and takes her hands, he isn't sure whether it's his palms, or hers, or both that are so sweaty.

More than a week ago, he had told Queenie that he wanted to be with her. She had said she felt the same way and was prepared to leave Mackey. That was as far as the conversation had gone, but now they sit, uncertain. They do not trust themselves to whisper. Queenie opens her mouth as if to speak, but he indicates that she should be silent. They sit, wait, listen to Mackey swearing. At last they hear him go through the gate.

Jeremiah peers through the window. "Him gone."

She does not respond.

"Me feel like a coward."

"Mackey is damn ignorant and fool-fool. We affi tink of a plan."

"Wha fi plan? Me wan yu as me woman," and to both their surprises, Jeremiah pulls Queenie to him and kisses her passionately. Queenie responds as eagerly and they hold each other.

"Stay in here all weekend wid me," Jeremiah demands.

"Ah can't do dat wid Mackey home."

"Yu don't ave to go back dere."

"But him will know."

"How him gwane know where yu is, if yu stay inside?"

"But wha bout me clothes? Wha we gwane eat?"

"Yu don't need anyting. Me will go buy food now."

Queenie looks up at him. She thinks about Mackey's threats to kill any man who looks at her. She nestles her head against Jeremiah's chest.

"Me couldn't bear it fi Mackey do anyting to yu."

250

"Wha him can do?" Jeremiah states, feeling confident. "If yu wan get anyting, yu betta get it now before me go to de shop," he says to her.

"Me ave everyting me need," Queenie replies, getting used to the idea of being with Jeremiah, with Mackey so close. "So yu gwane mek me yu prisoner dis weekend?" She smiles up at him. He kisses the top of her head. "Wha if Mackey still here Monday? Me can't stay prisoner fa eva."

"Me know. Me jus need little time fi figure it out."

While Jeremiah is out getting food and few other things, Queenie puts a clean sheet on his bed, and cracks the windows open. The room is very hot, and she fans herself with her hand. Just as she is about to turn on the radio, she hears the gate open and peers through the window. It is Mackey, so she ducks down, crawls on her knees to the bed and sits on its edge. She sees his shadow as he walks up to the window, and drops on the floor just before he gazes in through the slit of the window. She holds her breath, torn between hollering at him to get away and leave her alone, and dread about what he might do if he finds her locked in Jeremiah's room. Then he moves away, but just as she lets out her breath, she hears him banging on Jeremiah's door.

"Open up! Open up! Who in dere?"

Queenie sucks in air through her clenched teeth and thinks, *Him is real mad man fah true*. Right then and there she decides she doesn't want to deal with him any more. *As soon as him leave, me gwane move and go live wid Bulldozer.* Bulldozer is the nickname of her cousin who lives in Central Village who is an amateur boxer. *Mackey no match fah him.* She rolls over on her back and sinks onto the cool tile floor. She refrains from bursting out in laughter, at how funny she must look, lying on the floor in her lover's room, hiding from her man. Queenie cocks her head as she hears Mackey in their apartment, slamming down chairs, and no doubt searching through her things to see if he can find any clues to her whereabouts. She dozes and wakes, momentarily confused upon hearing Jeremiah's and Mackey's voices.

"Yu see me woman, yu see Queenie?" Mackey asks Jeremiah loudly.

"Afternoon," Jeremiah replies.

"Me no ave time fah no niceness," Mackey rejoins.

"Maybe dat why yu don't know whe Miss Queenie deh," Jeremiah replies.

"Wha mek yu tink yu can ave me woman name in yu mouth so familiar?" Mackey steps forward, his face close to Jeremiah's. Jeremiah stares at Mackey, but does not say anything. The two men try to outstare each other, and just when Jeremiah thinks he will have to drop his bags, including the one containing the soup he has bought for Queenie's and his lunch, they both shift their stare as the gate opens and Mabel, Stephanie and their children enter loudly. Mackey turns from Jeremiah and moves towards the sisters.

"Oonuh know whe Queenie deh?"

"Evenin, Mackey, is when yu come?"

"Evenin, Miss Mabel, Miss Stephanie," Jeremiah hollers.

"Manners to yu too, Jeremiah," responds Mabel, staring Mackey down. "Is good to know some people still have home training."

"Is worried ah worried bout Queenie," Mackey rejoins.

"Please don't address me wid any questions, if yu can't seh good day," Mabel says, turning away from him.

Jeremiah takes that opportunity to open the door to his room. Queenie is behind the door, and grabs hold of his arm, causing one bag to burst and the contents to spill on the floor. He slams the door shut, and she slumps on his chest. He stands there and holds her with one arm, the soup in the other. They listen to Mackey's and Stephanie's exchange.

"So yu know where Queenie is?" Mackey demands.

"Ah don't rightly know, yu know, Mackey. Ah did see her early dis morning, and ask her if yu was coming home dis weekend. She seh she didn't think so and she was feeling kinda lonely so she might go visit her sister in Bog Walk," Stephanie lies. She suspects, since Queenie and Jeremiah were together when she left, that Mackey has come home unexpectedly without Queenie having time to slip out. She figures if he buys the bait and goes looking for her at her sister in Bog Walk, that would give Queenie and Jeremiah time, and Queenie could have a story ready when Mackey returns.

"Yu sure she seh she going Bog Walk?" Mackey demands.

"De only thing me sure about is me name, but dat is wha me hear her seh dis mornin. When me leave, Queenie was still here; after all, me is not her *watchdog*." Stephanie emphasizes the watchdog part and places one hand on her hip. She doesn't like Mackey, not only because he is rude, but because he acts as if everyone owes him something. Here he is, she thinks, in the more than six months he has lived in the yard, never once giving any of the children any sweets, and seldom saying hello to her sister or her, and yet he feels the right to inquire about the whereabouts of his woman as if her carrying on is any of their business. She hopes he decides to go to Bog Walk. *Him deserve fi go on a wild pig chase*, she thinks, but smiles in his face. "Maybe yu can jus rest a while and see if she come back, but she might be in Bog Walk wid her sista. She always talkin bout her niece and nephew." Stephanie grins. "Anyway, Mackey, ah don't think yu ave to worry bout anyting."

"Is why yu seh dat? Is man come here come look fah Queenie?" he demands, querulously.

Stephanie places both her hands akimbo, and turns fully to Mackey. "It look like yu been in de sun too long! Don't drag me in yu confusion. Ah ain't mindin oder people's business, and no man don't come here lookin fah anyone. Yu mus excuse me now, ah ave to attend to me affairs," and she turns and walks away from Mackey, who swears under his breath.

Left alone, he opens the gate and stares both ways, up one way and down the other, hoping he will see Queenie. Stomping his feet, he slams the gate shut and returns to his apartment. He goes to the closet to see if all her clothes are there. He hears the radio in Jeremiah's apartment, and walks over to the wall by the barred door, and puts his ear to it. Thinks, *Queenie would neva ave anytin fi do wid dat idiot. Him so fraid of him own shadow, me don't know which woman would want be wid him*. He decides to get dressed and go to Bog Walk before it gets much later. He knows that Queenie is close to her sister, and in the past, whenever they quarrelled, that's where she has gone. He gathers his money and leaves.

Stephanie has been listening out for and watching Mackey. When she sees him leave, she surmises he has bought her bait, but she wants to make sure he isn't pretending to go, then wandering back. She hollers for her children and nieces and tells them they are going for a walk, and she will buy them treats. The children run in delighted expectation, and she saunters down the street, about five minutes behind Mackey. She stops at a few gates and exchanges greetings with her neighbours. The children run ahead, then double back. After about twenty minutes they arrive at the intersection where all vehicles pass, and she happens to see Mackey board a minibus, heading for Bog Walk she hopes. She buys the children sweets and ambles back home, this time without stopping. She slumps down noisily on one of the rocking chairs on the veranda.

"Mabel, Mabel," she hollers to her sister. "Ah just see Mackey get on a minibus. Ah think him gone Bog Walk go look fah Queenie," she says loudly enough for Jeremiah, and Queenie – if she is with him as she suspects – to hear.

"Ah hope Queenie sista set dog pan him," Mabel replies.

Stephanie continues to sit on the veranda, her eyes glued to Jeremiah's window and door, hoping to detect the slightest movement. Unless they are asleep, she is certain they heard her. All is quiet. She is anxious to know what is going on. She clears her throat. Still nothing. Unable to stand the suspense, Stephanie rises, goes to the side entrance and knocks on Jeremiah's door.

"Jeremiah, is me, Stephanie. Ah would like to have a word wid yu, please." She waits, then she hears light feet approach.

Queenie opens the door and says. "Ah would invite yu in, but de room well hot."

"Ah think Mackey gone Bog Walk look fah yu. Yu betta act quick."

Jeremiah appears behind Queenie. "Miss Stephanie, we tank yu fah lookin out fah we. Queenie and me need a few days fi figure tings out. Ah tink we gwane go to me country, go Yarmouth."

"When, Jeremiah?" Queenie asks, surprised.

"Right now; tonight. It just come to me."

"But how we gwane get dere? It getting late already."

"We will find a way. Go pack a few tings. We come back Monday and face Mackey den. Ah gwane need to pass by Mr. Davis so him know ah won't be at work come Monday." Jeremiah turns back into his room, while Queenie stands by the door, a puzzled look on her face.

"Ah tink yu should pack a few tings like Jeremiah seh," Stephanie says to her, guiding her out the door and leading her to her own apartment.

In less than thirty minutes, Jeremiah and Queenie are heading out the door, taking wide strides down the street. It is almost six o'clock. Queenie is doubtful they will get transportation at this hour to Yarmouth, and she is worried about where will they sleep. He has already told her about the church being burned down, and that he had to leave, and just two weeks ago, he'd showed her the letter from Mas Tomlin telling him that he had rented out his cottage. Queenie feels her heart pushing against her chest, and her head pounds. At the crossroads they cross the street; she stands back away from the road and allows Jeremiah to flag vehicles down. She prays Mackey is indeed on his way to Bog Walk and does not return and find them there. It is more than a hour before they climb into a bus that emits lots of exhaust, but it is not crowded. They get a seat together at the back. Only then does she let out her breath, and as the bus sets off and the cool evening breeze soothes her, she rests her head on Jeremiah's shoulder. He pats her hand which he takes into his lap and says, "Everyting gwane be alrite. Yu will see."

She nods, her head still resting on his shoulder and is soon sound asleep.

It is after eleven o'clock when they get to Jeremiah's village, after taking two different buses and a minibus, and walking close to three miles. Even though Jeremiah has carried both their small bags, Queenie is tired and wants the day to end. At Mas Tomlin's yard, three dogs rush towards and circle them, barking. Even though Jeremiah tells her not to be afraid, Queenie is terrified and clutches his arm. After what seems an eternity, Jeremiah quiets the dogs, who appear to remember him and are soon licking at his hands. They walk towards the house and bang on the door a long time before Mas Tomlin shouts, "Who dere dis time a night?"

"Is me, Mas Tomlin, Jeremiah."

"Jeremy, me boy, is yu fah true or me dreamin?"

Soon the door is thrust open wide and Mas Tomlin pulls

255

clumsily at Jeremiah and embraces him. Queenie stands uncertainly at the mouth of the door while Jeremiah and Mas Tomlin exchange greetings. Then turning towards her, Jeremiah holds her by the forearm, and leads her to Mas Tomlin.

"Mas Tomlin, dis here is Miss Queenie, de woman me intend to mek me wife."

Despite her fatigue Queenie grins. Mas Tomlin holds her firmly by both shoulders and gazes at her thoroughly. Still holding her he says, "Dis is a fine lookin oman, Jeremy, a fine lookin oman. Yu do well by me, boy, yu do well."

Queenie smiles, and when Mas Tomlin pulls her to him and embraces her, she hugs him in return.

He gives them tea from his thermos, fixes them bread and cheese, and although he only has one room and one bed, he insists that Queenie sleeps in there, assuring her that he and Jeremy can sleep on a pallet spread on the living-room floor. Queenie thanks him and turns in the room, grateful though a little disappointed; she had hoped to feel Jeremiah nestled next to her, still she is thankful that they are safe away from Mackey and that Jeremiah has taken her to meet the man he calls his father.

The following morning, after a breakfast of roasted breadfruit and salt fish, Jeremiah confides in Mas Tomlin about his and Queenie's relationship, and the threat that hangs over them with Mackey. Mas Tomlin listens silently, only shaking his head a few times. When Jeremiah is done relating the details of their meeting and attachment, Mas Tomlin looks at them both and says, "Love stranga dan hurricane. Yu neva know whe it gwane hit; yu jus ave to be prepared." Then he smiles at both of them, take their hands in his and blesses them. "May oonuh love be like de waves, and may oonuh abide wid one anoder like leaves pan tree."

Later, Mas Tomlin walks with Jeremiah and Queenie to the site that used to be the Rock, and there he leaves them. Jeremiah has told Queenie the story before, but now that they are standing there, he is flooded with memory.

"Even though ah didn't mean it, me responsible fah drownin dat girl," he whispers.

"Everyone meet dem own fate," Queenie replies.

"Ah know. Ah know. Dat's why a give up me robe."

"Den burn it." Queenie is surprised at her response.

"Why a mus burn it?"

"Because yu give it up. Done wid dat life. Yu no need live inside yu head any more."

Jeremiah holds onto this thought.

When they return to Mas Tomlin's house, Jeremiah finds the box in the shed in which he had stored the robe and other things belonging to his mother. He takes out the black robe, walks to the rear of Mas Tomlin's yard, lights a match and tosses it on the robe. Slowly, flames rise, along with a smouldering stench that blackens the air. Queenie sits with Mas Tomlin on the top of the steps and watches Jeremiah stare into the smoke as his robe disintegrates.

"Humble thineself, and the way will be made clear."

On Tuesday afternoon, Jeremiah and Queenie return. Everyone is at work, school, away. The only evidence of Mackey is Queenie's ripped clothes in heaps on the living-room floor, and tossed about their apartment. She salvages what she can and writes a note to him:

> Dear Mackey:
> Me hope you will accept this letter as a good bye and don't cause me no botheration. Ah sorry but ah don't love yu. Ah don't want to be yu wife and ah don't want yu child. You is a good man, but too, too jealous fah me. You was kind and generous to me, and ah tank yu fah dat. Ah only takin me clothes dat yu don't tear up. Ah leavin everyting else. Me know yu will find a woman who love yu and don't mind yu jealousy.
> Sincerely,
> Queenie

She leaves the note on the centre table, after she cleans up the apartment. She locks the door, and gives Jeremiah the key to give to Mackey. Jeremiah hires a car to take her to her cousin, Bulldozer, in Central Village, promising her that he will stop by after work. After she leaves, Jeremiah feels relieved. He puts on his work clothes, feeling giddily happy. He begins to whistle and

257

suddenly remembers Brother Jonah's caution about bodaciousness and Satan's temptation in the form of a woman. He chuckles and continues whistling as he hastens to work. Queenie is one temptation he doesn't plan to resist.

For the next several months the talk all over the community is about Jeremiah and Queenie. It is the biggest bram-bram – the most unexpected twist of events that any has witnessed.

Mackey is in prison for chopping up a man he thought was Jeremiah.

Queenie is pregnant and she and Jeremiah are building a house in the neighbourhood of the very community where they met. Everyone is invited to their wedding which is to be held in the Egg Woman's yard next week.

Allow thyself grace, and blessings will follow.

ABOUT THE AUTHOR

Opal Palmer Adisa is a Jamaica-born, award-winning poet, educator and storyteller. Her poetry, stories and articles have been anthologized widely.

She is the co-founder of Watoto Wa Kuumba, a children's theatre group that she directed from 1979-1991. Since 1993, Opal Palmer Adisa has taught literature and served as Chair of the Ethnic Studies/Cultural Diversity Program at the California College of Arts and Crafts in Oakland.

Her published works include: *Caribbean Passion*, Peepal Tree, 2004; *Leaf-of-Life*, poetry, Jukebox Press, 2000; *It Begins With Tears*, novel, Heinemann, 1997; *Tamarind and Mango Women*, poetry, Sister Vision Press, 1992; *traveling women*, poetry, Jukebox Press, 1989; *Bake-Face and Other Guava Stories*, Kelsey Street Press, 1986; *Pina, The Many-Eyed Fruit*, children's book, Julian Richardson Press, 1985.

ALSO BY OPAL PALMER ADISA

Caribbean Passion
ISBN 1 900715 92 9, price: £7.99, pp. 103, pub. 2004

Caribbean Passion is feisty, sensuous and thought provoking — everything one expects from Opal Palmer Adisa. Whether writing about history, Black lives, family, or love and sexual passion, she has an acute eye for the contraries of experience. Her Caribbean has a dynamic that draws from its dialectic of oppression and resistance; her childhood includes both the affirmation of parents that makes her 'leap fences' and the 'jeer of strange men on the street/that made your feet stumble'; and men are portrayed both as predators and as the objects of erotic desire. This vision of contraries is rooted in an intensely sensuous apprehension of the physical world. She observes the Caribbean's foods and flora with exactness; makes them emblematic metaphors that are often rewardingly oblique; and uses them as starting points for engagingly conversational meditations on aspects of remembered experience. There is a witty play between food and sexuality, but counterpointing her celebration of the erotic, there is a keen sense of the oppression of the female body. In her poem 'Bumbu Clat', for instance, she explores the deformation of a word that originally signified 'sisterhood' to become part of the most transgressive and misogynist curse in Jamaican society. In this doubleness of vision, the term 'womanist' was invented to describe Opal Palmer Adisa's work.

Over 160 Caribbean, Black British and South Asian titles can be bought on Peepal Tree's website on a secure server: www.peepaltreepress.com or by mail order from:
Peepal Tree Press, 17 King's Avenue, Leeds LS6 1QS
Telephone: (+44) 0113 245 1703 2
Email: hannah@peepaltreepress.com